FEEDING THE WHOLE FAMILY

Recipes for Babies, Young Children, and Their Parents

COOKING WITH WHOLE FOODS

CYNTHIA LAIR FOREWORD BY PEGGY O'MARA

SASQUATCH BOOKS
SEATTLE

Dedicated to Michael and Grace,
who light the candle and eat the food with me.

First edition published by LuraMedia, Inc, 1994.
Second edition published by Moon Smile Press, 1997.

The information in this book has been prepared thoughtfully and carefully. It is not intended to be diagnostic or prescriptive. Those who read the book are encouraged to use their own good judgment and to consult with their chosen health practitioner when planning their family's diet.

Printed in the United States of America
Published by Sasquatch Books
Distributed by PGW/Perseus
15 14 13 12 11 10   9 8 7 6 5

Cover illustration: Nikki McClure
Cover & interior design: Kate Basart/Union Pageworks
Interior illustrations: Robynne Hawthorne

Library of Congress Cataloging-in-Publication Data
Lair, Cynthia, 1953-
  Feeding the whole family : recipes for babies, young children, and their parents
/ by Cynthia Lair ; foreword by Peggy O'Mara. -- [3rd ed.]
     p. cm.
  Includes bibliographical references and index.
  ISBN-13: 978-1-57061-525-2
  ISBN-10: 1-57061-525-X
  1. Cookery (Natural foods) 2. Natural foods. I. Title.

TX741.L345 2008
641.5'636--dc22

                    2007044496

Sasquatch Books
119 South Main Street, Suite 400
Seattle, WA 98104
(206) 467-4300
www.sasquatchbooks.com
custserv@sasquatchbooks.com

CONTENTS

ACKNOWLEDGMENTS

I wish to acknowledge Jeff Basom, head chef at Bastyr University, for his incredible creativity with whole foods and for sharing his skills with me. His following recipes or recipe adaptations are proudly featured in this book: Jeff's Potato Pancakes, Lemon Basil Potato Salad, Golden Mushroom Basil Soup, Greens in Cashew Curry Sauce, Luscious Beet Salad with Toasted Pumpkin Seeds, Homemade Whole Grain Bread, and Homemade Curry Paste.

I am grateful to the faculty and staff at Bastyr University's School of Nutrition and Exercise Science, who have given me a place to teach and learn. In particular I wish to acknowledge Dr. Mark Kestin, Kathy Coffey, my creative colleague Mary Shaw and the two amazing women I teach with—Jennifer Adler and Becky Boutch.

I have learned a great deal from Seattle's own chain of high-quality natural foods markets—Puget Consumers Co-op. I have been a teacher for the PCC Cooks program for a couple of decades. The program is excellent, thanks to my friend Marilyn McCormick.

The lovely people at *Mothering* magazine have been very supportive of my work for many years. Ashisha and Peggy O'Mara—though I've never met you in person, I feel I know you and offer my gratitude. Many new additions to this version of the book came from articles I have written for *Mothering*.

My heartfelt thanks to:

Annemarie Colbin, my friend, colleague, and influential teacher.

Holly, Joy, and Matt for listening carefully and giving good counsel.

Jamie for greasing the wheels.

The talented performers in The Edge for keeping me sane and out of my mind at the same time.

Lura Geiger, who was brave enough to give this book its start.

I would also like to thank the following people and organizations for their various contributions of recipe ideas and expertise:

Birgitte Antonsen, Aunt Cathy, Carlie Bockelman, Michael Boer, Minx Boren, Karen Brown, Rita Carey, Goldie Caughlan, Mim Collins, Teresa Dowling, Connie Feutz, Dr. Bruce Gardner, Ronit Gourarie, Jack Kelly, Chris Lair, Buck Levin, Judy Loebl, Susan MacPherson, Kelly Morrow, Nina Petrulis, Nancy Rankin, Karen D. Seibert, Silence-Heart-Nest Restaurant, Gay Stielstra, Jackie Williams, Susan Wilson, and Rebecca Wood.

And, finally, I would never have started this journey without Michael and Grace and their perpetual support of who I am.

FOREWORD

Food is the new politics. In the past, it was enough to know whether or not you ate meat. Now, we also want to know where our food comes from, how it was grown, and if there was any exploitation involved. We're also beginning to think about the carbon footprint of our food and, therefore, to ask if organic fruit from New Zealand is really a sustainable choice. What we do realize now is that local food is best.

One of the reasons that I'm so interested in local food is that I want to support the farmers who live near me. I also know that local food requires less transportation, and thus less gasoline, than food shipped in from hundreds or thousands of miles away. And, in addition to being sustainable, local food is simply fresher and tastier.

There's no better place to get local food than at our farmers' market, and I rarely miss a Saturday there. Over the years, I've learned to bring my own baskets, even my own plastic bags, and, of course, cash. There are vegetables, fruits, meats, jellies, jams, baked goods, live plants, and music. A radio show may be broadcasting from one of the booths. There is chili simmering in the fall. I even noticed a cooking demonstration last Saturday. Going to the farmers' market is a refreshing experience of community; it never fails to cheer me up.

Buying local food and going to the farmers' market are both the result of a new awareness of our food choices. To lead us in making those choices, we need a guide, and there is no better one than Cynthia Lair. Cynthia has an outstanding constellation of talents. She is well educated in nutrition and brings subtle expertise to the luscious recipes in this book. Because she is also an excellent cook, the recipes are all delicious. Cynthia writes about food passionately, and with unusual clarity. And, because she is both a teacher and a mother, she has anticipated the questions her readers will have and has already incorporated the solutions into her offerings.

It is this outstanding combination of talents that has called the editors at *Mothering* back to Cynthia's articles again and again. For well over a dozen years she has been our primary food writer. She has an unequaled talent for writing about food and an enthusiasm for her subject that is contagious.

In this book, you will have the pleasure of reading astute food philosophy along with rich, tasty recipes that are responsive to your challenges as a parent. It's unusual, yet so rewarding, to find a cookbook that includes the breastfeeding years, early food for babies, and tips for feeding children. And there are menus! The book is very comprehensive and that is comforting. What we need as parents is just one book, a guide. *Feeding the Whole Family* is that guide.

—Peggy O'Mara
Editor and Publisher, *Mothering*
October 2007

INTRODUCTION TO THE THIRD EDITION

During the quiet, steady life of this book, I have had the honor of being a teacher of cooking and nutrition. Every week, every class, students ask questions that stump me, questions I find funny and annoying and stimulating. I am a naturally curious person; the queries I can't answer prompt me to keep learning. So when the opportunity came to give *Feeding the Whole Family* a third incarnation, I was ready and said let's go! A chance to incorporate new messages and recipes into the book sounded like fun.

The good news is that the basic whole foods premise with which this book began over a decade ago still holds strong. When I began writing, the very term "whole foods" was new-age-ish and alternative, but surprise, surprise, it has become all the rage. Good for all of us. Imagine my glee when the USDA food pyramid (and Oprah!) started singing the praises of whole grains. Yee haw!

So what did you change in this third edition, Cynthia? Over the years, I've realized that I really have to dig my heels into organic dirt not to sway with popular nutrition trends. We Americans (me too!) are very susceptible to the latest whatever. We are willing to drop whole nutrient groups for decades at a time (no butter? no bread?) because of a newly released study or fad diet. This shunning of staple foods (eggs, meat, butter, sugar, dairy, wheat, potatoes, you name it) does a lot to sell new products and little to improve overall health. Like a garbage disposal, our media grinds up the tried-and-true systems of eating that have supported generation after generation, leading us to revere fear-based consumerism over common sense. I work to be loyal to what has sustained us in the past while incorporating (cautiously) the latest research.

The "war on fat" dominated nutrition literature in the 1980s and '90s. Food with very little or no fat didn't taste right or feel right no matter what compelling anti-fat "facts" prevailed. And now we have a whole new bevy of pro-fat "facts" to add to the confusion. To gain some clarity, I looked at which fats add the most flavor while remaining stable when met with heat. I became more and more picky about what I would use in the teaching kitchen at Bastyr as well as in my home. So in this version of *Feeding the Whole Family*, I have used (almost exclusively) traditional, stable fats and oils that people have used for centuries all over the globe. I've used them in reasonable, but not restrictive, amounts. Healthful fats are crucial for the proper development of babies and young children, essential for the pregnant or nursing mother. Put organic butter on your baked potato. Olive oil makes fabulous salad dressing (and increases absorption of the vitamins in the vegetables!).

I'm sure you have heard stories of children who proclaim themselves "vegetarian" to their unsuspecting meat-and-potatoes parents. I experienced the reverse. When my daughter was about 8 years old, I brought home some raw beef chunks to give to my terriers. My daughter pulled the plastic-wrapped container from the grocery bag and begged to eat the beef. I shrugged and said "sure," suggesting that we cook it first. Being a mostly vegetarian parent raising a definitely carnivorous child and teaching hundreds of nutrition majors with different eating regimes, I strive to be open and accepting of everyone's food choices, and that flexibility is reflected in these recipes.

So you'll notice more recipes using animal protein. Now that it is easier (not easy) to get meat, dairy, eggs, and poultry from humanely raised, healthy animals, I feel easier about including more in my book. It is perfectly cool to be a vegetarian. It is also perfectly cool to be an omnivore. Every time we eat, it is costly; labor, resources, and lives are sacrificed to put delicious food on our tables. Who can say if the life of a chicken is more valuable than the lives of thousands of microbes and insects that are destroyed when a row of kale is harvested? Consciousness about this sacrifice, what we call "giving thanks" before eating, is worth practicing and teaching to our children.

There are other new buttons and bows in this edition. I've added over sixty new recipes that I just love. I put together some new ways to design meals that take into account not just nutrients and health, but color and flavor as well. The prevalence of food sensitivities in babies and children led me to offer additional help in making ingredient substitutions. What to give kids to drink seems to confound most parents, so I've provided some options. And since what is served at the table starts with choices at the grocery store (or farmers' market), I thought I'd better get pretty detailed about what deserves a spot in the grocery cart.

Feeding the whole family is not just about what you and your spouse and your offspring ingest for dinner. It's also about all the ripples that result from your need to eat, the whole mother earth family. We are little links in an enormous, complex food chain, and our lives depend on our appreciation and support of other links in the chain. When we buy organic green beans from a local farmer, we not only support our family's vegetable intake and the farmer's pocketbook, we support microorganisms in soil, plankton in water, less junk in the landfill. Conscious grocery cart choices support the sustainable future of all.

Our children deserve to be fed well so that they can pursue their dreams. Poor health due to eating poor-quality food is fixable! When we help children learn to eat well, we nourish our grandchildren and their children. Remind them that the earth is the provider of food. Instill in children that no box, no powder, no concoction from a laboratory offers the same vitality and beauty as a direct offering from nature.

Sitting down together and sharing food has enormous power. This ritual is an essential element in the spiritual glue that holds us together as families and communities. Learning to prepare and eat simple, whole foods that the earth naturally provides can transform lives.

—Cynthia Lair
October 2007

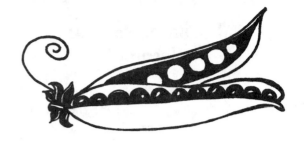

Wholesome Family Eating

When my daughter was young I read aloud to her several books that were set in the late 1800s in this country. Only 100-plus years ago, our great-grandparents created a dinner plate very different from what is typical today. Food on the table was, for the most part, grown, raised, caught, or shot. The only fresh fruits and vegetables available were what grew in season in one's climate. Often, folks ate the same foods day after day. Corn mush and rabbit stew was a regular hit on the prairie. Day after day, Laura and Mary, in *Little House on the Prairie*, ate corn mush. I felt so relieved when summer came, and they got to go blackberry picking.

In the summer I sometimes visit Wichita, Kansas, to see my family. My sister's house is near a big suburban supermarket. This place has everything! There is every imaginable kind of food available. People push giant grocery carts piled high with packages of every color, shape, and size. Besides a vast array of food, there's a post office, a paperback book section, video rentals, a banking facility, dry cleaners, a prescription drug counter,

and free colon cancer screening tests—all in the same store! The number of choices and amount of stimuli are overwhelming. The question, what should we eat for dinner? has ten thousand answers. And there are several thousand more choices of what to do after dinner.

If I don't have my priorities in place, a trip to the grocery store can be like getting lost in the woods. Not only do I function better with a list in hand, but I need a clear concept of what is healthy and wholesome and what isn't. I want our hard-earned family dollars to buy food that will vitalize our bodies, minds, and spirits.

In this book I have carved out my own interpretation of the more-than-ample information available about nutrition. I have used research and data from today, as well as some of the simple common sense of yesteryear. The information isn't meant to be the final word for you or for me. I encourage you to start your own journey with food and health. Once you truly understand the power you hold as you stroll down a grocery store aisle, your dinner plate may never look the same.

What Do We Mean by Wholesome?

The word "wholesome" conjures up lovely images. We think of rosy-cheeked children running and playing in the sunshine, or a tidy house where there are clean cotton sheets on the beds, a simple wood table for meals, and the smell of homemade bread. The word can also suggest something about a person's character, hinting at openness, honesty, and a wealth of common sense. When the word "wholesome" is linked to food, the adjectives "health-giving," "fresh," and "naturally produced" come to mind. We might picture a pot of freshly made vegetable soup, a basket of apples, or the local farmers' market with its bounty of colorful produce. Sounds good.

As parents we want our children to have a wholesome upbringing to establish a steady base from which they can eventually contribute to the world. The most primary way to fulfill that intention is by providing nourishing food for our children to eat. Yet most of our information about how to do that is conflicting. The latest scientific research is sometimes at odds with common sense. The American diet lacks history. Aside from apple pie and hot dogs, we don't seem to have an undercurrent of traditional foods and flavors that have built our children and our children's children to be strong. And so we are easily swayed by facts, figures, and the latest fad diets. Food manufacturers leap on evidence uncovered in a research project, identify a microscopic substance, and get their media machines to make us believe that we won't survive without it. The fear factor has been set in motion. The quality and integrity of the original food source is usually lost in exchange for quantity. Money is made, but I don't believe anyone's health is preserved.

In our culture we maintain a very mechanistic view of nutrition. We dissect food in an attempt to quantify its contents. Charts are formed to show us how an average carrot contains a certain number of calories, so many milligrams of this, international units of that, and grams of such and such. Then we take an "average" 8-year-old weighing so many pounds and walking this many kilometers a week and decide how many units of each of these macro- and micronutrients he or she will use up. After the data is gathered, someone attempts to crunch the numbers and make recommendations about how many units of each of the nutrients need to be poured into the model child to make sure the machine works. That's one way of thinking about it.

It is true that knowing something about the nutrient content of food can be helpful in determining what is wholesome. Be aware, however, that we have identified and named only a tiny percent of all the miraculous nutrients that foods are composed of. In the early nineteenth century, protein, carbohydrates, and fat were named as compounds all foods were composed of. The second wave of discovery about nutrition came when vitamins and minerals were identified. We found that for the macronutrients to metabolize in the body, certain vitamins and minerals had to also be present. Recently, another set of nutrients in food plants were uncovered, polyphenols. There are hundreds of these compounds, and they give plants the things they need to manufacture not just vitamins, minerals, and various antioxidants—but also flavor!

Consider, too, that feeding a family must be more than a math quiz. Vitamins and minerals and grams of whatever are good to know about, but we have to take their presence on faith—they are invisible to us. When you eat kale, your taste

WHAT IS A WHOLE FOOD?

To determine whether a food is whole or not, we must be conscious when making food choices. Before we put a bite of it in our mouths, before we heat it up, before we even decide to toss it in our grocery cart, there needs to be a moment, a second, when we consider where the food came from. What was its life like before it came to be on this grocery store shelf? Foods that are in boxes can be pretty mysterious. For simple whole foods, foods that don't need a list of ingredients, imagining what their journey was like is easier. I have found that the best way to determine whether a food is whole or not is to ask these questions:

Can I imagine it growing?

It is easy to picture a wheat field or an apple on a tree. Tough to picture a field of marshmallows. I know of no streams where one can scoop up a bucket of diet soda, no trees where one can pick Froot Loops.

How many ingredients does it have?

A whole food has only one ingredient—itself. No label of ingredients is necessary on simple foods like apples, salmon, and wild rice.

What's been done to the food since it was harvested?

The less, the better. Many foods we eat no longer resemble anything found in nature. Stripped, refined, bleached, injected, hydrogenated, chemically treated, irradiated, and gassed, modern foods have literally had the life taken out of them. Read the list of ingredients on the labels: if you can't pronounce it or can't imagine it growing, don't eat it. If it is not something that you could possibly make in your kitchen or grow in a garden, be wary. For example, you can make tofu, but you can't make isolated soy protein.

Is this product "part" of a food or the "whole" entity?

Juice is only a part of a fruit. Oil is only part of the olive. When you eat a lot of partial foods, your body in its natural wisdom will crave the parts it didn't get.

How long has this food been known to nourish human beings?

Sounds rough, but my criterion is a thousand years. Okay maybe a couple of hundred. Putting something on my toast or in my tea that the FDA approved last month warrants caution. Time and again the rush to put a new drug, supplement, or food additive on the market has had questionable long-term effects. Most whole foods have been on the dinner table for centuries.

buds can't compute how many milligrams of calcium, vitamin A, and vitamin C are present. We need to expand our criteria for how to choose and ingest food, employing not just data and research reported by the media, but also our senses. Sight, smell, touch, taste, and intuition are equally important.

Study a raspberry. Who could make such a voluptuous, tasty thing? Who designed it to gently pull off the vine when it is ripe to perfection, to have all those succulent rosy red pockets of juicy flavor? Only sun, water, and fertile soil can make this good fruit. Humans depend on simple whole foods like the raspberry, as well as other plants and the animals that eat the plants, to create the tissue and blood and milk that form our children and our children's children. Let's begin by defining the concept of a "whole food," for this will lead us to wholesomeness.

WHY CHOOSE WHOLE FOODS?

Until the last century, humans have survived on whole foods found in nature. As industrialization and agribusiness made headway, refined foods became not only available, but also popular. Our attraction to these fractionated foods may be out of habit and convenience rather than true appetite. A whole food harvested in season, with very little transportation time to the market, is at its peak in flavor. The good taste and rich color of food is an indication that nutrients are present. The fiber that comes as a natural part of whole foods makes us feel fuller and more satisfied with smaller serving sizes. Deep in our cells we know that whole, fresh, natural foods are the best nourishment for body and soul.

Our children deserve the best

One need only look at the health statistics of our children to realize that changing the way we eat is critical. Of our children ages 6 to 19, 30 percent are overweight and 15 percent are obese. These are staggering figures. With obesity comes a higher prevalence of diabetes, hypertension, and orthopedic complications in our children, not to mention the devastating psychosocial effects. Among 3- to 17-year-olds, 8 percent have a learning disability (7 percent have ADHD). And 12 percent of our children have been diagnosed with asthma. Children under 6 years of age get an average of 6 to 8 colds a year. Some sources put the figure at closer to one a month for school-age children! All of these maladies cannot be ascribed to diet alone, but why not feed our children the best food possible and create a better chance for good health?

This country produces 3,900 calories of food each day for every person. This represents a huge excess of food that advertisers coax us to consume. Obviously, we need to eat less and move more, but we also need to serve our children higher quality food. Empty calories from highly refined foods like high-fructose corn syrup (Americans eat 83 pounds a year per person of this!) contribute to weight gain and little else. Synthetic sweeteners (such as aspartame and splenda), pesticides, hormones, antibiotics, preservatives, dyes, fillers, stabilizers, and other chemical concoctions found in our food are used to increase profits, not health. Optimistically they are just foreign substances the body has to eliminate or store. Realistically they can set the stage for malfunction. Nutrient-dense, fiber-rich whole foods are more nutritious and filling per calorie. Every calorie of a peach or a piece of

A WELL-BALANCED WHOLE FOODS DIET

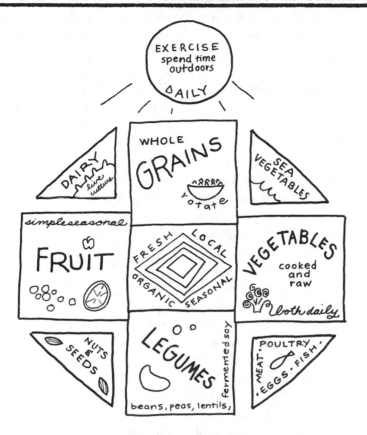

MAIN DISHES (squares):
Whole Grains, Vegetables, Legumes, Fruits

SIDE DISHES AND TOPPINGS (triangles):
Dairy, Sea Vegetables, Eggs, Fish, Meat or Poultry, Nuts and Seeds

For most, having these foods take a supporting role in the meal is best. However, they can be emphasized more in the diet of those with elevated needs, such as women who are pregnant or nursing, persons who participate daily in hard physical labor, and children or adults who are regularly involved in athletic competition.

At least two of the four foods represented by triangles should be included in the diet; so for those choosing to be vegan it is important to include nuts and seeds (for fats) and sea vegetables (for minerals) on a regular basis.

broiled salmon is usable by the body in a positive way. Home cooking represents another less measurable, but important form of quality. Make a commitment to the future and teach children to enjoy the very best at the kitchen table.

The desire for wholeness comes from within

Eating whole foods can help feed the desire for wholeness within ourselves. This spiritual benefit is magnified when the entire family partakes of nature's bounty together. Not only are the individuals of the family enriched and nourished, but the family is strengthened as well. In one of my classes, a student asked me if a chicken leg was a whole food. "Don't you have to eat all of the chicken for it to be a whole food?" she asked. I posed the question to my friend and mentor Annemarie Colbin, founder of the Natural Gourmet Institute and author, who wisely told me that yes, you would have to eat the whole chicken . . . over time. She reminded me that when Native Americans killed a buffalo, the whole buffalo was used, much of it as food, the rest for other practical needs. The sharing of this whole animal by a group of people was part of what held them together. It is not just the ritual of a shared meal that is important here. Each member of the tribe had consumed a part of something that had recently been a powerful whole. On some level this helped hold the tribe together. It is a unifying force.

The intention of this book is to encourage families to share meals consisting of whole foods. That is why I recommend that babies and children eat the same foods that their parents are eating. There is ample support in our world for developing individualism. What is sometimes missing, what we often long for in the depths of our soul, is that connectedness to the whole. We have an opportunity to help satisfy this yearning every day at the dining table by choosing whole foods and by sharing those foods as a family.

Shopping for Sustenance

High-quality food is more expensive, but consider this: in the 1960s American families spent 18 percent of their income on food and 5 percent on health care. Nowadays this is reversed: we spend just 9 percent of our hard-earned dollars on food and 16 percent on health care. Which would you rather spend your money on?

FRESH, LOCAL, ORGANIC, SEASONAL

This could easily be the mantra guiding whole foods eating. If you purchase a food that was grown locally and organically, and is fresh and in season, that's as good as it gets.

Fresh

Fresh is best. The chemical composition of food changes radically a few hours after harvest simply because it is cut off from its food and water supply. Fresh food, particularly fresh produce, gives us maximum nutrients and flavor.

Frozen food can be good too. Most of the nutrients are retained in foods that are frozen; however, some of the enzymes, color, and flavor will have disappeared. If purchasing frozen fruits and vegetables, you will notice that the texture will have changed. The foods are much less crisp than fresh foods because the cell structure is damaged by crystallization of water.

Canned foods have most of their nutrients present, but the flavor, color, and texture suffer. One exception is tomatoes, which are picked at maximum ripeness and canned the same day. Often a canned tomato will be superior in flavor to a fresh tomato purchased in February that was flown thousands of miles.

Local

Did you know that 86 percent of our fruits, nuts, and vegetables are grown on farms surrounding America's cities? Most farmers who sell their food locally don't artificially treat crops to withstand shipping and extend their shelf life. Have a conversation with some of the nonorganic vendors at your local farmers' market and you may find out that some local farmers do not use synthetic fertilizers or pesticides, but lack the size or profits to go through the rigorous process of attaining organic status. Many farmers will sell their eggs, beef, and pork directly to the consumer. The same is true for milk and milk products from healthy cows and goats. Check out www.eatwild.com and click on your state. Consider subscribing to a CSA (Community Supported Agriculture) for a box of fresh, locally grown produce delivered or picked up every week. The site www.localharvest.org has listings. As novelist Barbara Kingsolver pointedly reminds us in her essay "Lily's Chickens"—"Even if you walk or bike to the store, if you come home with bananas from Ecuador, tomatoes from Holland, cheese from France, and artichokes from California, you have guzzled some serious gas. This extravagance that most of us take for granted is a stunning boondoggle: Transporting 5 calories' worth of strawberry from California to New York costs 435 calories of fossil fuel." Buying locally supports your community, supports your health, and supports the intention of conserving global resources.

Organic

Buying organic products is a form of voting. Your organic purchase says that you support the growers and manufacturers who are producing food without the use of the synthetic fertilizers, insecticides, fungicides, herbicides, or pesticides that pollute your body and your world. Buying organic produce, especially locally grown produce, also helps keep you in tune with the seasons. Many believe that organic produce tastes better and contains more nutrients.

We have national standards for labeling food "organic." A label that says "100 percent Organic" must contain all organic ingredients. If the label simply says "Organic," at least 95 percent of the ingredients are organically produced. When the label reads "Made with Organic Ingredients," at least 70 percent of the ingredients are organic, and the use of the USDA Organic seal is prohibited. Organic produce label codes start with the number 9.

Please be aware that before there were national standards set for labeling a food "organic," the term meant that the product had been grown according to strict uniform standards, verified by independent state or private organizations. In constructing national regulations, the standards have been watered down some. Now that superchains like Wal-Mart are carrying organic produce, the standards may be changed to benefit large producers over individual consumers. The large corporations have more lobbying power to get the regulations changed to suit their need for lower prices and bigger profits. This trend may put the small, local farmers out of business, so whenever possible, buy organic produce at your local farmers' market or natural foods co-op rather than at chain supermarkets.

Make a special effort to use organic products when preparing food for pregnant or nursing moms, infants, and children. Toxins found in the mother's food can cross the placenta to the growing fetus or wind up in breast milk. What may be tolerated by a mature adult may prove harsh to the immature system of a fetus or an infant. Regulatory practices used to control pesticides in foods are based on studies of pesticide exposure to the general population, without regard to the special needs of infants. Some of the most pesticide-saturated foods are ones that we routinely give children to snack on, including peanut butter, peanuts, raisins, and potato chips. Nonorganic apples, peaches, strawberries, and celery can contain as many as eighty pesticide residues. Use your power as a consumer to demand the best for our children, our planet, and the future of both.

Seasonal

Choosing food that is in season gives the year rhythm and ritual. It is exciting to wait for local strawberries to appear—they are sweeter and fresher than eating Mexican-grown berries in January. Anticipation is a wonderful feeling. I can't wait for corn to be in season locally because it is so sweet it hardly needs to be cooked. By waiting for produce available locally only during windows of time, our eating has a cyclical feeling keeping us in tune with the seasons.

Eating seasonally also puts your body in tune with the climate you are living in. The stereo-typical Southern Californian preference for raw salads and avocados has sense to it. The lighter diet that includes lots of raw foods is perfect for living in a sunny, warm climate. Pacific Northwesterners need the density of frequent servings of salmon, for example, to survive the cold damp of rainy winters. Traveling north of our continent, an even fattier diet is appropriate for surviving the cold. Where do you live? What did the ancestors who inhabited your community grow and eat?

THE MAIN DISHES

Whole grains, beans, vegetables, and fruit are central to the whole foods diet and essential to the vegetarian or vegan diet. Humans have eaten these staple foods for centuries. They represent the beginning of agriculture; planting, tending, and harvesting created stability and community in our species. Later, their consumption became an economically viable source of calories and protein. We return to these humble foods at a time when we need a diet that is nutrient dense and fiber rich for better health.

Whole grains

For daily consumption whole grains are superior to refined grains because the whole product contains protein, fiber, B vitamins, calcium, iron, vitamin E, and *life* (the germ of the grain is the live part). Eating grains in their whole, natural form is satisfying and beneficial. Whole grains can also be ground into flours or cereals, made into pasta or noodles.

As you discover the benefits of whole grains, remember to rotate grains in your diet. When you eat the same grain every day, you are more likely to develop sensitivity to it. If you have brown rice on Monday, try quinoa on Tuesday. Each grain has something unique to offer the body.

Most cereal grains and beans have a phosphorus-containing compound in the outer layers called phytic acid. Phytic acid can bind with certain minerals like calcium, iron, and zinc in the intestinal tract, preventing their absorption. Most people eat a wide variety of foods, and this is not an issue. According to Sally Fallon's book *Nourishing Traditions* (ProMotion Publishing, 1995), many traditional societies soaked or fermented their whole grains before eating them. Soaking grains and beans activates the seed embryo, which neutralizes the phytic acid.

Many natural foods grocery stores offer whole grains and legumes, as well as other products, in bulk. Purchasing foods this way is less expensive than buying them in packages. There is no difference in the quality. Whole grains can be stored in airtight containers on the shelf. I prefer to keep ground grains and flours in the refrigerator or freezer. Their germ has been exposed as a result of grinding, making them more vulnerable. Consider buying some large mason jars for keeping grains and beans. That way you can see what you have and create an interesting display. If you are keeping grains and beans in glass jars, don't store them in direct sunlight; find a dark, cool place.

Whole grains used in this book:
  Amaranth
  Brown rice
  Buckwheat (toasted is kasha)
  Hulled barley
  Millet
  Oats
  Quinoa
  Spelt
  Sweet brown rice

Ground grains and flours used in this book:
  Barley flour
  Cornmeal
  Kamut flour
  Polenta
  Rolled oats
  Soba noodles
  Spelt flour
  Steel cut oats
  Udon noodles
  Whole wheat flour
  Whole wheat pastry flour

Legumes

For centuries cultures have combined legumes (beans, peas, lentils, and soy products) with whole grains to create delicious daily fare. Most grains are lacking the amino acid lysine, while most beans lack methionine. Beans have plenty of lysine, grains ample methionine. Together they are complete. They do not have to be combined at the same meal to get the benefit of complementary amino acids. You carry an amino acid pool of some 80 to 90 grams of complete protein in your body that can be called upon to fill any gaps. Setting aside science, grain and bean combinations are the base of some of the most exciting and delicious cuisine in the world.

Beans are rich in protein and complex carbohydrates, high in fiber, low in calories, and they contain appreciable amounts of calcium, iron, and other nutrients. Beans accept herbs and spices graciously to create hearty, mouthwatering dishes.

And beans are inexpensive and available everywhere—what more could you ask from a food?

You can choose from traditional beans such as kidney and pinto or try one of the offbeat varieties such as Christmas limas or cranberry beans. Whole dry beans can be purchased in bulk or packaged. Many brands of canned beans are fine, though the flavor and tenderness may be superior if you cook the beans yourself. Tips for reducing the properties in beans that can cause gas are on page 68.

Soy foods

When the media began reporting scientific research showing health benefits from eating soy products, Americans hopped on the soy wagon. Hence not only the gulping of soy lattes, munching of soy-based candy bars (referred to as "energy bars") and slicing of Tofurkey at Thanksgiving, but the broad acceptance that anything with soy anything in it is good for you. Good news for the soybean farmers who were subsidized $1.6 billion in 2005 by our federal government.

Soybeans have some great things to brag about. Farmers like that they are a versatile, inexpensive, and easy-to-grow. They are a good noncholesterol protein source, a natural source of lecithin, and concentrated in essential fatty acids, including omega-3.

Soybeans are also a difficult food for humans to digest. They contain more phytic acid than most grains or beans, which can affect mineral absorption. Some feel that their natural enzyme inhibitors can block protein absorption. Kaayla T. Daniel, PhD, CCN, in her book *The Whole Soy Story: The Dark Side of America's Favorite Health Food* (New Trends Publishing, 2005) takes more punches at the bean, citing allergies, sexual dysfunction, adverse affects on hormone development during puberty, thyroid deficiencies, and retarded growth in children as symptoms of eating too much soy. I'm not confident that soy is that sinister, but it's definitely overused and overrated.

Soybean derivatives such as soy flour, textured soy protein, partially hydrogenated soybean oil, and soy protein isolate certainly raise some concerns. These highly processed soy products, a result of multistage chemical processes, have become a major ingredient in many prepackaged or fast foods. Products made from soy derivatives, such as cheese, margarine, burgers, hot dogs, and bacon, are a staple in most vegetarian and vegan diets. To me, these products do not seem any livelier or healthier than their animal-based counterparts. Less so in most cases.

The traditional Japanese diet, through centuries of trial and error, found ways to use soybeans in a healthful manner. The Japanese mainly ate carefully crafted, fermented soy products in small amounts. Tamari, shoyu, miso, and tempeh add flavor and digestibility to meals. Cultures that traditionally used soy products in their diets also included sea vegetables. If there is any worry about mineral absorption or thyroid deficiencies from eating soy, the plethora of minerals, including iodine, in sea vegetables counters it. The various soy products are discussed in greater detail in "Identifying, Purchasing, and Storing Whole Foods" in Appendix B.

Beans used in this book:
   Black beans
   Brown lentils
   Cannellini beans
   Christmas limas
   French lentils
   Chickpeas (garbanzos)
   Kidney beans

Navy beans
Pinto beans
Red lentils
Split peas

Fermented soy foods used in this book:
Miso
Shoyu
Tamari
Tempeh
Tofu*

Vegetables

Choose to eat both cooked vegetables and raw vegetables every day. Cooking vegetables lessens some of their nutritional value yet makes the food more digestible and easier to assimilate. Raw vegetables are rich in nutrients and some enzymes that can't be found in cooked vegetables; however, some vegetables, such as broccoli and cauliflower, are harder to digest eaten raw. You need both. One way to approach this is to eat mostly cooked vegetables and use raw vegetables as a condiment in the cooler months of the year and reverse this when it is warm.

Eat all colors. Don't form prejudices. Try dark green, light green, white, purple, red, yellow, orange, gold, black, brown; eat vegetables you've never had before. Lean toward nutrient-dense dark green and orange vegetables, giving them a daily appearance on your plate. These are supernutritious vegetables that contain vitamins and minerals you can't get too much of. Buy organic and/or locally produced produce whenever possible (check out www.localharvest.org).

I attended a talk given by one of our renowned nutritionists, Marion Nestle, when her book *What to Eat* (North Point Press, 2006) appeared on the shelves. She spoke about shopping on the outskirts of the grocery store as a way to choose healthier food. That's where you will find vegetables and fruit. Use your senses to choose vegetables and fruits: touch avocados, smell melons, look for bright, perky greens. Avoid produce that appears wilted or moldy or has edges that are turning brown.

Store dark, leafy greens in open plastic bags in the refrigerator, where they will stay moist but will still be able to breathe. Keep storage vegetables like onions, garlic, squashes, and potatoes in a cool, dry, dark place—the refrigerator can sometimes be too moist. When in doubt, get clues from where and how the grocery store displays the item.

Dark green and orange vegetables used in this book:
Arugula
Beet greens
Bok choy
Broccoli
Cabbage
Carrots
Chinese cabbage
Collards
Kale
Mustard greens
Spinach
Sweet potatoes
Swiss chard
Watercress
Winter squash
Yams

---

*   *Tofu is not a fermented soy product; however, it is usually served with other fermented soy products. The phytic acid of the soybean is mostly found in the fiber, which is not included in tofu making.*

Fruit

In-season fruit is the least expensive and most delicious. It's sometimes hard to decipher what is in season because we import fruit from many parts of the world. Eating local produce solves the dilemma. Buying produce seasonally helps remind you of the rhythm of the passing seasons and keeps you in tune with nature: strawberries every June, plums in September. Eat fruit in its whole, fresh state. Include some cooked fruits and dried fruits in your diet, especially in winter.

Drinking juice is not the same as eating a piece of whole fruit. Juice lacks fiber, which slows the rate of sugar absorption. Plus juice is not a whole food. Children can get the equivalent of a sugar "high" on straight fruit juice. They may crave juice for quick energy and fill up on it instead of eating more nutritious food. Avoid serving juice with meals. I recommend diluting juice for children, one-half juice and one-half filtered water. Buy organic fruit, especially for babies, children, and pregnant moms.

Store tropical and subtropical fruits like pineapples, melons, bananas, lemons, limes, oranges, grapefruits, avocados, and tomatoes on the counter. These fruits usually originated in a hot or warm climate, and refrigeration can be too cold, causing them to lose flavor.

Fruits used in this book:

- Apples
- Apricots
- Avocados
- Blueberries
- Cranberries
- Dates
- Grapes
- Kiwis
- Lemons
- Melons
- Oranges
- Pears
- Plums
- Raisins
- Raspberries
- Strawberries
- Tomatoes

SIDE DISHES AND TOPPINGS

Using foods that are more concentrated in fat and protein as side dishes keeps them in healthful proportion. A small serving of sea vegetables now and then will keep your family's diet mineral-rich.

Dairy

Many cultures throughout history fermented or cultured dairy foods to use as part of their diet. They did this because milk from other mammals can be a difficult food for humans past the age of weaning to digest. Yogurt, laban, kefir, crème fraîche, clabber, and aged cheese are a few examples of milk products that utilize separated, cultured milk. Souring milk or adding live cultures breaks down both the milk sugar (lactose) and the milk protein (casein), which are responsible for most digestive problems. Naturally cultured or fermented dairy products from soured milk not only add fat, protein, and minerals to the diet but also friendly bacteria, which can help with your digestion of other foods.

The choice to include or exclude dairy products can be confusing, especially when it comes to children. I have been schooled in the ill effects of eating dairy as well as the importance of including this very nutrient-dense food. The practice of drinking homogenized, pasteurized milk is fairly recent and seems to have caused some health problems for some individuals. For me, the evidence seems to validate that including small amounts of cultured or fermented whole dairy products in the diet can be quite healthful. I feel it is important to include dairy in dishes that include nightshades (tomatoes, potatoes, eggplants, and peppers) for balance as mentioned on page 21. For more discussion on dairy foods and children see "Food Allergies and Intolerances" (pages 36–38) or "What Should I Give My Child to Drink?" (pages 47–50).

Because antibiotics, hormones, and pesticides often get stored in the fat of the animal, which is then transferred to the milk, it is wise to purchase organic dairy products. I prefer not to use nonfat or reduced-fat dairy products. These products are no longer whole, natural foods. Their nutritional composition has been altered, leaving a disproportionately high protein content. Parents should be aware that using low-fat or nonfat milk is inappropriate for children under 2 years of age. Children need healthy fats in their diet for physical growth and mental development. I would rather see folks, young and old, consuming a small amount of satisfying full-fat organic dairy than large amounts of products with little or no fat.

Cultured and fermented dairy used in this book:
  Blue cheese
  Cultured butter
  Feta cheese
  Ghee
  Parmesan cheese
  Sour cream
  Whole milk yogurt

Sea vegetables

These jewels from the ocean are unknown to most American palates. The sea vegetables used in this book include only a sampling of the variety to be found. Each kind is unique, offering the cook an array of varied tastes and textures.

Sea vegetables have a rich and diverse nutritional profile. Ounce for ounce sea vegetables are higher in minerals than any other class of food because they are grown in sea water where minerals are constantly being renewed. They are a rich source of vitamins A, B, C, and E, as well as calcium and iron. Many trace elements and some key minerals such as zinc and iodine are difficult to obtain in land vegetables today because modern farming methods have badly depleted our soil.

The taste may seem strong or unfamiliar at first, so using a recipe that includes other foods you enjoy in the dish can be helpful. Many sea vegetables (such as nori) can be toasted and crushed or ground into a powder that can be put in a salt shaker and used as a condiment.

You may wonder about the pollution factor. Harvesters of sea vegetables conscientiously seek out chaste waters to grow and forage their crops. As with other ocean vegetation, sea vegetables won't flourish in polluted areas.

Sea vegetables are purchased dried in bags in the ethnic or macrobiotic section of natural foods grocery stores. They can be kept indefinitely in a sealed container in a cool, dry, dark place. Most sea vegetables, with the exception of nori, are reconstituted in water prior to using.

Sea vegetables used in this book:
Agar
Arame
Dulse
Dulse flakes
Hijiki
Kombu
Nori
Wakame

Eggs, fish, poultry, and meat

Ample protein is needed for growth and repair in the body. Consequently, protein is particularly important for pregnant or nursing mothers, active children, anyone participating in athletics, and people who do heavy physical labor as part of their employment. Some people can derive all the protein they need from vegetarian sources of protein, while others don't feel right without some flesh foods in their diet. For most people 3 to 4 ounces of eggs, fish, poultry, or meat daily is ample, and these foods can be used as a side dish rather than being the star of the meal. For those with elevated needs, as listed previously, more may be needed.

Label reading and questioning your fish monger or butcher has never been more important. We do not want to support the inhumane, unhealthy processing plants where animals are treated as simply "product." Finding high-quality, respectfully produced meat, poultry, fish, and eggs requires investigation and education. Remember the saying, "You are what you eat"? Well in this case you are what *they* eat. When buying healthy eggs, fish, birds, or animals, it is best if they have had access to their natural diet and have not been given antibiotics or hormones. Visit www.certifiedhumane.com to learn more.

Eggs

The natural diet for a chicken is bugs, worms, and some grains, seeds, and greens. When birds eat this food they produce incredible eggs. The yolks are golden-orange and naturally rich in omega-3 fatty acids, and the whites are viscous, not runny.

Conventional eggs (which have no special labeling) come from factories where two to four pullets as young as 19 weeks old are put into a wire cage with an area of approximately 2 feet square. A barn full of these cages is known as a battery of cages. Feeds are allowed to contain antibiotics and are mostly made up of bioengineered corn. Battery cages are banned in some places in Europe.

Though the terms "cage free," "free run," "free roaming," and "free range" sound more appealing, they simply mean that there are no cages in the chicken house and/or that the birds have access to the outside. It doesn't mean they necessarily go outside, nor do the terms tell us anything about the bird's diet. "Omega-3" on the label means the feed given to the birds contains 10 to 20 percent flax seed, which increases the omega-3 value in the nutrient content of the egg. Organic eggs are pricey, but they guarantee that flocks have access to an organic outside area year round and are fed at least 80 percent organic non-GMO feed. There are no meats or meat by-products, antibiotics, or hormones allowed in the feed, and each bird must have at least 2 square feet of floor space.

"Pastured" is a new term coined to explain the regimen of keeping birds in a moveable enclosure with nests and roosts that are moved once or twice daily to a new piece of grass. The chickens get at least 20 percent of their diet from foraging and eating insects. These are probably the highest-quality eggs you can purchase. You may find pastured eggs at a local farmers' market or by making friends with a neighbor that keeps chickens.

Fish

The best-quality fish are wild, line-caught fish. This means that the fish lived a relatively normal life, ate a natural diet, and was caught in a sustainable way. The Monterey Bay Aquarium (www.mbayaq.org) is the watchdog organization in the seafood industry. It does a superb job of letting consumers know which fisheries are doing a good job of maintaining our precious oceans and the sea life that live in them.

Fish farming, also known as aquaculture, uses a variety of methods to grow or breed fish or shellfish in marine or fresh water. Fish farms currently provide one-third of all seafood. However, this amount will increase in the future to help meet a growing global demand for seafood that can't be met by wild fisheries alone. Popular seafood such as salmon and shrimp are farm raised in addition to being fished in the wild. Other popular seafood items such as tilapia, catfish, and mussels are almost always farm raised.

The upside of farm-raised fish is that more people are eating fish because of its availability and price. The downsides cause concern. Much of our farm-raised fish, particularly "Atlantic" salmon, is genetically modified. Because of the sameness of the fish, disease spreads rapidly, and antibiotics must be used. The PCB levels are higher because the fish live in their own waste in a limited area. Farmed salmon are fed pellets to which coloring has been added to get the red color in the flesh.

Fish farming can be done responsibly. Trout, for example, are farmed by blocking off a section of river. The water is flowing, allowing natural waste control and providing the trout with more of their natural diet.

Buy fresh or frozen-at-sea (and still frozen) fish caught in a sustainable way. Look for fish that has a shiny semigloss sheen, a fresh smell, and tight flesh. Gaps in the flesh or yellowing are an indication of age. Cook and eat what you have purchased within 48 hours if it is not frozen. Store fresh fish in its packaging resting on a pan of ice in the refrigerator. Do not attempt to buy fresh fish and freeze it yourself, as the temperature on home freezers does not get low enough, and the slow growth of ice crystals will negatively affect the texture.

Poultry

Many of the terms used on egg cartons are also used for labeling poultry. "Free range" or "free roaming" means that the poultry are not caged, and need only mean that the bird has had some access to the outdoors each day. The outdoor area must be 50 percent of the size of the barn area. How long the bird or animal spends outside depends on the producer and the climate. Claims are defined by the USDA but are not verified by third-party inspectors. The USDA also allows producers to label meat and poultry products with the claims "no antibiotics administered" or "raised without antibiotics." Again, claims are defined by the USDA but are not verified by third-party inspectors.

The term "organic" on poultry lets us know that the birds are fed organic feed are not administered any antibiotics, and no irradiation or genetic modification takes place. They are raised under conditions that provide for exercise, access to the outdoors, and freedom of movement, though most birds have a very short life and rarely have the time or inclination to hang out in the outdoor area provided. Organic labeling claims are verified by third-party inspectors.

Another option is to research your local community to see if any small farmers are raising poultry to sell. Sometimes purchasing the birds may require a trip to the farm or to a farmers' market.

Always store raw meat or poultry on the bottom shelf of your refrigerator to avoid any cross-contamination that may occur from dripping juices. Wash, rinse, and sanitize the cutting surface and all the utensils (knives, etc.) every time you finish cutting raw meat, fish, and poultry. Household bleach is a good sanitizer. Use a capful (1 teaspoon) for each gallon of *cool* water.

Meat

The natural diet of cows is grass. Their whole anatomy and physiology is set up to graze and digest grass. Cows that are allowed to be raised and finished on grass have more omega-3 fatty acids (anti-inflammatory) in their fat. If instead cattle are fed corn or soy meal, they are not as healthy, often requiring antibiotics to cure their ills. So by far, the healthiest beef comes from meat products bearing the label "grass-fed."

Cows like to move around a lot to graze. It's better for them and better for the acreage they live on. Some ranchers offer their cattle hundreds of acres to roam, and it would be quite difficult to maintain all that land as "organic." So while it is certainly preferable to see the organic label guaranteeing that no hormones or antibiotics were given to the cattle, organic beef is not the only wholesome game in town. Another good label to shop for is "certified humane raised and handled," which means that cattle have sufficient space and shelter and must have access to fresh water at all times. They must not be fed hormones or antibiotics and must be treated and handled according to Humane Farm Animal Care standards. Claims are verified by third-party inspectors. See www.certifiedhumane.com. Again, checking out your local community may reveal some excellent sources (www.eatwild.com).

Nuts and seeds

Nuts and seeds are delicious whole foods that contain many beneficial nutrients: for example, almonds are rich in calcium; pumpkin seeds are high in iron. Nuts and seeds contain high-quality fats. The added calories and healthful fats can be useful for pregnant or nursing moms and active children. Buy organic nuts whenever possible.

The shell protects the nut or seed from heat, air, and light. Nuts in the shell are not very widely available, however. After you purchase raw, shelled nuts or seeds, it is a good idea to keep them in a sealed container in a dark, cold place. I keep mine in the freezer.

Nuts and seeds used in this book:
Almonds
Cashews
Hazelnuts
Peanuts
Pecans
Pine nuts
Sesame seeds
Sunflower seeds
Walnuts

KITCHEN STAPLES FOR WHOLE FOODS COOKING

Whole grains, beans, vegetables, and other whole foods can lack flavor on their own. They need salt, fat, spices, and other natural condiments to bring out their beauty—sort of like how the basic black dress needs the right pair of shoes.

Salt

I call salt the "Merlin" of the kitchen because when you understand how to use it, it can be quite magical in how it affects food. Salt is essential for bringing to life bland foods like grains, beans, and starchy vegetables. Eggs, fish, poultry, and meat don't taste right without salt. So the question is, what to buy?

A really good sea salt should have no other ingredients on the label other than salt—no iodine, anti-caking agents, or bleaches. Better to get your iodine in its natural form by including seafood and sea vegetables in your diet. In good sea salts you can usually see tiny flecks of gray or black. These are minerals. Celtic sea salt boasts that 16 percent of the salt is minerals. Another clue is moistness. Solar-evaporated sea salts with minerals still present have a slight moistness to them that is different from more processed bone-dry salts.

There are many excellent brands. One resource for salt worth mentioning is the Grain and Salt Society, purveyors of ingredients of uncommon quality (www.celticsalt.com).

Tamari, shoyu (natural brewed soy sauces), and miso have a high salt content and can be used to add salt and flavor.

Fats and oils

This has to be the most confusing ingredient to choose for most consumers. For many years, Americans were told that hydrogenated fats like margarine were better for us. Then polyunsaturated vegetable oils were given the big thumbs up as an answer to high cholesterol. We hear butter is good, then it is bad. So far no one has bashed olive oil. What is right?

In the Bastyr Nutrition Kitchen we prefer to cook with traditional fats and oils that have nourished populations for thousands of years. Historically, most cultures have cooked with saturated and monounsaturated fats, which are stable and less likely to go rancid. Following are our top picks for use in the whole foods cooking classes at Bastyr and for this book. Whenever possible, organic is preferred.

▶ **Butter** is stable, has fewer rancidity problems and maintains its integrity when cooked. Butter contains lauric acid, lecithin, and vitamins A and D. If the butter comes from cows allowed access to pasture, the possible presence of omega-3 fatty acids increases.

▶ **Coconut oil** is a saturated fat that is solid at room temperatures lower than 76°F. Its antifungal, antibacterial properties make it the perfect fat for rapidly decomposing foods in tropics; it is definitely not a local or seasonal food. Coconut oil has a long shelf life and is a very stable fat. It works nicely in baked goods and holds its integrity during medium temperature frying.

▶ **Cold-pressed extra-virgin olive oil** must be mechanically produced with no heat according to standards set by the International Olive Oil Council of Madrid. Extra-virgin oil comes from the first pressing of the olives and is only 1 percent acid or less. Olive oil contains monounsaturated fats, which are cholesterol-free and help with its stability. The deeper the color, the more intense the flavor will be.

▶ **Unrefined sesame oil** is a traditional oil from the Asian culture. It is 46 percent monounsaturated and 41 percent polyunsaturated. The poly part is protected from rancidity by sesamol, an antioxidant naturally present in the seed. This oil has a distinct, delicious flavor.

- **Cold-pressed, unrefined oils** are fine for salad dressings and recipes that have low or no heat involved. These oils are fragile, making them unsuitable for baking or high temperatures. They are also usually fairly expensive. Rapunzel and other food companies produce high-quality cold-pressed, unrefined oils from a variety of food sources; two examples are hazelnut oil and pumpkin seed oil.

For occasional high-heat cooking we use refined, expeller-pressed grape seed, safflower, sunflower, or peanut oil. I don't use or recommend refined vegetable oils for regular consumption. Most of these oils employee solvents to help extract the oil from the seed. The oil is filtered, refined with alkaline chemicals, steam deodorized at 460°F, and filtered again. This creates oil with few nutrients, no aroma, and very little taste that has a long shelf life.

Sweeteners

I prefer to use the following sweeteners in baked goods and desserts because they are a little less processed and have a more distinctive flavor. Further instructions for how to replace white sugar with natural sweeteners are described in Appendix A, "Have It Your Way: Flour, Fat, Milk, Sweetener, and Egg Substitutions" (page 273). Occasionally I use a bit of white sugar to sweeten something when I don't want the brown color of Sucanat or maple syrup, but the amounts are quite small.

- **Agave nectar** comes from the juice extracted from the cactuslike agave plant.

The juice goes through an enzymatic process to transform the polyfructose into simple fructose and dextrose syrup that is 1.4 times sweeter than sugar. It is less viscose than honey, doesn't crystallize, and has a two-year shelf life. Like honey and maple syrup, it retains moisture in baked goods. Agave nectar doesn't stimulate digestive insulin secretion as other sugars do. It comes in three grades—light, amber, and dark.

- **Unrefined cane sugar** is the juice that has been extracted from the sugar cane, then dehydrated and granulated. This product is less refined than white sugar because some of the mineral-rich molasses is not removed. It resembles brown sugar in appearance and taste, though it is slightly less sweet. Sucanat and Rapadura are brand names for organically grown, dehydrated sugar cane juice.

- **Barley malt** is a complex carbohydrate sweetener made from barley that has been soaked, sprouted, and cooked until the starches in the grain are broken down and converted into maltose. Barley malt is dark and thick like molasses and has a maltlike taste.

- **Brown rice syrup** is made from rice that has been soaked, sprouted, and cooked with a cereal enzyme that breaks the starches into maltose. Rice syrup has a light, delicate flavor and looks similar to honey but is less sweet. Both barley malt and brown rice syrup cool to a harder, crispier texture than other sweeteners.

- **Honey** is simply nectar collected from flowers by bees. It is then pumped out of the body into a hive cell. The cell is sealed and the honey ripens in three weeks. A strong hive will have one queen and a few hundred males and about 20,000 female workers. It is a very visible sweetener with a distinct flavor. Honey adds a moister quality to baked goods because it loses water to air more slowly than sugar. Do not give babies raw honey (see page 35).

▶ **Maple syrup** is made from the boiled sap of sugar maple trees. Forty gallons of sap (from nine trees) make 1 gallon of syrup. Maple syrup is available in two grades: A and B. Grade A is the lightest in color and flavor, good for topping pancakes and waffles. Grade B is made toward the end of the season and has a darker color, stronger flavor, and a slightly higher mineral content. It is nice for baking and flavoring.

Herbs and spices

To get the full aromatic flavor of herbs and spices, they need to be as fresh as possible. Fresh herbs release their essential oils when they are chopped or rubbed. The tender green plants not only add flavor, but also the nutrients that other green vegetables have. Most fresh herbs need to be added at the end of cooking time or used raw. Spices are usually the dried barks, buds, and seeds of plants. Buy them whole and grind them in a small electric coffee grinder before adding to food. The flavor will be about three times as intense as preground spices. Spices respond to heat and fat; it is good to toast or sauté them to increase their potency. If you do buy herbs and spices dried or preground, be sure to date the package. Throw them out and replace them after six to twelve months as they will have little flavor left.

Vinegars

A splash of high-quality vinegar can add sparkle to soups, salads, grains, and vegetables. There are many exciting choices: balsamic, rice, wine, and herb-infused vinegars. Try raw unfiltered apple cider vinegar to add friendly bacteria to your foods.

Sharing a Nourishing Meal

Once you have made a commitment to be conscious about where your food comes from and realize that eating whole foods will give you the most bang for your buck, you can begin to plan meals. Not only is it important to decide how to put dishes together to create a nutritionally sound, yet flavorful meal, it is also important to contemplate the setting of each meal. A child that sits with his siblings for a full 10 minutes to enjoy a bowl of warm oatmeal receives gifts that far outweigh the half a bagel wolfed down on the carpool ride to school. For meal plan ideas, see Appendix C, "Meal Plans Using Recipes from This Book" (page 285).

PLANNING THE WHOLE FOODS MEAL

I have taken many nutritional concepts from the East and the West and funneled them into some very simple structures that can be used to plan simple, whole foods meals. The proportion of nutrients sidesteps faddish diets and focuses more on the long-term needs of nourishing families living in current times. Here's the plan:

Vegetarian meal plan:
　　Whole grain
　　Legume or soy food
　　Vegetable (green)
　　Vegetable (any color)
　　Digestive (raw, fermented,
　　　　cultured, pickled, bitter)
　　B12 source

Meal plan with animal protein:

- Fish, eggs, chicken, pork, or beef
- Starchy vegetable or whole grain
- Vegetable (green)
- Vegetable (any color)
- Digestive (raw, fermented, cultured, pickled, bitter)

Vegetarian meal plan

The vegetarian meal features the combination of a whole grain and a legume. The combination provides the full array of amino acids so that protein needs can be met. The vegetarian plan also asks for a B12 source. B12 can only be reliably found in animal products. If you include dairy products or eggs as a part of your meal plan, you're covered. If you are vegan, you will need to include a regular supplement.

Meal plan with animal protein

The meal plan with animal protein has many of the same elements as the vegetarian meal plan. The main difference is that instead of legumes as a protein source, an animal protein is present. With the presence of animal protein no inclusion of additional B12 is necessary.

Another variation is "starchy vegetable or whole grain." I call this the "brown rice and steak" concept. The combination sounds rather unappealing, yes? That's probably because they are both pretty heavy foods. One student informed me that in Australia they say a good meal is meat and three vegetables. That makes sense to me. For a meal with animal protein, the denser the protein, the lighter the starch or grain can be. For example beef goes nicely with potatoes, fish with quinoa salad.

Commonalities of both plans

There are two vegetables in each meal plan, with one of them being a leafy green. This provides lots of nutrients and very few calories. The green vegetables are some of the more nutrient-dense, especially dark, leafy greens, so they are emphasized. A fruit can replace a vegetable in either menu structure.

Each meal plan asks for something called a "digestive." These are foods that are raw, pickled, fermented, or cultured. Most ethnic cuisines include these as a traditional part of the meal. Good examples are pickles, miso, sauerkraut, chutneys, yogurt, sour cream, slaws, and salsas.

If you are not eating foods that are enzyme-rich or that contain healthy bacteria, your digestive system may not be at peak performance. Without adequate healthy bacteria and enzymes, food sensitivities, indigestion, bloating, gas, constipation, diarrhea, belching, cramping, or bad breath may occur.

It is estimated that more than four hundred species of bacteria inhabit our digestive tracts, weighing up to 3½ pounds. It is important to have enough healthy bacteria to maintain optimal health. They help keep the intestines clean and free of parasites. They manufacture omega-3 fatty acids, vitamin K, and the B vitamins. In addition, healthy bacteria make up about 75 percent of our immune cells. This good bacteria is depleted by consuming prescription antibiotics, meat or dairy from animals fed antibiotics, or fluoride and chlorine in our water. It is important to replenish good bacteria on a daily basis by including foods such as miso and yogurt. The digestive foods not only add enzymes and friendly bacteria, they also add flavor and texture to any meal!

For some sample meal plans, see Appendix C, "Meal Plans Using Recipes from This Book" (page 285).

GOOD MARRIAGES

There are three whole foods couples that have been paired together in dishes for ages, with good reason. Whenever possible, keep these couples together in the same meal:

Whole grains plus legumes

Most grains are lacking the amino acid lysine, while most beans lack methionine. Together they provide all eight amino acids.

Nightshades plus dairy

The nightshade plants (tomato, potato, eggplant, and peppers) are high in alkaloids, which according to some may subtly remove calcium from bone. Dairy products have enough calcium to make a baby calf double its bone structure in six months—maybe more calcium than we smaller, slower-growing humans need. Perhaps the two have been kept together in dishes to balance their effects. Those who eat no dairy products need to be wary of eating too many nightshade vegetables.

Soy foods plus sea vegetables

The cultures that have utilized carefully crafted soy products in their diet have also included plants from the sea. Soy foods are thought to possibly be demineralizing and possibly lower thyroid function. Sea vegetables are amazingly rich in minerals, including iodine, which stimulates the thyroid. That may be why they're usually found together in traditional cuisines.

Setting the Table, Setting the Scene

In his stellar book *The Omnivore's Dilemma* (Penguin Press, 2006), Michael Pollan talks about cooking as a way of honoring the things we eat. It is a way of paying respect to the animals and plants that have been sacrificed to gratify our needs and of acknowledging the people who have produced the food so that we can enjoy it. Not only should we choose and cook our food thoughtfully, but it should be served and eaten with care, in a spirit of gratefulness.

SIT DOWN AND BREATHE

The way in which you eat is just as important as what you eat. For a comprehensive discussion of this, read *The Slow Down Diet* by Marc David (Healing Arts Press, 2005). Digestion is remarkably enhanced if one actually sits down, relaxes, and enjoys the food one is eating. When digestion is improved, metabolism and uptake of nutrients are improved. Often we stuff our faces with something, anything, in a hurry to get to the next task. This not only takes all of the joy out of eating, but also our bodies aren't relaxed enough to take in the nutrients and we are left hungry for more, which can lead to overeating. Consider not only what you consume at your meals, but *how* you consume it. It makes all the difference. Rule number one for children is that they need to sit down to eat their meals. Even fidgety children can be taught to do this. Insist on it.

EATING IS A VISUAL EXPERIENCE

We eat with all of our senses. In fact, when we look at or think about food, often our mouths begin to salivate, which begins the secretion of enzymes, preparing for the digestion of our food. Looking at colorful, artfully arranged food also nourishes our soul and inspires our own creativity. Give your children beauty. Setting the table can be an artistic task that very young children are capable of doing. Let them pick flowers to put in a vase, draw place mats, tie ribbons on napkins, and decide what color of candles would be just right. This makes them feel that their artistic sense is important.

It does not require a huge wallet to set a beautiful table. I attended an outdoor wedding where the couple had dyed sheets a beautiful lavender tone to fashion matching tablecloths. Mason jars with colored ribbons tied round the top held our beverages, and a potpourri of floral plates from the thrift shop with a cloth napkin that matched each completed the look. The food was fabulous too, but boy was our desire for the food heightened with the picture painted by those table settings. Even if the best you can do is order in some Chinese food to go with your leftover brown rice, take the time to set the table. Lay a bright tablecloth on the table. Eat on colorful plates.

Not only can beauty be offered by the table design, but the way in which food is arranged on the plate is also important. When you dine out at a fancy schmancy restaurant and a plate of gorgeous food arrives looking like a painting, everyone at the table says "AHHHH" before they have even tasted it. Arrange food on the plate in a pleasing way. Choose foods that have several colors so that your plate is not all brown and beige. Garnish! Many plain-Jane dishes can look like a million dollars with chopped green basil, white sour cream, orange zest, or a sliver of red pepper placed just right. Avoid the flowered shirt with plaid pants error and make sure that visually all of your dishes aren't confetti mixes. The eye needs solid colors alongside a more mixed palette, so serve vegetable beef stew with simple corn bread, not wild rice salad. Make sense? The stomach sees too and recoils from food that looks too busy or overwhelming.

SHARING THE MEAL

At a time when families are dealing with two careers, longer working hours, and children with numerous extracurricular activities, the fate of the shared, home-cooked family meal seems in jeopardy. But the fact is that many families juggle commitments in order to eat together as often as possible. We know that eating meals together increases the enjoyment of the meal, solidifies family bonds, and encourages communication about the day's activities among family members. If we are willing to make the extra effort required to share common meals, then our lives are richer as we break bread together, and family solidarity is built.

Children love the predictability of positive family events that occur daily, and shared family meals are very beneficial to them. Family dinner conversation helps expand children's vocabulary skills and increases success in learning to read.

Mealtime is also where children learn many of their social skills, including table manners and the art of conversation.

Much of family history relating to culture and race is passed on to children by parents at the dinner table. Food rituals may illuminate a family's ethnic heritage when traditional meals are served. These things help stabilize the child's identity as a member of a particular group. Studies show children who participate in regular family meals and other rituals have more emotional resilience to help them handle stress and chaos in other areas of life. Marooning babies in high chairs or plopping children in front of the tube while they are being fed robs them of what could be an otherwise enriching experience.

If all that doesn't convince you, consider this. The National Center on Addiction and Substance Abuse at Columbia University released a study showing teens who regularly dine with their families have a smaller chance of smoking, drinking alcohol, and using drugs; they also earn better grades in school. Set a firm foundation of shared meals when your children are young.

There are also nutritional advantages to eating meals together. Children who dine without parents or siblings eat fewer servings from the necessary food groups. This is partly true because when parents are present they can monitor a child's food intake, ensuring nutritional adequacy. Eating together also gives parents the opportunity to model good eating habits such as choosing healthy foods, chewing food well, and stopping when full.

Keep conversation pleasant at mealtime. If you have touchy subjects to bring up with your spouse or children, don't do it while dining. Unpleasant news will tighten the stomach, taking your mind off the enjoyment of eating, and the potential benefit of the meal will have been wasted.

MAKE CHANGES SLOWLY

The first step in changing the way you eat is to become conscious of what goes in your mouth. Think about what you are buying at the store. Does this product deserve your hard-earned money? What's in it? Are you buying it out of habit or because the label looks attractive? Think about your food as you prepare it, as you eat it. Where did this food originate? Will it add to your vitality? For a while observe what you eat without changing anything.

Take baby steps. Pick one thing to change, such as switching from white bread to whole grain bread or learning to eat the fast-cooking grain quinoa. Make small changes over weeks and months, and create the time and space needed to give your family deeply nourishing food a little at a time.

In order to modify old habits, you must feel an intrinsic desire to change. Many people change their diets for health reasons, often the result of a live or-die situation. But there are reasons to make changes before a crisis occurs. In my classes, I have heard many stories of children who are influencing their parents to eat better.

Sometimes people tell me they can't change their family's food because one family member simply won't have it. If you're in this situation, talk to the person who objects. Let them know that your motivation comes from love. Perhaps the reluctant family member will agree to one small change—for instance, having a fresh green salad every evening or maybe brown rice instead of white rice once in a while. Go slowly, slowly. Make changing what you eat a gentle, healing process. There is no rush. Lasting changes require the intention to evolve and a lot of patience.

Including Baby

When I was a brand-new mother, I had a 2-week old infant who liked to curl her fists up in tight balls and scream for several hours straight every evening. Her condition was relegated to the catchall term "colic." I worried about my breast milk being okay. I worried about her tiny digestive system. I was exhausted. I felt lost.

I chose to stay right with Grace during her long tirades. I held her, walked with her, bounced her and hung in there with her. When I could get past my own frustration, I would think about how difficult her transition must have been—from spirit to water baby in my womb to infant out in the world. It must be so hard to suddenly find your soul in a helpless, tiny body; a body that requires ingesting food and eliminating waste and wearing clothes and seeing lights and hearing noise. My heart would go out to this tiny child who seemed to be quite angry about making this transition. Often silent tears would slide down my cheek.

Most of us are searching for a sense of belonging and wanting to be loved all our lives. Giving food is one of our primary means of expressing love. There is nothing that can duplicate the reassurance that is conveyed when a baby's food is accompanied by the face, hands, voice, breast, or chest of a loving parent.

Start with the Best, the Breast

There is no better food you can give your newborn child than breast milk. Every year a new study appears discovering some nutrient or immunological factor found in breast milk that cannot be duplicated in the laboratory. Breast milk is designed by nature to help our species thrive. We have only begun to discover the myriad ways in which breast milk nourishes and protects both mother and child.

The first substance from the mother's breast after birth is thick liquid called colostrum. Colostrum does just what is needed immediately after birth: it helps the baby pass meconium, a substance in the baby's bowels that needs to come out before ordinary digestion can begin. Colostrum contains half of the immunological properties the newborn needs, ensuring immediate protection. Colostrum also decreases the absorption of bilirubin, reducing the chance of jaundice. The colostrum decreases as mother's milk matures in the ten to fourteen days following birth.

Breast milk is the only food your baby will need for six months. No extra water, juice, tea, or anything else is needed. Giving your baby a bottle of anything during the first few weeks of breastfeeding can cause nipple confusion. The breast and bottle require different sucking styles. Going from one to the other can result in frustration for mother and baby. When well-meaning relatives and friends encourage you to feed the baby something else, thank them for their advice. They may be unaware of the bonuses Mother Nature included in breast milk. (See "Breastfeeding Bonuses" on pages 29–30.)

In researching breastfeeding and breast milk, I was awed by one discovery: the biological communication established between mother and baby during nursing. The milk responds to the needs of the baby. Formula is static, but breast milk is not. It is a living, constantly changing food.

For example, the milk produced for a premature baby is different than the milk that comes in for a full-term infant. Breast milk even changes within a single feeding. The milk that comes out of the breast at the beginning of the feeding is more watery and satisfies thirst quickly. Toward the end of the feeding, the milk (called the hind milk) becomes richer in fat. Both are vital for baby.

The interaction between the baby's mouth and the mother's nipple signals the mother's body to increase certain nutrients in the milk if needed or restrict substances that appear dangerous. No human-made substance can duplicate the sensitive response of human breast milk. It's truly a miracle of nature.

The flavor of a woman's breast milk changes in response to what she has eaten. Formula is always the same. My good friend Susan, a post-partum doula, wonders if breastfed babies may respond to and accept new foods more readily as they have already been receiving a variety of tastes.

Cultural influences have led women to believe breastfeeding is a hardship. Even when women choose to nurse, their husbands, relatives, and friends may pressure them into early weaning because they are socially uncomfortable seeing the child and the mother's breast together. Social conditioning from advertisements by formula manufacturers and guidance by healthcare practitioners unfamiliar with the advantages of breastfeeding perpetuate this message. To raise children strengthened by breastfeeding requires the courage to ignore such outdated social stigmas.

If you are pregnant, contact your local La Leche League before the birth for additional support. This amazing international organization offers meetings, counseling, and literature that promote and support breastfeeding. The International Childbirth Education Association (www. icea.org) provides breastfeeding classes and early mothering support classes. Breastfeeding is not simply a matter of doing what you've seen many women in your family do before. We are isolated, no longer privy to the shared wisdom of the greater family. Natural ways often need to be explained and justified. Nevertheless, the resources to bolster our innate wisdom remain within our reach.

In instances where breastfeeding may not be possible, such as adoption, formula is the preferred second choice. Formula makers continue to try to mimic breast milk. Recently formula companies have begun adding long-chain fatty acids that are important for the development of brain and nerves, probiotics that help baby have healthy bowel flora, and beta-carotene, which is a precursor for vitamin A. These three components are naturally present in breast milk.

No single brand of formula appears to be any better than another. Most commercial formulas contain sugar, salt, and cheap fats such as refined oils. There is no evidence that soy formula is a better choice than cow's milk formula. Recent studies claim that there is no evidence showing decreased risk of developing allergies if soy formula is used. It is important that parents do not give their baby soy milk or soy beverages as a replacement for breast milk or formula.

Some companies are producing organic formula, which is a step in the right direction. Creative nutritionists, naturopaths, and other health-care practitioners have attempted to invent more lively homemade formulas that usually combine some form of milk with high-quality vitamin and mineral supplements. Sally Fallon's book *Nourishing Traditions* (ProMotion Publishing, 1995) has a couple of recipes for homemade formula that use raw milk and very high-quality fats. You might explore your community and see if there is a reasonable alternative that you and your health-care practitioner can agree upon.

Parents have an instinctual need to nourish their children. The premise of this book is based on that drive. I encourage you to make whatever changes you require, in your lifestyle or in your head, in order to experience the power of breastfeeding in your family. It is a part of womanhood we need to reclaim and pass on to the next generation.

FOODS FOR BREASTFEEDING MOMS

Sometimes women who have been very careful about their eating habits during pregnancy may forget, during nursing, that their bodies are still the source of nutrition for their child. Continuing good eating habits is important during breastfeeding, though sometimes harder to remember with a wee one in tow. The substances taken in by the nursing mother have a strong effect on the milk she produces.

For instance, the alcohol from a single drink consumed by a nursing mother appears in the breast milk in the same concentration as the mother's blood within 30 minutes. Nicotine ingested by a nursing mother who smokes cigarettes passes into the breast milk as well. Foods eaten by mom sometimes disagree with the breastfed child; especially high-dosage vitamins, supplements high in iron, artificial sweeteners, caffeine, heavily spiced foods, and occasionally dairy products. Colicky or fussy babies may improve if the nursing mother's diet is changed. Consult with your health practitioner or lactation counselor.

GREAT FOODS FOR BREASTFEEDING MOMS

Following are foods that have above-average levels of one or more of the following nutrients: protein, calcium, iron, folic acid, vitamin A, and vitamin C. Needs for these nutrients are elevated for nursing mothers.

WHOLE GRAINS	Quinoa, millet, sweet brown rice
LEGUMES	Chickpeas, pinto and navy beans, lentils, split peas, fermented soy foods
VEGETABLES	Anything dark green or orange
FRUITS	Oranges, lemons, berries, grapes, grapefruit, apricots, peaches, melons
NUTS AND SEEDS	Almonds, flaxseed, pine nuts, sesame and pumpkin seeds, walnuts
SEA VEGETABLES	Dulse, hijiki, arame
DAIRY	Organic yogurt, kefir, sour cream and aged cheeses from grass-fed cows if possible, fresh goat milks and cheeses
FISH	Wild line-caught fish, especially salmon and halibut. A good cod liver oil supplement can also be beneficial if access to wild fish is limited.
POULTRY	Free-range or pastured poultry and eggs from them
MEAT	Beef, lamb, and pork from humanely raised animals

Many women feel rushed to get rid of weight gained during pregnancy. The nursing period is not an appropriate time to diet. Dieting can compromise the mother's stamina and her milk supply. Environmental contaminants stored in the mother's body fat can be released into the milk if she loses over 4 pounds a month. Over-indulging in caffeine found in coffee, diet soft drinks, or over-the-counter drugs can result in an overstimulated baby. Breastfeeding as long as is comfortable, eating regular nutritious meals, and exercising are the most important factors in finding your way back into your old jeans.

The postnatal diet of tribal women throughout the world reveals a consistency of custom. Tribal diets focus on grain-vegetable soups, soft-cooked grains and vegetables, greens, and fish soups. Women drink large quantities of warm water and tea to encourage the flow of milk. At one time African women used a grain called "linga-linga" when nursing. The same grain used in Peru was called "quinoa." This grain has an especially high mineral content. Quinoa has been rediscovered and is now grown and sold in this country. I use this delicious grain in several recipes in this book. Another grain purported to aid in producing a good milk supply is sweet brown rice, a cousin of brown rice that has a higher fat content. This grain is often eaten in the form of mochi or amazake. To get those beneficial long-chain fatty acids into mother's milk, it is wise for mom to consume fish, eggs, poultry, and meat from healthfully raised animals, fermented full-fat dairy products, and nuts and seeds. Breast milk rich in beta-carotene as well as other vitamins and minerals requires mom to stock up on lots of dark green and orange vegetables and fruits. All signals point toward whole foods prepared in simple, satisfying ways.

Departing from cultural wisdom and returning to nutritional math, we see that the Recommended Dietary Allowances from the National Academy of Sciences propose that lactating women need an extra 70 to 80 grams of carbohydrates, 20 to 25 extra grams of protein, and 3 to 4 extra grams of fiber, as well as additional vitamins A, C, E, folate, and vitamin B12. By eating ample nutrient-dense whole foods, such as the ones listed in the following chart and used in the recipes in this book, meeting the additional requirements of nursing a child is simple and satisfying. Consuming foods that contain only empty calories, such as soft drinks, candy, pastries, and salty snack foods, will not add necessary nutrients to your milk, but will add inches to your hips! Keep these foods to a minimum.

High-quality breast milk doesn't require you to eat perfectly balanced, home-cooked meals each and every day. Nature provides plenty of leeway. Do your best to eat well and sensibly throughout the day, drink plenty of liquids, sleep when you can, and love yourself and your baby. Your milk will be blessed food.

BONUSES FOR BABY

▶ Colostrum, the first substance from the mother's breast, helps baby pass meconium, reduces the chance of jaundice, and supplies your baby with immunological properties.

▶ Breast milk contains antibodies to illnesses the mother has had, protecting baby against infections and reducing the risk of allergies.

▶ Your baby can easily absorb the iron in breast milk thanks to the presence of specialized proteins and vitamin C.

- Sucking at the breast enhances good hand-eye coordination and promotes proper jaw and teeth alignment.

- Breast milk naturally contains the long-chain fatty acids necessary for the development of brain and nerves, and beta-carotene, which is a precursor for vitamin A, an important vitamin for the healthy growth of cells.

- Probiotics (friendly bacteria) are naturally present in breast milk. These help babies develop healthy bowel flora and protect against infections. Their presence may help prevent eczema, hay fever, asthma, and food allergies

BONUSES FOR MOTHER

- After birth, immediate breastfeeding helps contract the uterus and reduce the risk of hemorrhaging.

- The hormone prolactin, which appears in the mother as a result of breastfeeding, is a relaxant. It is the hormone thought to help new moms feel "motherly."

- Breastfeeding aids in natural weight loss by using up an extra 500 calories a day.

- Studies show that breastfeeding for at least twenty-five months total during a mother's life reduces the risk of breast cancer (which now strikes one out of nine women in this country).

- Recent studies also show reduced risk of developing diabetes or becoming obese in mothers who breastfeed.

BONUSES FOR EVERYONE

- Breastfeeding gives mother and child a deep sense of security and love, and encourages physical closeness.

- Breastfeeding saves time and money. Formula feeding is very expensive!

- Outings with baby are easier using naturally hygienic breast milk: no bottles, no sterilizing, no heating things up, no formula, no fuss.

Starting Solids

Parenthood begins with extreme closeness. The baby is inside the mother. Even if children are adopted, infants are held against the chest of mom or dad more hours of the day than they are not. We let go of our children slowly, giving them nourishment of every sort to help them get on their feet. We want to provide the best food possible for them so that they can grow healthy bodies capable of fulfilling their dreams.

When we give babies separate meals made of factory-created food that is bland and full of fillers, we do them a disservice. This trains them to expect separate meals and prefer bland empty calories. Do your children a favor and introduce them to food with flavor. Let them recognize a variety of simply prepared whole foods as the familiar tastes that trigger "home" in their mind and bodies. Feed them what you eat. Make what you eat good enough to feed your baby.

WHEN

There is no hurry. Look at your baby, not the calendar. Your baby will let you know when it's time to start. When your baby is around 6 or 7 months old, he or she will give visible signs of readiness for solid foods. Here's what to watch for:

- **Can your baby sit up unattended?** Sitting upright is necessary for swallowing thicker substances.

- **Is your baby able to pick up small objects?** This indicates that babies can put a small bit of food in their mouths.

- **Does your baby show interest in what you're eating?** Mimicking your chewing, watching food go in your mouth, or even grabbing for your food are all signs of interest. At www.pregnancy.org they like to say that babies are ready for solids when they begin to intercept the food between your plate and your mouth!

- **If you offer baby a little taste of food, is she or he able to swallow it, or is it pushed back out with the tongue?** There is some practice involved here; the tongue-thrusting reflex is a physiological protection device that begins to diminish around 6 months of age. Note that some babies may gag or choke easily when first learning to eat. This is not abnormal. If this happens, try diluting the food so that it is more like thick milk or thin cereal.

- **Has your baby begun teething?** Some cultures regard the appearance of teeth as a sign of readiness for solid food.

Your baby's digestive enzymes are not fully developed for several years; however, at 6 months of age they are developed enough for experimental feedings. Starting solids too early has no benefits unless there are clinical signs that early feeding is critical. Baby's delicate digestive system may become unbalanced by introducing food too soon. Don't be fooled into thinking your baby will sleep through the night if you start giving solid foods. This is a myth in our "hurry up" society. Trust your observations. Wait until your child is physically prepared for solids before introducing them.

HOW

The introduction of solids is formative in how children establish their relationship with food. Make it a joyful occasion, not one approached with fear or trepidation.

Again, there is no hurry; the initial step is to introduce new tastes and textures. Your baby is still getting all the nutrition needed from breast milk or formula. The transition to solid food as the primary source of nutrition should be long and slow.

Once you feel your baby may be ready to experiment with solids, here's how to start:

- **Use one, simple, whole food, and begin with only a teaspoon of food.** A soft fruit or a cooked sweet vegetable is a good choice. Purée the food in a blender or processor, or mash with a fork. Start with a consistency that is similar to thick milk or thin cereal. Mix the food with a little breast milk or formula. This will give your baby a familiar taste. Choose a quiet time of the day that isn't a regular nursing or bottle time.

- **Talk to your baby about the food and the eating procedure.** Later your baby will be able to respond to cues such as "Open your mouth!" or "Bananas, Henry?" Don't coax baby into eating something that you wouldn't dream of eating. Tell the truth. Approach the task as a fun experiment.

- **Taste a little of the food yourself.** You can model eating for your baby. Homemade baby food will be much appreciated here. Offer the food from your finger or from a spoon, or allow baby to grab (messier for you, fascinating for baby).

- **Wait about three to four days before introducing another new food.** With each new food tried, be aware of allergic reactions such as rashes around the mouth or anus, diarrhea, skin reactions, lethargy, or unusual fussiness. Eliminate, for the time being, any food that causes a reaction and try it again when baby is several months older. See "Food Allergies and Intolerances" on pages 36–38 for information on common allergens and other potentially disruptive foods that should be avoided.

▶ **After several weeks of one small meal a day, you can increase to two small meals a day.** If your baby doesn't seem to enjoy eating solid foods, stop the feedings until baby is more receptive.

WHAT

Around the globe, a variety of foods are used as baby's first solid food. In Oceania babies are given prechewed fish, grubs, and liver. The Polynesians prefer a puddinglike mixture of breadfruit and coconut cream. Inuit babies are started on seaweed and seal blubber, while Japanese health-care providers recommend a thin rice porridge, eventually made thicker and topped with dried fish, tuna, tofu, and mashed pumpkin.

In our culture, whether your baby's first solid food should be a cereal, a fruit, or a vegetable is debated. If your child is labeled underweight, a health-care practitioner or a relative may encourage you to start with cereals. Others recommend starting baby on fruits and vegetables because they digest more easily and quickly than grains. There is some thought that grains are too complex, and introducing cereals too early can give babies digestive trouble or lead to allergies. I feel this is largely due to the overuse of highly refined, flaked baby cereals and grain fillers (such as modified corn starch and flour) added to jarred food. Adverse reactions are less likely if freshly made grains are served. It is reasonable to suggest that we may be exacerbating the infant's sensitivity to foods in this culture by early use of antibiotics, disinter-

est in breastfeeding, and other choices (see "Food Allergies and Intolerances" on pages 36–38).

You may notice that other cultures include fats and proteins as part of baby's beginner foods, whereas American practitioners tend to guide parents toward carbohydrates as starter foods. I haven't provided hard and fast rules about which foods to introduce when. I believe that starting solids must take into account the food culture that the parents come from and the current health of the infant. Collect information from various sources and choose what makes sense to you. I feel that if parents serve beginner foods that stay within the realm of simple, whole, fresh foods, avoiding the list of "'Not-So-Good' Food for Infants" on pages 34–35, the dangers are minimal.

Start with puréed fruits and vegetables

A safe plan is to serve simple fruits and vegetables for the first few weeks of starting solids. My favorite beginning fruits and vegetables are applesauce, avocados, bananas, carrots, sweet potatoes, peas, and winter squash. Begin with a mashed fruit or vegetable that is the consistency of thick milk or thin soup. Babies will let you know what their favorite foods are.

Begin to add nonallergenic cereal grains

After a few weeks of serving puréed fruits and vegetables, you might try cereal. The least allergenic grains, the ones I recommend starting with, are brown rice, sweet brown rice, quinoa, and millet. For instructions on how to make your own Toasted Whole Grain Baby Cereal, see page 74. Begin with grain cereal that is the consistency of thick milk or thin soup.

Include beginner fats and proteins

After a month or two of baby's successful eating, you might begin adding some easily digested, high-quality proteins and fats. Just a teaspoon or two daily is fine. There are many good choices. Soft-cooked egg yolks or organic plain whole milk yogurt are two. Eggs from pastured or free-range hens are best. Excellent yogurts should only have organic whole milk and a variety of live cultures in the ingredients list. Putting a dab of organic butter in cooked vegetables or grains that you serve to baby is another way to begin adding fats. Or purée vegetables and grains for baby with homemade soup stock that has been made with bones (see "Take Stock" on page 136).

Homemade vs. commercial

Be aware that many commercial baby food manufacturers replace real food with thickening agents (like flour or starches) in their products. This helps their profits but does little to nourish your baby. Commercial baby foods are very high priced compared to similar regular foods, especially foods such as baby food juices and applesauce. Baby food manufacturers encourage a mystique about their products, making parents believe that commercial baby food has special properties that can't be duplicated in your own kitchen. This is clearly untrue. Why pay high prices for nutritionally inferior food for your baby? Parents can easily prepare safe, nutritious, and economical foods for their infants at home.

Certainly occasional organic jarred food can be used for baby as a convenience, but it definitely lacks freshness and flavor. Instead of training baby to eat bland food, help him develop a repertoire of flavors and textures of food your family regularly enjoys. This makes the transition to eating family meals seamless. Adaptations for how to take part of the meal that the rest of the family is eating and mash some for baby are given at the end of most recipes in this book. Any time you see "*For babies 6 months and older*" at the bottom of a recipe, an idea follows for taking part of the dish and making food for a baby just starting solids. Usually a tablespoon or two of food is adequate for a baby just starting to eat. Amounts can increase with baby's size and desire.

Safety tips for homemade baby food

▶ Before using any equipment to prepare baby food, wash it with hot water and soap.

▶ Never serve your baby food hot off the stove. Room temperature or slightly warm is fine. Hungry baby, but cereal's too hot? Stir it with an ice cube for quick cooling.

▶ Microwaving sometimes heats food unevenly. This can create "hot spots" in baby's food or in a bottle that can burn your baby's mouth. Use caution if microwaving or avoid it.

▶ If you've made a large batch of food, remove a small portion to a separate dish to serve your baby.

▶ Discard leftover food that has had spoon-to-mouth contact.

▶ Store leftovers that have not had spoon-to-mouth contact in the refrigerator and use within two or three days.

- Freeze extra puréed food in ice-cube trays. Frozen cubes can then be stored in the freezer in plastic bags. For a quick meal, place a cube or two of frozen food in a small dish and heat in a covered pan of boiling water. Use frozen baby food within four weeks.

- Store ground grains for cereals in sterile jars in the refrigerator or freezer (canning jars or jelly jars work fine).

- Label all stored food.

Should I give my baby iron supplements or iron-fortified cereal?

My first response to this question is "How could we have survived as a species so long if babies can't thrive without artificial supplements?" Many parents are encouraged to give their baby iron supplements or iron-fortified cereals starting at around 6 months. I never blindly accepted that I needed to supplement my baby's diet with iron or other nutrients. Ferrous sulfate, the most common iron supplement, is poorly absorbed and can cause indigestion and constipation. The type of iron used in commercial baby cereals is one of the least absorbable. It is used because it sticks to the flakes and won't discolor the cereal.

Your baby was born with a good store of iron that came from the mother during pregnancy. This is one reason why hematocrit levels are monitored in pregnant women and women are encouraged to increase their iron intake during pregnancy. During the past century, it became common practice to clamp the cord about 10 seconds after the baby's shoulders were delivered. However, there has been little scientific research to justify such rapid clamping. Just a 2-minute delay in clamping a baby's umbilical cord can boost the child's iron reserves and prevent anemia for months. This was reported by nutritionists at the University of California, Davis from a 2005 study done in Mexico City, though I was aware of this fact over a decade ago thanks to information from savvy midwives.

Breast milk contains a small amount of absorbable iron to meet baby's needs. Babies can absorb up to 50 percent of the iron in breast milk, but only 4 percent of the iron in fortified formula. Vitamin C in breast milk increases the absorption of the iron. Lactoferrin and transferrin, two specialized proteins in mother's milk, regulate the iron supply to baby. As long as the mother was not anemic during pregnancy and the umbilical cord was not cut too early, the breastfed baby should have adequate iron for the first year of life.

Around 6 months, when solid foods are introduced, your baby begins to get iron and other nutrients from sources other than breast milk or formula, or stores accumulated in utero. With the transition to a simple, whole foods diet, most babies need no supplements. Serve your baby whole grain cereals, freshly prepared fruits and vegetables, and protein from good vegetable or animal sources, giving your baby naturally occurring iron in the proportions his or her body needs. For extra iron, add sea vegetables to baby's diet and use cast-iron cookware.

"NOT-SO-GOOD" FOOD FOR INFANTS

A true food allergy is a reaction by the immune system to a specific protein. Peanuts, cow's milk, and egg whites are the most common, but fish, shellfish, soy, and wheat are also problems for some people. If you suspect a food allergy or have a family history of food allergies, it would be prudent to forgo the common allergens listed above.

See "Food Allergies and Intolerances" on pages 36–38 for more on this topic.*

▶ **Caffeine** is a stimulant, not a food. Soft drinks and cocoa not only contain sugar; they have as much caffeine as coffee. Caffeine can cause elevated blood sugar and stimulate the heart and lungs. This kind of stimulation can be detrimental for babies.

▶ Avoid **chemical additives** such as aspartame, saccharin, Splenda (sucralose), other chemical sweeteners, BHT, artificial flavors and colors, MSG, nitrates and other additives. The effect of chemical additives on adults is not entirely known. There certainly can be no benefit to introducing chemicals to your baby's immature system. Read labels.

▶ **Cow's milk** given in a bottle or cup as a replacement for formula or breast milk is not appropriate for babies under 1 year of age. It can cause bleeding in the intestines that is difficult to detect, resulting in iron-deficiency anemia.

▶ **Honey** and **corn syrup** sometimes contain botulism toxins in amounts that are detrimental to infants under 1 year of age. Barley malt or brown rice syrup can be substituted for honey or corn syrup.

▶ Heavily **salted foods** can stress baby's immature kidneys. Salted food can also interfere with your baby's natural appetite. Sufficient salt (sodium) is readily available in many foods in their natural state. Adding sea salt to cooked foods that will later be served to baby is fine. This is a very negligible amount. Avoid processed packaged foods, which often contain large amounts of sodium to give the lifeless food flavor, and salty snack foods such as pretzels or potato chips.

▶ A prime source of empty calories, **sugar** has almost no nutritive value. Eating large amounts of sugary foods can displace more nutritional foods, resulting in vitamin and mineral deficiencies. Refined sugar consumption, including corn syrup, fructose, high-fructose corn syrup, and cane sugar, has been linked with tooth decay, heart disease, atherosclerosis, diabetes, obesity, learning difficulties, and behavior problems. Why let your baby develop a taste for it?

Foods Babies Often Choke On

To prevent accidents, never give the following foods to babies under 1 year of age. When trying any new snack, be sure that your baby is close by so that you can be quick to help if a problem develops. Have children sit down when eating, as choking most often occurs when children are walking or running.

Apple chunks or slices
Dry cereal
Grapes
Hard candy
Hard cookies
Hot dogs
Meat chunks
Peanut butter or other nut butter sandwiches
Popcorn
Potato chips
Raw carrot sticks or slices
Rice cakes
Whole nuts and seeds
Whole or unseeded berries

---

* *Some may wonder why carrots didn't make this list. The incidence of nitrate poisoning from carrots and other vegetables is very rare and is typically traced to ground water contamination from private wells. Babies over 6 months of age have a digestive system mature enough to handle nitrates.*

Food Allergies and Intolerances

Some long-standing foods in the human diet, like wheat and eggs, have recently become suspect of causing a wide range of symptoms. Following is a brief overview of this trend and some suggestions on how to take preventative action.

FOOD ALLERGIES

A food allergy is a reaction by the immune system to a specific protein in food. The diagnosis can be confirmed by a skin or blood test. The allergy can be expressed in a variety of ways, everything from rashes, vomiting, or wheezing to anaphylactic shock (in rare cases). A true food allergy is actually quite rare (6 to 8 percent of children under 1 year and 2 percent of the adult population) although nearly 20 percent claim they have a food allergy. When children are suspected of having a food allergy, usually a parent or family member suffers from the same problem. If you discover your child has a food allergy, the food needs to be avoided. Except in severe cases the child may outgrow the allergy by 2 to 3 years of age, and the food can be tried again with a health practitioner's supervision.

If members of your family have food allergies and you feel your baby may be at risk for developing them, there are a few things you can do.

Breastfeeding is recommended because of its many beneficial effects. Aim for exclusive breastfeeding for six months and continue breastfeeding for the first year. There are special formulas that may be useful in preventing allergies as well; check with your health care practitioner.

In some recent studies babies with a positive skin test or blood test for a food allergy, expressed as eczema, showed a great improvement when given the gentle probiotic Lactobacillus GG supplement. The results of the study (April 2005, *Allergy*) are promising and support the idea that good digestion is imperative for preventing food allergies and intolerances.

When you introduce solid foods at 6 months old, start with low-allergy foods such as rice, millet, squash, sweet potato, and pear. Wait to introduce cow's milk, egg whites, soy, fish, and wheat until the child is 12 to 18 months old. Children whose parents are allergic to these foods should wait until 2 to 3 years old to be introduced to them. If there is a high risk of peanut or shellfish allergy, delay trying these foods until the child is 3 years old and then do so with supervision from your health care provider. Do not avoid these foods unless there is a clear reason for doing so.

FOOD INTOLERANCES OR SENSITIVITIES

A food intolerance or sensitivity is not a true food allergy. This diagnosis is more common, yet it is not well understood why the intolerances occur. The skin and blood tests that can be used to determine an allergy to a food protein cannot reveal the more subtle intolerance to a food. Symptoms of food intolerance are quite varied. They include skin reactions such as eczema, breathing problems such as runny or stuffed nose, and for some people headaches, muscle pain, and general irritability. The most common way of determining food sensitivity is to go on a diet that avoids all of the likely foods and then gradually add the foods slowly to determine which ones are causing the symptoms.

If you find that your child has a food intolerance, by noticing that symptoms improve when certain foods are avoided, here are a few things to consider.

Babies are born with a fairly primitive immune system. How the immune system develops and reacts to new foods is influenced in part by gut flora. Things that destroy the friendly bacteria in our gut include antibiotics (taken directly or from our food supply), chlorinated water, and stress. In our ultraclean society we sometimes don't develop enough friendly bacteria in our gut to aid with digestion and support the immune system, potentially making us more hypersensitive to foods.

Breastfed babies have the benefit of receiving the friendly bacteria present in mother's milk. Another way to improve gut flora is to include small amounts of yogurt that contains live cultures with baby's food (just a half teaspoon will do). Also, allowing baby to interact with nature, other children, and tame animals exposes them to a variety of bacteria, strengthening their immune system. This was borne out by a study that uncovered that children raised on farms tend to have stronger immune systems than city kids (*The Lancet*, October 6, 2001).

If your child has recently taken a round of antibiotics it might be prudent to follow it with a round of probiotics to reestablish his or her intestinal flora. The antibiotic kills all bacteria—harmful and friendly—leaving the gut void of the cultures it needs to properly digest food. Check with your health-care provider to find the right probiotic food or supplement to include in your child's diet.

Some food sensitivities may simply be a symptom of poor digestion. Improve your children's ability to digest their food by making sure that they eat at regular times and sit calmly while they eat, chewing well. Include some cultured or fermented foods in their diet such as high-quality yogurt, miso soup, or pickles to give the friendly bacteria in their digestive system a boost.

Food sensitivities may also be reflective of overdoing certain foods. Because of the overproduction of soy, corn, and wheat crops in our country, food producers have found ways to stretch their profits by adding cheap oils, sweeteners, starches, and fillers made from highly refined versions of these foods. As a result they are in virtually every processed food product that we purchase. This certainly can lead to consuming the same foods, in unwhole, unfresh forms, over and over and over. Read labels, eat a variety of grains and legumes, and avoid refined forms of soy, corn, and wheat.

Cow's milk is a common food sensitivity for young children. Most often the symptoms are skin or sinus related. Sometimes babies and young children with frequent runny noses or ear infections improve their symptoms after eliminating dairy from their diets. Avoiding pasteurized, homogenized cow's milk and focusing on fermented and cultured dairy products may be one solution. These products have some of the more problematic proteins and sugars broken down by friendly bacteria, making the food easier to digest. Some parents have good luck with serving raw cow or goat milk in which some of the helpful enzymes are still present. If you choose to do this, you will want to know the farmer (and the cow) well and purchase the milk as fresh as possible. Raw milk is fragile, and when it has to be transported and stored it is susceptible to contamination. Be wary of replacing everything that comes from a cow (milk, cheese) with products that come from the soybean (see page 10).

Take time to contemplate how your child is doing on an emotional level. Food intolerances are more common in children who are under stress, either emotionally, physically, or both.

Once their life becomes more balanced, the sensitivity may go away

Food sensitivities are a snapshot representing a period of time, not a life sentence. Some children simply outgrow food intolerances as their bodies get larger and more mature.

Gluten intolerance, or celiac disease, is a much more serious problem. This is a genetic disorder where symptoms may include diarrhea and weight loss. Those affected suffer damage to the villi in the intestines when specific grains are eaten, especially wheat, barley, and rye. Visit www.celiac.com, where there are many formulas for creating gluten-free flours for baking in the recipe section, or use the simple replacement formula found on page 273 in this book.

The good news is that this book is actually very friendly for families that have food allergies or sensitivities! Besides using a wide variety of grains, legumes, and nuts, this book provides simple instructions for how to make substitutions in "Have It Your Way: Flour, Fat, Milk, Sweetener, and Egg Substitutions" on page 273.

Expanding the Diet of the Older Baby

Babies who have been eating puréed vegetables, fruits, and cereals for a few months may be ready for more food choices. Ground nuts and seeds, the smaller beans (lentils and peas), soft-cooked fish, and meat can be added to your baby's diet. As your baby begins to take less breast or bottle milk, these new foods fill in the nutritional spaces. Occasional small quantities (a teaspoon or less) of sea vegetables can provide additional vitamins and minerals for your baby.

With the addition of a few new foods to baby's diet, moms, dads, and other caretakers will have no problem finding items from their wholesome meals to offer baby. My child became less interested in puréed foods around 11 months old and wanted foods she could pick up herself. This is where the list of finger foods that follows can come in handy.

Food ideas for older babies are given at the end of most recipes in the recipe section of this book. Any time you see "*For babies 10 months and older*" at the bottom of a recipe, an idea for taking part of the dish and making food for a baby follows. Babies who have been eating solids for several months can be served about one-third to one-half cup of food at a sitting.

IDEAS FOR FINGER FOODS

Around the time babies start walking, they become interested in picking up food with their own hands and feeding themselves. Use your judgment about what your baby can handle. Keep the food soft enough that it could be "gummed" and stay within earshot. These snacks are generally okay for babies 1 year old and up:

BAKED OR ROASTED VEGETABLES

Red potatoes

Squash

Sweet potatoes

BLANCHED OR STEAMED VEGETABLES

Broccoli

Carrots

Cauliflower

Edamame

Peas

Zucchini

DRIED FRUIT
(soak in water to make it softer)

STEAMED FRUIT

Apples

Pears

RIPE FRUIT

Avocados

Bananas

Mangoes

Melons

Nectarines

Peaches

Plums

BEANS
(make sure they are well cooked)

NORI
(tear into small pieces)

WHOLE GRAIN CRACKERS
(read labels carefully)

WHOLE GRAIN NOODLES
(cut in pieces)

FISH
(small, well-cooked pieces; remove tiny bones)

TOFU
(cut in cubes)

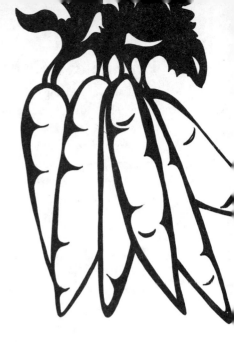

Raising Healthy Eaters

When I would pick my daughter up from kindergarten, she usually wanted to stay and play until all the other children were gone, so I often watched the children in her class.

One year, there was a mischievous elflike boy named Jonathan in her class. He would run and hide when the teachers wanted him to come in. He would dart outside without putting his shoes on. Once, he sat down in the mud. He delighted in testing boundaries. I formed opinions about him. I thought of him as a "handful." One time I thought that they probably needed an extra teacher just for Jonathan.

I was invited to school to make lunch with the children one Friday. I brought pinto beans, whole wheat tortillas, brown rice, avocados, salsa, cheese, and lettuce and proceeded to make the fixings for a burrito lunch. The kitchen is near the classroom, and the children were welcome to help. Some would stop by and assist for 10 or 15 minutes and then drift on to play.

One child stayed right by my side all morning—Jonathan. He mashed beans, peeled avocados, and squeezed lemons. He followed instructions and was not only helpful, but gleeful about making guacamole. I was humbled. This little elf reminded me about respect, a word that means "to look again." Children are remarkably malleable. As soon as we label them, thinking that we can predict their behavior in some way, they surprise us by doing the opposite. Children invite us to experience the world with awe. They remind us that we do not know what will happen next. Don't presume that Fred will never eat lima beans and Judy will always want her apple peeled. Stay open to the little bits of magic lurking in every corner.

Maybe you'll discover an elf in your kitchen.

Parents as Role Models

What are your eating habits like? Children model themselves after their parents. The tiniest baby notices every move you make, every forkful that goes into your mouth. A well-intentioned friend I once knew carefully prepared homemade, whole grain baby cereals and organic purées for her baby while she and her husband dined on fast-food takeout and doughnuts. As soon as the child could walk and grab, the baby wanted what mommy and daddy were eating. As much of a cliché as it may sound, the primary job parents have is to set a good example. This gravitation toward the parent's eating habits will wax and wane. Children hit many rebellious stages where rejecting whatever parents do is the course of the day, but the underlying patterns they were shown about food remain. Here are four suggestions to help you become models of healthful eating habits for your children.

BECOME AWARE OF HOW YOU FEEL ABOUT FOOD

What are some of your favorite foods? What kind of feelings would surface if you could never have them again? What are some foods you hate? Do you know why you hate them? Many hated foods have their roots in our childhood. How closely have you modeled your parents' eating habits? Are vegetables something you're supposed to eat or do you really like them? Is sugar something you deserve if you've been good, had a bad day, or finished your plate?

These unspoken attitudes are clearly transmitted to children. We may not be able to change our feelings about food just because we become parents, but we can become aware of how we think, feel, and act about various food choices. Take stock. Figure out which attitudes you may be

unconsciously acting out, and decide if they are beneficial to pass on to your children.

SET BOUNDARIES ABOUT FOOD CHOICES AND MEALTIME

Many child-rearing books encourage parents to set gentle but firm boundaries with children to help them feel safe and protected. This concept applies to eating as well. Be sure to set boundaries that you can follow too. It's not fair to have a strict "no ice cream" policy and keep pints in the freezer just for the parents. Helpful boundaries for feeding children that offer ways to instill nutritious eating habits with minimum stress are outlined in "Setting Boundaries" on pages 44–46.

Setting boundaries to provide security also includes creating fun rituals. I sometimes listen to *This I Believe* on NPR. Recently a woman with five children who was going through medical school and a divorce talked about "Sweet Fridays," a ritual she learned about in the Republic of Georgia and brought to her family. Every Friday afternoon they invite the neighbors to come have cake in their home. She says, "It is not just the extravagant sweetness of the afternoon or the regularity of the occasion that qualifies this as a tradition. It is the attention to detail and the anticipation—always a tablecloth (if maybe not ironed) and always a centerpiece (pine boughs, a pumpkin, or some flowers from the garden). My children and I fantasize about the event all week long. And then, walking home from school on Fridays we round up everyone we pass." Having your own food rituals can provide stability to ride the ups and downs of family life.

TAKE TIME TO EDUCATE AND SPREAD THE JOY

As soon as your children can talk, you can begin to communicate information about food. Try not to nag them about how they need to eat specific (invisible) micronutrients, such as having to drink their milk to get enough calcium. This can create fear or invite stubbornness about eating. You can offer brief reasons for why you don't want them to eat certain foods, such as "This soda has things in it that your body can't use, let's buy something else to drink." With school-age children you can reflect back to them how it seems that they act or look when they've eaten foods with a poor nutritional profile. Preteens can be very influenced by how better food keeps their skin clearer. Gently help children notice how they feel when they have skipped meals or eaten too much. Just as often let your children see your appreciation of a ripe summer peach, your pleasure as you dip into just-made guacamole, savor grilled halibut, or enjoy mouthwatering home-made Apple Pie with Butter Crust (page 257). Infect them with the pleasure and enjoyment of eating fresh, wholesome food.

I have the pleasure of performing regularly with The Edge, an improvisational theater group. One of the pillars of improvisational acting is practicing the "Yes and" rule—where every idea, good or bad, is greeted enthusiastically and added on to. It is a great life lesson. Practice it in your home, around food. Instead of turning away from what may be disliked or unfamiliar, foster adventurism.

Take your children shopping with you. As your children get older, let them play detective in the store: present them with a challenge, such as finding a jar of tomato sauce that's organic or juice without high-fructose corn syrup. Encourage your children to help you cook by slowing down and allowing for the longer preparation time necessary to include a willing participant. Check the section called "Involving Your Children in the Kitchen" on pages 51–52 for ideas. As children get older, talk to them about how the more nutritious foods can help them attain some of their desires (clearer skin, more stamina in the second half of the soccer game, better concentration). They may not accept everything you tell them, but occasionally they will see and feel results, and that can be powerful!

LET GO

Learning to bend rules, be flexible, and let go are perhaps the most important lessons of parenting. Relaxing around birthday parties and other social gatherings where junk foods are offered is a lot easier if you know what's served at home is nutritionally sound. A woman in one of my classes proudly announced that she bakes no-sugar, whole wheat birthday cakes for her child to take to parties instead of allowing the child to share the cake being served. Rules that cause a child to feel uncomfortable in social situations are unnecessary and can be more unhealthy than sugary cake. Watch out for setting up too many "forbidden fruits." Highly restricted foods may become irresistible and take on more power than they warrant.

We need to respect our child's food preferences and choices to a certain extent. Children have a lot to teach us. Have you ever had the experience of offering food to your child all day, having the offer repeatedly refused, then realizing later that he or she was coming down with a cold? The child's intuition not to eat at that time was right on the nose. My child used to regularly come home from a birthday party and ask to eat nori strips. How did she know that one of the consequences of too much sugar is that it creates a mineral debt in the body, and that seaweed contains more minerals than any other food? Many children intuitively select what their bodies need.

Children have a lot to teach us about simplicity, too. You may notice young children tend to dislike casseroles or salad dishes containing many different ingredients. They'd rather have simpler, plainer food. A child's preferences can set a good example for parents to follow.

Be a model, not a critic. It would be so much easier to glibly express platitudes and warnings to our children as we merrily indulge in our addictions and whims. Let's let our children see us be grateful for and eat nourishing food with the knowledge that whole foods make us healthier on many levels.

Setting Boundaries

All children need and want boundaries. When we set boundaries, we are saying we care about them. When they're infants, we keep our children very close to our bodies. With each year we give them a little more space to roam and a few more choices to make, even as we continue to provide limits to protect them. This concept also applies to food. An infant is given the simple security of breast or bottle. Preschoolers may be able to clearly tell you if they would prefer an apple or a rice cake. A 10-year-old can help plan the dinner menu. Keep the choices simple and limited for the younger ones while allowing older children more input.

PROVIDE EXCELLENT CHOICES

Stock your cupboards and your refrigerator with fresh, healthful, whole foods products. When all of the food in your home is food you feel good about serving your children, you can eliminate many battles around eating. It won't matter what your child chooses or asks for. You can't expect to keep junk foods and sugary items around the house and not be badgered, especially if your child sees you eating those items.

If you pack a lunch box for your child, make sure the choices inside are good ones. When there are candies and soft drinks and such in the lunch box, children often eat or drink the sweets and skip the rest; however, if each item is substantial and nutritious, you don't need to worry about what your child eats or doesn't eat.

For a very convincing story on just how much of an impact food can have on the health and behavior of young people, check out www.michaelfieldsaginst.org/programs/food/case_study.pdf. The online file gives a report on the school lunch program at Central High School in Appleton, Wisconsin, where upgrading the quality of the food had a dramatic, positive effect on the students.

HONOR MEALTIMES

Commit to sharing at least one common meal with your whole family each day. The family meal is not only a time for nourishment, but also an opportunity for children to experience social education. Emphasize social patterns with rituals: lighting candles, saying a verse, setting the table with care, serving food a certain way. Consider keeping a regular time for the evening meal. For some pretty convincing reasons why sharing meals benefits children, check out "Sharing a Nourishing Meal" on pages 19–21.

WHAT'S SERVED IS SERVED

Do not make the mistake of preparing a separate meal for your child. Let each person receive some portion of each dish that has been prepared. If your children refuse to eat one of the foods, encourage them to sample one or two bites, and then say no more. A child sometimes refuses food because of appearance and then appreciates it when tasted. I like what my friend Kathy Coffey uses as a simple dinnertime rule for her two boys: "Eat something of everything, all of something."

Children who refuse to eat anything on the plate should be asked to excuse themselves and told that no other food will be served until breakfast or until 8 p.m. that night or whatever seems reasonable according to your child's age. If they come whining for food later, consider offering the leftover dinner. One way to avoid the "untouched meal" syndrome is to make sure that each meal has a sure winner: a simple side dish you know your child will like (see "Include a winner at every meal," which follows).

Incorporate a "no-critics-at-the-table" rule. Teach your children that it is inappropriate for any participant at the table to offer harsh and cruel reviews such as, "I hate everything!" or "This looks awful!" Remind such reviewers that their words are unkind and ask them to excuse themselves from the dinner table. Suggest alternative ways for expressing dislike of the dinner menu. Let them know they will be welcome at dinner the next night, where they can practice being more considerate. I find that children who help prepare the food for a meal are less critical at the dinner table.

INCLUDE A WINNER AT EVERY MEAL

Children usually like simple food and will sometimes refuse foods that have several ingredients. Let your child learn to appreciate simple foods by regularly offering them. There is nothing wrong with plain carrots, plain baked squash, plain noodles, or plain brown rice. Sometimes it takes an elaborate salad to please me, whereas a 5-year-old is happy with sliced cucumbers or shredded lettuce without dressing. When planning meals, include something simple that you're certain your child will like, even if it's just a side dish of sliced bread or carrot sticks or applesauce.

DON'T BRIBE, REWARD, OR PUNISH WITH FOOD

Offering or withholding sweets or any other "forbidden" food in exchange for good behavior is not a good idea. This sets up hard-to-reverse psychological attachments to food. Food is something you eat in order to get energy to play and to grow. Eating is a primal need that can be a joyful daily ritual. Find an arena besides the dinner table to work out power struggles with children.

Avoid tension and save money by not serving desserts every day. Save home-baked goodies occasionally for snacks or special occasions and avoid constant negotiation about dessert. Let's say doughnuts are the favorite food, and you, the parent, feel it is not in the child's best interest to serve them routinely. Instead of forbidding doughnuts or using them as a trade for finishing math homework (bad idea), set a schedule and stick to it. Doughnuts can be the Saturday breakfast treat. That way there is a rule in place, and when battles arise you can simply restate the rule.

BE FIRMER DURING STRESSFUL TIMES

When your child is ill or has an infection, remove foods known to be stressful to the system. Enforce your greater knowledge and forbid candy, soda, salty, and fried foods. Bodies recover from illnesses much quicker when they are given nourishing foods that are easy to digest, such as soups and broths. Explain what you're doing in a way your child will understand.

Holidays can be stressful, too. Most holidays we celebrate seem to center around sugar. Provide some reasonable rules to curb the heavy intake of sugary foods at these times. When my child was given a bag of candy at a birthday party, we let her choose one piece a day to eat. This worked, as she sometimes lost interest after a few days. If your child is over age 8, let them help create the rules.

LISTEN TO YOUR CHILD

Children have good instincts. If they are being offered excellent foods, they will eat exactly what their body needs. Children create a balanced diet over many days rather than within one day. Watch. Often they will hit all the food groups during the week. To eliminate worry about sufficient nutrients, offer a variety of whole foods steadily and consistently.

But children's wonderful intuition can go awry. Refined sugar and flour, foods with chemical additives, and highly salted foods can be addictive, and excessive amounts of them can mar your child's natural good judgment. When heavy doses of unnatural foods have been consumed and children begin expressing cravings for more, parents need to intervene and restore balance.

When setting boundaries remember to respect your child's individuality. Children who are very sensitive to certain foods may benefit from firmer boundaries. Others may show so little interest in food that you may not need to set many limits. Some children are natural vegetarians, while others may want or need some animal protein. Listen to your children's requests and guide them toward the healthier, whole foods way of fulfilling them.

For Parents of Picky Eaters

▶ Have your child help plan, shop for, and prepare meals. See "Involving Your Children in the Kitchen" (pages 51–52).

▶ Don't be tempted to make separate meals for your picky eater. What's served for the meal is what's served. Include a small "no thank you" helping of each dish that has been prepared for the meal.

▶ Include one healthful dish at each meal that you know your child will enjoy. Something as simple as applesauce or bread is fine.

▶ Try new ways of presenting the food. Examples abound in "Presenting Food So It Appeals to Young Children" (pages 52–53), "My Child Won't Eat Vegetables" (pages 54–55), and at the bottom of some of the recipes in the recipe section.

What Should I Give My Child to Drink?

A commitment to giving your child only breast milk, or, in some cases, formula to drink during their first six months is easy. After infancy the question of juice and milk arises: when? And what kind? And as soon as the media grabs your child's mind, Squirt, Gatorade, even Frappuccinos are requested.

There is a plethora of liquid refreshment choices to buy at the grocery store. Even if the health-conscious parent skips by the soda pop aisle, there are hundreds of choices in the fruit juice aisle, even more on the bottled water shelves. Let's sort out why and how much children need to drink and then survey some of our choices.

WHY PARENTS NEED TO BE MINDFUL OF THEIR CHILD'S HYDRATION

All human beings need to drink water. Water is important to many bodily functions, such as regulating temperature, transporting nutrients and oxygen to the blood, removing waste, and lubricating joints. Every day our bodies lose water through sweating, exhaling, urination, and bowel movements. This water needs to be replaced. Even mild dehydration—as little as 2 percent loss of body water—can sap energy and make a child feel tired.

If a child is told to "move your big toe" and then moves his or her big toe, the accomplishment of this tiny task by the body is made possible by a series of nerve impulses that travel through the brain, down the spinal cord to the toe. The smooth functioning of the electrical transmissions of our nervous system is highly dependant on water. Our brains are composed of about 90 percent water. Hydration is not only key for physical activity, but for thinking and learning as well.

Surprisingly, thirst is not a reliable indicator of the need for hydration in children. The human thirst mechanism doesn't kick in until a person has lost a significant amount of fluid. At this point decreased performance has already become evident. By the time your child is thirsty, he is already dehydrated. Drinking water according to a schedule or a routine is the best insurance against dehydration. Encourage your child to drink water before, during, and after play.

HOW MUCH SHOULD CHILDREN DRINK?

There is not an easy answer to this question as there are many variables. The more active your child is, the more he or she needs to drink. Hot weather or heated indoor conditions cause more moisture loss. Illnesses that involve fever, vomiting, or diarrhea require considerably more fluid replacement. The age, size, and general constitution of the child are also factors.

Not all fluid replacement comes from drinking liquid. There is more water value in a diet that includes simple wholesome foods like cooked grains, fresh fruits and vegetables, organic yogurt, and milk. The more highly processed foods, like candy, chips, crackers, and even energy bars, have less available fluid. A child who eats fresh, whole foods is being partially hydrated by his diet, whereas a child who eats more manufactured food will need to drink more water.

Children ages 6 to 11 need to ingest at least 3 to 4 cups of fluids a day, 5 to 6 cups for more active children or children participating in sports. Recommendations escalate during hot weather.

WHAT IS APPROPRIATE FOR A CHILD TO DRINK AND WHAT IS NOT?

Read the label on the can or bottle of any liquid refreshment that you buy for your child. Avoid any beverage that contains caffeine. Caffeine acts as a diuretic, which is unhelpful when the goal is to rehydrate, never mind the short-term jolt of nervous energy. Whenever possible pick beverages that have low or no refined sugar content. This includes drinks with highly refined high-fructose corn syrup. Be sure that you recognize each ingredient in the drink as something you feel good about giving your child.

Liquid candy

One fifth of 1- and 2-year-old children consume carbonated soft drinks. The average American child age 6 to 11 drinks at least 15 ounces per day; teenage boys consume upwards of 28 ounces a day. There is much evidence that Americans' addiction to soda is a component of the rise in childhood obesity and diabetes. The high-fructose corn syrup used to sweeten most soft drinks converts to fat more quickly than sugar. These drinks are also high in phosphoric acid, which causes calcium to be excreted from the bones. Parents can help stop this national addiction. Make a pledge not to buy them at the store or in a restaurant, and don't drink them yourself. Set limits for older children, maybe one soft drink a week, and stick to the rules you set.

The good news is that there are some health-conscious companies producing soft drinks that have pretty good ingredients in them, like R. W. Knudsen's fruit spritzers and Santa Cruz Organics sparkling beverages. These contain mostly sparkling water and concentrated fruit juice. Sweet!

Only one calorie

Some parents who have children with weight problems, or who want to prevent weight problems, may suggest that the child drink diet sodas. Please read the labels of these products and engage your common sense. A typical list of ingredients for these chemical cocktails is carbonated water, caramel color, aspartame (NutraSweet), phosphoric acid, artificial flavors, potassium benzoate, citric acid, and caffeine. Google each of these ingredients and read a little bit about each one. The reason manufacturers use these ingredients has little to do with health.

Just do it, just drink it

Many parents forgo Coke and Pepsi and buy their kids sports drinks—even if their kids don't play sports. Most sports drinks are basically expensive, diluted soft drinks. The bright colors produced by food coloring do nothing to enhance health or fluid replenishment. It is true that children will drink more water if it is slightly flavored or sweetened, but this can be accomplished in a variety of simple ways, like diluting fruit juice or adding a little lemon juice to water.

I like coffee, I like tea

As mentioned above, drinks that contain caffeine are inappropriate for children. Caffeine acts as a diuretic, which inhibits the reabsorption of water in the kidneys, causing more water to be lost in the urine. There are some children who are soothed by a cup of warm herbal tea. Brew it weak for children under 6 years old (twice as much water per bag) and use gentle herbs like chamomile, hibiscus, and mint.

Peel me a grape

Fruit juice contains a significant amount of calories. Filling up on juice can decrease your child's appetite for other more nutritious, whole foods. If your child is a picky eater, overweight or underweight, has digestive problems, or is prone to dental cavities, consider limiting the amount of fruit juice consumed. Infants under 6 months of age do not need juice. Children aged 1 to 6 years should only have 4 to 6 ounces a day, preferably diluted with water by half. Instead of juice, encourage your children to eat whole fruits. When you do buy juice, purchase 100 percent organic fruit juice and avoid juice "drinks," which usually contain refined sweeteners.

Got milk?

Organic whole milk or raw milk from cows or goats that have not been given antibiotics, pesticides, or growth hormones can be a wholesome food in a child's diet. Even though milk contains a significant amount of water, I consider milk to be a food, not a beverage, because of its high calorie content, as well as its ample supply of protein and fat. Use milk as a mini-meal, not a fluid replacer. It is contraindicated to give children under 1 year of age cow's milk or soy milk to drink. When you do introduce milk, especially cow's milk, note any difficulties in assimilation. Signs of intolerance include runny or stuffy noses and chronic ear infections.

Many parents who feel that their child may be sensitive to cow's milk begin giving their child bottles or glasses of soy milks and soy beverages. It is good to remember that soy milk straight from the soy bean tastes very different from what people currently buy in aseptic packages. It has a strong, beany flavor and a bitter aftertaste. Soy milk producers have to do a lot of doctoring up to make a good-selling crowd-pleasing beverage. To give the soy milk the "mouthfeel" of dairy milk, many commercial brands add things such as seaweed and sweeteners to add thickness and help the flavor. Also many soy milks are supplemented with mass-produced calcium and vitamin D—but are these supplements in the right balance with other nutrients so they're absorbable? I'm not sure. I know that these nutrients are not naturally occurring in the soybean.

Neither processed soy milk nor homogenized, pasteurized cow's milk are particularly easy to digest. That is why historically soybeans and dairy milk were fermented or cultured. These natural processes break down some of the components of the food, which aids digestion.

Cool, clear water

The simplest choice is the best. Begin encouraging your child to drink water when he is a toddler. Make it a ritual by offering a glass of water before and after play or before meals. Filtered or bottled water is a good choice, although most tap water is safe.

There are also myriad specialty waters on the grocery shelves these days, including vitamin waters, enhanced waters, energy waters, and flavored waters. As they say, it's your nickel. Do read the labels regardless. Highly refined sugars like high-fructose corn syrup and crystalline fructose, or chemical sweeteners like NutraSweet or sucralose are best left out of your child's bottled water.

One of my daughter's primary school teachers had little ones who were upset take ten sips of water to calm down before reporting their trauma to her. Hydration and stress relief in one glass!

Children who depend on sodas or large quantities of fruit juices to satisfy their body's need for liquids are compromised. They run the risk of replacing healthful calories with more or less empty carbohydrates. This paves the path for weight problems and other maladies associated with poor nutrition. Help your child develop the habit of replenishing his or her body with water by offering it regularly.

WHAT MAKES DRINKS SWEET, AND ARE THESE SUBSTANCES OKAY FOR CHILDREN?

Years ago I used to be a real Carrie Nation about sugar and soda, the evils of which were ruining the health of our children. Plain old cane sugar seems more benign these days compared to the numerous chemical concoctions that sweeten beverages. Below is a list of sweeteners found in drinks that I feel you should avoid purchasing for children.

► **Acesulfame** is a synthetic chemical that our bodies can't metabolize. This substance needs more testing to determine safety.

► **Aspartame** is also known as Equal, NutraSweet, and NatraTaste. It is a synthetic derivation of a combination of the amino acids aspartic acid and phenylalanine. There are few if any non–industry funded studies that have been done to resolve this sweetener's safety issues. A recent European study links consumption of aspartame with cancer in rats.

► **Crystalline fructose** is high-fructose corn syrup that has been further processed to crystallize it (see high-fructose corn syrup).

► **Dextrose** is a refined sweetener which is also called corn sugar or grape sugar. It is usually obtained by the hydrolysis of starch into glucose.

► **High-fructose corn syrup (HFCS)** is a product that can be cheaply produced because of excess corn production due to government subsidies. Corn syrup initially does not contain much fructose. Through a multistage process of mixing corn syrup with bacterial enzymes, a dramatic increase in fructose is produced, making it much sweeter (and cheaper) than cane sugar. Americans consume 83 pounds per person per year. HFCS metabolizes into fat faster than sugar, and overconsumption of this caloric sweetener is someimes linked to weight issues. Other effects of consuming such high doses remain unclear.

► **Saccharin** is a synthetic chemical that was discovered in 1879. It is also known as Sweet'N Low. Our bodies can't metabolize saccharin, and there is much evidence that it is unsafe for human consumption.

► **Sucralose** is also known as Splenda. Sugar is chemically combined with chlorine to produce a sweetener that our bodies can't use as fuel, making it noncaloric. Americans consume 14 pounds of artificial sweeteners per person each year.

Involving Your Children in the Kitchen

Children need to feel a sense of belonging. It is one of their primary drives. In the days of farms and big families, children were a natural part of daily activities. Every child was needed to do chores in order for food to get to the table. Today, children often lose the opportunity to be needed, to contribute to the daily work routine of house and family. Meals are something prepared for the children, not by the children.

Even children who have just begun to walk can help out in the kitchen. They can learn all sorts of things about food, cooking, nutrition, math, science, and recycling by helping prepare food. Kitchen participation helps teach self-reliance and the importance of contributing to the functioning of the household.

Most 3- to 6-year-olds can handle the following tasks. Match the task to your child's skill level. If the task seems too difficult at first, let it go and try again in several months. Remember to use simple, short sentences to describe how the work is done and do the task slowly as you show and tell your child how it is done. Be patient, and pretty soon you'll have an ace helper in the kitchen.

HELPING YOUR HELPER

▶ Clear out a low cupboard for your child. Keep spare pots and pans there so your toddler can play near you, copying you.

▶ For your preschooler, use the space to store unbreakable dishes that they can serve with or use for playing "house." Older children may enjoy having their own kitchen tools or ingredients to make simple snacks on a reachable shelf.

▶ Get a sturdy stool or small chair that your child can move in order to reach the counter and sink.

THINGS YOUR CHILD CAN DO TO HELP WITH MEALS

Preparing
Help with menu selection
Carry groceries into the house
Unload grocery bags and put things away
Retrieve items from the refrigerator
Pick herbs, fruits, or vegetables
  from the garden
Wash fruits and vegetables
Stir wet or dry ingredients
Sift flour
Knead dough
Peel carrots, cucumbers, potatoes
Grate carrots, cheese
Grind grains or nuts in a grinder
  or food processor
Crack nuts
Cut vegetables or fruit (if your child
  is at least 4 or 5 years old)
Measure and pour liquid ingredients
Measure and add dry ingredients
Turn blenders and food
  processors on and off
Use mixer with supervision
Roll out dough with rolling pin
Form cookies with hands
Cut out cookies with cutters
Put muffin cups in muffin tins
Oil pans and cookie sheets
Tell you when something is boiling
Tell you when the timer goes off
Spin the salad spinner
Tear lettuce or greens into small pieces
Toss a salad

Put spreads on breads, crackers,
  rice cakes, or tortillas

Pour pancake batter with cup

Flip pancakes

Serving

Set the table with place mats, silverware,
  cups or glasses, and napkins

Put candles on table and light
  candles with assistance

Pick flowers and put them
  in a vase with water

Make place mats with construction
  paper, crayons, or pens

Roll napkins into napkin rings

Make place cards for guests

Call the family to dinner

Cleaning

Carry dishes from table to sink

Wash dishes

Dry dishes

Load dishes in dishwasher

Unload dishes from dishwasher

Sweep the floor (a child-size
  broom is helpful)

Wipe table or place mats with a sponge

Put recyclable items in bins

Take food scraps to a worm
  bin or compost pile

Sort clean silverware into compartments

Presenting Food So It Appeals to Young Children

Beauty is in the eye of the beholder. Presentation is very important for young children. Your child may refuse a sandwich unless it's cut a certain way or has the bread crusts cut off. You may be able to delight a child into eating something new by putting a face on it or cutting it into a heart shape. Dust off your imagination and expand on the following ideas for creative food preparation for youngsters.

Good-looking food is not just about glamour. When the eyes see something colorful and tantalizing, the mouth begins secreting enzymes to digest the food. Good digestion and assimilation begin with presentation!

DECORATE FOOD

▶ Stock a variety of cookie cutters and use them to cut sandwiches and pancakes. Find cutters in the shapes of your child's favorite animals. Asian markets sometimes have small, strong cutters for making vegetables into beautiful shapes. These can be fun for turning zucchini or carrot slices into flowers.

▶ Serving brown rice, potatoes, or other foods with a large ice cream scoop makes miniature mountains on your child's plate.

▶ Make food friendlier by using raisins, small pieces of vegetables, small crackers, or whatever you can dream up to put a face on the food. Bowls of soup, mashed potatoes, or plates of rice suddenly become funny personalities for your child to devour. Apple slices make sweeping smiles, olives make 3-D eyeballs. I once cut a sheet of nori into paper dolls for my 3-year-old. Decorating food will bring humor and light to your day and your child's.

USE DELIGHTFUL DINNERWARE AND PLAYFUL PACKAGING

▶ You might try buying a special plate, cup, or even silverware for your child. This can be as extravagant as a complete Winnie-the-Pooh set or simply "Jack's yellow plate." Having personal dinnerware can enhance your child's enjoyment of meals. Children also derive security from being able to count on the same bowl or spoon every day. Serving red zinger tea in a special cup or plopping a crazy straw into a smoothie can make all the difference.

▶ Lunch box packaging can have charm too. Your child may love having lunch packed in a recyclable paper bag with a silly face drawn on the outside. Another child may prefer a basket with a lid and ribbons tied on the handle. Asian markets sell interesting merchandise designed for packing food to go. Sometimes you can find beautiful container boxes in pretty colors that have little compartments inside.

▶ Fun surprises hidden inside a lunch box need not be sweets. How about a marble, a seashell, an envelope with a note or stickers inside, a little pad of paper, and a tiny pencil? There are many ways to convey a loving message.

TELL A STORY

▶ Can you turn a plate of spaghetti into a pail of hay for a pretend lamb in your kitchen?

▶ Can a bowl of yellow split pea soup be a bowl of melted gold for your pirate?

Pretend play is very important to young folks. Why not use it to everyone's advantage in the nutrition department? Make up a wild story about what you're serving that will make it impossible not to devour (or at least taste).

"My Child Won't Eat Vegetables"

In almost every class that I have taught for parents someone raises their hand to say, "My (husband, daughter, son) hates vegetables. What should I do?" This is a common worry, especially since the USDA began its emphasis on including more fruits and vegetables in the diet.

First, check out your own thoughts about vegetable eating. Make sure that you love them, like them, or at least appreciate them before asking your children to eat more of them. What you are thinking has an effect.

Next, help your child create a relationship with vegetables. One excellent way to improve your child's interest in vegetables is to let him or her help you plant and harvest a small vegetable garden. If you don't have space for a garden, go visit one. Let them see, touch, and even smell vegetables being grown.

Bring your children with you to the grocery store and let them pick out fruits and vegetables that look good to them.

Invite your child to help you prepare vegetables. Look at "One-Trick Vegetables" (pages 184–186) to find plain-Jane, but tasty vegetable dishes your child can help make. Let your child make beautiful arrangements on the plate using the bright colors of vegetables.

With children who eat their fair share of whole grains, fruits, and beans, you can relax some; these foods contain a wide variety of vitamins and minerals. However, parents are right to be concerned if their children subsist mainly on sugar and white flour products. Vegetables are rich in vitamins not found in refined foods.

Don't make a big fuss if your child refuses vegetables. Instead, eat them yourself and regularly offer them to your child. Remembering that beauty is in the eye of the beholder, here are some ways to prepare and serve vegetables that may appeal to your child.

▶ **Juices:** Students who take my classes report great success in getting children to drink various vegetable juices. Carrot juice is a favorite, especially mixed with a little apple juice. But remember, juice is not a whole food; the fiber is gone and the sugars become highly concentrated. Dilute vegetable and fruit juices; one-half juice, one-half water.

▶ **Dippers:** You can use raw vegetables as dippers for your child's favorite dip. Bean dips, guacamole, and tofu dips can be scooped up on a carrot stick, celery stick, or a slice of zucchini. To make vegetables easier to chew and digest, as well as enhancing their flavor, blanch them (see page 184).

▶ **Soups:** Children who refuse a serving of vegetables will often eat the same vegetable in a soup. If vegetables in their whole form are a turn-off, purée the soup (see Rosemary Red Soup, page 128 or Golden Mushroom Basil Soup, page 129).

▶ **Muffins:** You can add vegetables to muffins and other baked goods (as in Sweet Squash Corn Muffins, page 218 or Halloween Cookies, page 248). Zucchini, corn, squash, carrots, and sweet potatoes taste great in a muffin mix.

- **Sandwich spreads:** When you're purée-ing beans or tofu or avocado into a tasty sandwich spread, add vegetables. Parsley, cilantro, fresh basil, red pepper, or scallions work well to enhance flavor and nutritive value. Sometimes I add corn, grated zucchini, or chopped green peppers to burritos. Amid the beans, salsa, tortillas and all, they are hardly noticed.

- **Salads:** Sometimes it's just the sight of combined ingredients that turn kids off to salads. Experiment by offering a single raw vegetable or raw vegetables in separate piles, not mixed together. Try different shapes and sizes. Grated beets or radishes, finely sliced cabbage, zucchini, summer squash, daikon (white radish), or even plain lettuce bites can be fun for small fingers to pick up.

Basic Grain and Bean Cookery

Brown Rice
Bulgur
Millet
Couscous
Kasha
Rolled or Steel-Cut Oats
Polenta
Quinoa
Wild Rice
Basic Small Beans
Basic Big Beans
Basic Pressure-Cooked Beans

COOKING WHOLE GRAINS

For tips on shopping and storage, see Appendix B, "Identifying, Purchasing, and Storing Whole Foods."

Washing

Brown rice, millet, and quinoa, bought in bulk, are whole grains that need to be washed prior to cooking to remove chaff, dust, or other debris. Grains that have been partially milled, steamed, or toasted, such as polenta, steel-cut oats, bulgur, or kasha, do not require rinsing. The best way to wash grains is to place the grains in a pan with a generous amount of water. Swirl the grains in the water with your hand. As you touch the grain, remember your gratefulness to the earth for providing this food. Pour off the water through a fine strainer. Repeat this process again until the water you pour off is clear.

Cooking

To begin, it is usually necessary to bring the water and grain up to boiling. Be sure to lower the heat immediately once the water has reached the boiling stage and establish a gentle simmer. If the heat on your stovetop is not flexible, using a "flame-tamer," or heat diffuser, a perforated metal plate with a handle, placed between the pan and the heat source, can be helpful. When grains turn out too stiff and separate, usually the grain was cooked at too high a temperature for too long. If the grain turns out mushy or clumped together, the heat may not have been high enough, or you may have used too much water.

Sea salt brings out the sweetness in grains and helps the grain to open up. Grains cooked without salt will taste very flat. The only time you don't use salt is when preparing grains to be deep-fried; in that case, the grains are usually served with a salty dipping sauce or gravy.

Don't stir cooking grains! Whole grains create their own steam holes from the bottom of the pan to the top so that they cook thoroughly. Stirring them disturbs the steam holes. Whole grains that have been ground or cereals are another matter. They can be stirred.

To test for doneness without disturbing the steam holes, remove the lid and gently tip the pan to one side. If even a tiny bit of liquid pools, replace the lid and return grains to heat. You want all of the liquid to be absorbed to get a properly cooked grain.

Brown Rice

Rice is the principal food for half of the world's people. Rice with the hull, bran, and germ removed is white rice. Rice with just the hull removed is brown rice. Brown rice comes in a variety of types: short-grain, long-grain, and basmati are three. All of these varieties can be prepared according to the directions below.

Boiled Brown Rice

Prep time: 55 minutes
Makes 2½ to 3 cups

> **1 cup brown rice**
> **½ teaspoon sea salt**
> **1¾ to 2 cups water**

Rinse and drain rice. Place rice in a 2-quart pot with salt and water. Bring to a bubbling boil. Lower heat and establish a nice simmer: movement but no bubbles. Cover the pan and let the rice simmer for 45 to 50 minutes, or until all the water is absorbed. Don't stir the rice while it is cooking. Test for doneness by tilting the pan to one side, making sure all of the water has been absorbed.

Pressure-Cooked Brown Rice

Prep time: 45 minutes
Makes 2½ to 3 cups

> **1 cup brown rice**
> **½ teaspoon sea salt**
> **1½ cups water**

Pressure-cooking makes chewier, stickier rice, which many people find satisfying. Rinse and drain rice. Put rice, salt, and water in the pressure cooker. Lock the lid and turn heat to high until pressure gauge comes up. Then lower the heat and begin timing for 35 to 40 minutes. Remove from heat and allow pressure and gauge to come down naturally or by running a small stream of cold water over the top of the cooker.

For babies 6 months and older: Make rice cereal by taking a small amount of cooked brown rice and blending it with a little breast milk or water until smooth.

Bulgur

Bulgur is parboiled, dried, and cracked whole wheat. Wheat was grown as a crop as far back as 7000 BC! Bulgur can be used as a base grain for a variety of bean and vegetable dishes.

Prep time: 15 minutes
Makes 2½ to 3 cups

> **1 cup water**
> **½ teaspoon sea salt**
> **1 cup bulgur**

Bring water and salt to a boil in a 2-quart pan. Add bulgur. Cover pan and remove from heat. Let stand for 10 minutes. Fluff grain with a fork before serving. Add a few drops of oil to the cooked bulgur to keep it loose.

Millet

Millet is a small, round, yellow grain that is one of the oldest foods known to humans; it is also one of the least allergenic grains. It is still a staple food in parts of Africa. Millet has a sweet, earthy taste that is enriched by dry-toasting the grain before cooking.

Prep time: 45 to 50 minutes
Makes 2½ to 3 cups

> **1 cup millet**
> **2 to 3 cups water**
> **½ teaspoon sea salt**

Wash millet and drain. Repeat the rinsing 2 or 3 times.

Dry-toast millet for a better flavor and texture (this is optional). To do this, heat the washed grain in a 2-quart pot, stirring constantly until it is toasted dry and gives off a nutty aroma, about 5 to 7 minutes.

Add water and salt to toasted millet. Use 2 cups of water for a fluffy grain. Use 3 cups of water for a creamier, breakfastlike grain. Bring water, millet, and salt to boil, lower heat, cover, and simmer for 30 to 40 minutes, until all the water is absorbed.

🥣 **For babies 6 months and older:** Blend cooked millet with a little water or breast milk to make an excellent baby cereal.

Couscous

Couscous is actually tiny pasta made from coarsely ground and steamed wheat. It is usually made from refined grain, although whole wheat couscous is becoming more widely available. Couscous can be used as a base grain for beans and stews, and it also makes a nice salad when fresh vegetables and a dressing are added to the cooked grain.

Prep time: 15 minutes
Makes 2½ to 3 cups

> **1 cup water**
> **½ teaspoon sea salt**
> **1 cup whole wheat couscous**

Bring water and salt to a boil in a 2-quart pan. Add couscous. Cover pan and remove from heat. Let stand 5 to 10 minutes. Fluff grain with a fork before serving. Stir in a few drops of oil to keep the couscous from clumping.

Kasha

Kasha is roasted buckwheat groats. Buckwheat originally grew wild in Asia and was carried by migrating tribes to Eastern Europe where it is still a significant food for humans. Look for a brown, angular-looking grain. Kasha has a strong and hearty flavor; it is an excellent grain to eat during cold weather.

Prep time: 25 minutes
Makes 2½ to 3 cups

> **1 tablespoon butter or olive oil**
> **1 cup kasha**
> **2 cups water**
> **½ teaspoon sea salt**

Heat the butter in a 2-quart pan. Add kasha and sauté until coated. Bring water to a boil in a tea kettle or separate pan. Add boiling water and salt to kasha. Cover the pan, reduce heat to low, and let simmer 15 to 20 minutes.

🥣 **For babies 6 months and older:** Blend cooked kasha and water to make a cereal for baby. Kasha is one of the least allergenic grains.

Rolled or Steel-Cut Oats

In North America oats are chiefly used for animal feed; only 5 percent are used for human consumption. Oat groats that have been thinly sliced with steel blades are called steel-cut oats or Irish oatmeal. Oat groats that have been heated until soft and pressed flat are called rolled oats.

Prep time: 25 to 35 minutes
Makes 2½ to 3 cups

> **1 cup rolled or steel-cut oats**
> **½ teaspoon sea salt**
> **3 cups water**

Place oats in a pot with salt and water. Bring to a boil, reduce heat, cover, and let simmer on very low for 20 to 25 minutes (steel-cut oats will take 30 to 35 minutes), stirring occasionally. Add raisins or other fruits and spices during the last 10 minutes of cooking if desired.

For a quicker version, soak oats overnight in water and add salt in the morning (some cinnamon and raisins are nice, too). Bring heat up to a simmer and cook about 5 minutes, stirring constantly.

> **For babies 10 months and older:** Oatmeal is a fine food for babies. I have suggested 10 months and older because it is not my first choice for a beginner grain; however, many babies do fine with it. If using steel-cut oats, blend the cooked grain before serving it to baby, as it can have a rather coarse texture.

Polenta

Polenta is coarsely ground cornmeal that is cooked and served as a kind of mush or, if allowed to set, can then be sliced. You can use broth instead of water as a cooking liquid or add cheese, vegetables, or chiles to the cooked polenta to enliven the taste.

Prep time: 50 minutes
Makes 8 slices

> **5 cups water or vegetable or chicken stock**
> **½ teaspoon sea salt**
> **2 teaspoons extra-virgin olive oil or butter**
> **1 cup polenta or corn grits**
> **2 to 3 tablespoons Parmesan cheese (optional)**

Bring water to rapid boil in a 4-quart (or larger) pot. Add salt and oil. Slowly add polenta, stirring continuously with a whisk. Lower heat and continue stirring in a clockwise motion, making sure that the heat is at a temperature where polenta puckers but does not boil.

Practice mindful meditation and stir for 30 minutes, or until grains become less individualized and the mixture is thick and creamy. If using cheese, stir in at this point.

Lightly oil a pie plate or 8 x 8-inch pan. Pour polenta into pan and smooth the top. Let cool to room temperature. Slice and serve.

If you wish to reheat the polenta slices, brush with oil and place under broiler or on the grill for a few minutes. Serve immediately.

☞ **For babies 10 months and older:** Corn is one of the top food allergies in our country, mostly because of the overuse of highly refined forms of it in processed food products. That is why I have suggested using it for the older baby. Reserve a portion before placing in pan to cool and serve as a mush, or let set, cool, and serve in small chunks as a finger food to your toddler.

Quinoa

Quinoa (keen-wah) comes from the Andes Mountains in South America, where it was once a staple food for the Incas. It has a deliciously light, nutty flavor. When it cooks the grain opens up to make tiny spirals. Quinoa contains all eight amino acids (proteins) and therefore has better protein value than most grains. A nutrient-dense grain, perfect for those who have elevated needs, such as pregnant or nursing mothers.

Prep time: 20 to 25 minutes
Makes 2½ to 3 cups

> **1 cup quinoa**
> **½ teaspoon sea salt**
> **1¾ cups water**

Rinse quinoa with water and drain. Place rinsed quinoa, salt, and water in a 2-quart pot. Bring to a boil, reduce heat to low, cover, and let simmer 15 to 20 minutes. Don't stir the grain while it is cooking. Test for doneness by tilting the pan to one side, making sure all of the water has been absorbed. Fluff with a fork before serving.

For babies 6 months and older: Quinoa is an excellent beginner grain. Simply add a small amount of breast milk or water to the cooked grain and run it through the blender

Wild Rice

Wild rice is a native North American whole grain harvested from an aquatic grass plant. It has a higher concentration of B vitamins, magnesium, and zinc than regular rice and is especially rich in lysine—the amino acid most grains lack.

Prep time: 70 to 80 minutes
Makes 3 cups

> 2½ **cups water or vegetable or chicken stock**
> 1 **tablespoon butter**
> ½ **teaspoon sea salt**
> 1 **cup wild rice (black grains, ½ inch long)**

Bring water to a boil in a 2-quart pan. Add butter, salt, and rice. Bring to a boil again, cover, lower heat, and simmer 60 minutes or more. Check to make sure all the liquid has been absorbed by tipping pan to the side. Continue simmering until no liquid is left.

For babies 10 months and older: Wild rice has a strong flavor but is nonallergenic and suitable for all ages. Blending it with a sweet vegetable, such as baked sweet potato or roasted carrots, would be nice for baby.

COOKING BEANS

Selecting which beans to cook

Buy beans at a store that has a rapid turn-over of dried beans, and use them within a few months. If your beans are older than six months, they will take much longer to cook. You can tell if dried beans are a bit aged by their appearance: the color will be faded, not rich, and the outside of the bean will be dull instead of shiny. Sort through beans bought in bulk and pick out any stones or bits before soaking. Smaller beans, such as peas and lentils, do not require soaking. However, all beans benefit greatly from being soaked. Soaking reduces cooking time and aids digestibility. Because beans require a little extra thought and time, make a double recipe and freeze half for a busy day. Below are lists of favorite small and big beans.

Small Beans

Adzuki beans
Black-eyed peas
Green or brown lentils
Green or yellow split peas
Mung beans
Red lentils

Big Beans

Black beans
Cannellini beans
Chickpeas (garbanzos)
Christmas limas
Great northern beans
Kidney beans
Lima beans
Navy beans
Pinto beans
Swedish brown beans

How to soak beans

Place beans in a large bowl. Cover with twice as much water as beans (e.g., for 2 cups beans use 4 cups water) and let stand 8 hours or overnight. Rinse off the soaking water and cook beans according to recipe.

You can also quick-soak beans by bring-ing the same proportion of beans and water to a boil, turning heat off and letting beans soak for 2 hours. This will decrease cooking time but will not give the beans the increased digestibility that a long soak does. Rinse off the soaking water and cook beans according to recipe.

Notes on cooking beans

A long soak and a slow cook renders the most tender, digestible bean. Pressure-cooking is my favorite way to cook beans. It gives the beans a creamy texture and deep flavor, and you can get a tender bean in less time.

If you soak beans shorter or longer than 8 hours, simply adjust the cooking time. If using a pressure cooker, you will also need to adjust the amount of water: less if the beans were soaked too long, more if the time was shortened. Beans that have sat in water longer than 24 hours may begin to sprout. Then you can't cook them because they have morphed into a new food. If you've soaked them for a day, don't have time to cook them, and want to keep them from sprouting, drain off the soaking water and store them in the refrig-erator. Cook as soon as possible.

I have always been taught that salting beans while cooking toughens the bean's outer layer. Others claim that adding salt during cooking makes the beans explode. I have found neither extreme to be true, but I generally recommend salting beans after they have been cooked. I like to taste the warm, cooked beans for texture, then I salt the beans, taste again, and add more if needed. Beans need a lot of salt to bring up the flavor. For 1 cup dry beans add at least 1 teaspoon of salt after they are cooked.

Buying canned, cooked beans is fine when you're in a hurry. Be sure to read labels carefully. Choose organic products and products that don't contain unwanted ingredients such as preservatives, MSG, or high amounts of sodium. Cooking your own beans is less expensive than buying canned beans and the taste is fresher. Flavorings such as garlic, chiles, and onion are more deeply absorbed if added during cooking. Remember that you can cook a big batch of beans and freeze part for another day, another recipe.

Basic Small Beans

Green, brown, or red lentils, green or yellow split peas, black-eyed peas, mung beans, and adzuki beans can all be considered small beans. I have suggested that beans be cooked with kombu. This sea vegetable has a property that tenderizes beans and helps prevent flatulence. The kombu also adds minerals to the beans.

Prep time: 20 to 60 minutes
Makes 6 cups of cooked beans

> **2 cups small dried beans, soaked 6 to 8 hours**
> **4 to 5 cups water**
> **2-inch piece of kombu, soaked 5 minutes in cold water**
> **1 to 2 teaspoons sea salt**

Drain off soaking water or rinse and drain beans. Place beans, water, and kombu in a 3- or 4-quart pot; bring to a boil. Reduce heat, cover, and simmer. Most of these smaller beans take 45 to 50 minutes to cook, with the exception of adzuki beans, which take an hour, and red lentils, which cook in 20 to 25 minutes. Don't salt the beans until the end of cooking time, when you are satisfied with their texture.

For babies 10 months and older: Purée a small amount of cooked beans with water and serve as a thick soup.

REDUCING FLATULENCE CAUSED BY EATING BEANS

Oligosaccharides, molecules consisting of three, four, and five sugar molecules linked together, in beans are responsible for producing gases. Oligosaccharides accumulate in the final stages of seed development, which is why green, immature beans are much less troublesome. Human digestive enzymes do not easily handle oligosaccharides, which can leave the small intestines unchanged and move to the lower intestines. The digestive job is then left up to the large bacterial population in the lower intestines. In the process various gases, primarily carbon dioxide, are produced as waste products. Navy and lima beans tend to cause the most problems, peanuts the least. Here are tips on preparing beans that may help reduce the likelihood of flatulence.

1. Soak beans overnight and replace the soaking water with fresh water for cooking.

2. Cook beans with a piece of kombu seaweed. Kombu contains glutamic acid, which acts as a natural bean tenderizer. The kombu also adds vitamins and minerals, especially trace minerals.

3. Two tablespoons of the herb winter savory or 4 tablespoons of the Mexican herb epazote added to beans as they cook will reduce the effects of raffinose sugars. Other seasonings that help are cumin and fennel.

4. Let beans cook slowly for a long period of time so they are very tender. Can you easily mash the bean on the roof of your mouth?

5. Don't add baking soda to soaking water. It destroys nutrients, particularly thiamine, and imparts a slight acrid flavor and mealy texture.

6. Parboil beans as a pretreatment. Bring beans to a boil, then scoop off and discard foam, which accumulates on top, before continuing cooking.

7. Use a salt seasoning—sea salt, miso, soy sauce—at the end of cooking time.

8. Eat more beans. You can expect a digestive adjustment when beans are new to the diet. Eat small amounts frequently to allow the body to get used to digesting them.

9. Improve your overall digestion. Chew foods slowly and thoroughly. Avoid washing foods down with liquids. Eat fewer kinds of foods at the same meal. Drink plenty of water between meals.

10. For persistent gas, try pouring a little apple cider vinegar or brown rice vinegar into the cooking liquid during the last stages of cooking. Vinegar softens legumes and breaks down the protein chains and other indigestible compounds. Another option is to marinate the cooked beans in a solution of two-thirds vinegar and one-third olive oil, creating a salad-type dish. Marinate while still warm.

Basic Big Beans

Chickpeas (garbanzos), pinto, black, lima, navy, kidney, great northern, Swedish brown, cannellini, and Christmas limas are some favorite varieties of big beans. See Appendix B, "Identifying, Purchasing, and Storing Whole Foods" for an explanation of why kombu is added. Kombu can be found in natural foods stores in the macrobiotic section.

Simmered Beans

Prep time: 60 minutes
Makes 6 cups of cooked beans

> **2 cups dried beans, soaked 6 to 8 hours**
> **6 cups water**
> **2-inch piece of kombu, soaked 5 minutes in cold water**
> **1 to 2 teaspoons sea salt**

Drain off soaking water. Put soaked beans, fresh water, and kombu in a pot; bring to a boil. Lower heat and let simmer, covered, until beans are quite tender (55 to 60 minutes). A well-cooked bean can be easily mashed on the roof of the mouth with the tongue. Add water during cooking if needed. Salt beans at the end of the cooking time.

Slow-Cooked Beans

Prep time: 8 hours
Makes 6 cups of cooked beans

Using an electric slow cooker allows you to sleep or work while your beans cook. Soak beans overnight. Drain off soaking water, and then follow directions that apply to your slow cooker. This typically requires 8 hours on high. A thick, folded towel placed on the lid of your slow cooker helps conserve heat.

LEFTOVER GRAINS AND BEANS: FOOD FOR BABY AND COMPANY

My friend Mary Shaw used to teach a class for the Puget Consumer's Co-op cooking program (PCC Cooks) called "A Pot of Grain, A Crock of Beans." In the class she would show how to prepare a large amount of one whole grain and one bean and then proceed to make 5 or 6 different dishes out of the two beginning staples. This is a very practical task for busy families that want to eat well.

Most cooked whole grains can be run through the blender with a little water or breast milk to make high-quality cereal For babies 6 months and older. Cooked beans can be puréed or mashed into food for babies who have been eating solids for a few months.

Leftover grains and beans make wonderful salads with the addition of some fresh vegetables and a vinaigrette. Leftover grains can be stir-fried with fresh vegetables and a little tamari to make a simple, warm lunch. Beans can be puréed with fresh herbs and spices to make tasty sandwich spreads or added to salads to increase the protein value of the dish.

Following are lists of dishes that can be made from leftover cooked grains and beans using the recipes in this book.

Leftover brown rice? Use it to make:
Dilled Brown Rice and Kidney
  Beans (page 102)
Rice Balls Rolled in Sesame Salt (page 111)
Savory Lunch Box Roll-Ups (page 120)
Whole Wheat and Rice Bread (page 214)
Nut Burgers (page 155)

Leftover millet? Use it to make:
Deep-Fried Millet Croquettes (page 144)
Orange Millet Raisin Bread (page 214)
Gracie's Yellow Birthday Cake (page 258)

Leftover polenta? Use to make:
Pan-fried polenta with maple
  syrup as a breakfast treat
Brushed with olive oil and
  grilled for the lunch box

Leftover quinoa? Use it to make:
Quick Lemon and Garlic
  Quinoa Salad (page 110)
Mediterranean Quinoa (page 143)
Red Bean and Quinoa Chili (page 151)
Quinoa Garlic Herb Bread (page 215)

Leftover beans? Use them to make:
On the side with Huevos
  Rancheros (page 95)
Dilled Brown Rice and Kidney
  Beans (page 102)
Hummus (page 114)
French Lentil Dijon Spread (page 113)
Santa Fe Black Bean Salad (page 103)
Savory Lunch Box Roll-Ups (page 120)
White Bean and Kale Minestrone (page 132)
Golden Spice Rice with
  Chickpeas (page 142)
Mexican Bean and Corn Casserole (page 154)
Three Sisters Stew (page 157)
Black Bean Tostados (page 161)
Spice Island Beef Stew (page 172)
Susan's Succulent Supper Salad (page 203)
Romaine Chop Salad with Basil
  Dressing (page 195)
Bean Apple Rye Bread (page 216)

Basic Pressure-Cooked Beans

No matter how hot the heat source, boiling liquid in the presence of air can never reach a temperature of over 212°F. Pressure cookers have a locking, airtight lid and a valve system to regulate pressure. Steam builds up inside the pot so that temperatures as high as 250°F can be maintained, which shortens cooking time. Nutrients and flavors are also conserved.

Prep time: 45 to 50 minutes
Makes 6 cups of cooked beans

> **2 cups dried beans, soaked 6 to 8 hours**
> **4 cups water**
> **2-inch piece of kombu, soaked 5 minutes in cold water**
> **1 to 2 teaspoons sea salt**

Drain off soaking water. Put soaked beans, fresh water, and kombu in pressure cooker. Lock the lid in place and turn heat to high until pressure gauge comes up. Then lower the heat and begin timing for 40 to 45 minutes. Add more time and liquid if the beans were not soaked. Reduce time and liquid if the beans were soaked over 10 hours. Keep the heat at a temperature where the gauge remains up and you hear a soft hissing sound.

At the end of the cooking time, remove from heat and allow pressure and gauge to come down naturally or by running a small stream of cold water over the top of the cooker. Add salt after cooking.

☞ **For babies 10 months and older:** Use a few well-cooked beans as a finger food.

Bustling Breakfasts

Toasted Whole Grain Baby Cereal
Soaked Whole Grain Baby Porridge
Ancient Grain Raisin Cereal
Five-Grain Morning Cereal
Steel-Cut Oats with Dates and Cinnamon
Homemade Applesauce
Sunny Millet with Peaches
Orange Hazelnut Muesli
Maple Butter Nut Granola
Kasha Pilaf with Poached Eggs
Jam-Filled Mochi
Jeff's Potato Pancakes
Essene Bread and Fresh Fruit
Goldie's Whole Grain Pancake Mix
Buttermilk Banana Pancakes
Blueberry Sauce
Tofu Vegetable Breakfast Burritos
Healthy Home Fries
Green Eggs (No Ham)
Ben's Friday Pancakes
Tempeh Bacon
Huevos Rancheros

Toasted Whole Grain Baby Cereal

Making your own baby cereal is nutritious, economical, and quite delicious. The grains listed below were chosen because they are the least allergenic and the easiest to digest. For babies just starting solids, the cereal should be the consistency of soup. Make the consistency thicker as baby gets older. I don't like calling this "baby cereal" because this cereal is for everyone!

Prep time: 5 to 15 minutes for toasting, 5 to 12 minutes to cook cereal
Makes 1 cup toasted grains; 4 adult-size servings

Toasted Cereal Grains

1 cup short-grain brown rice, millet, quinoa, or sweet brown rice

Place grains in a fine strainer; rinse and drain. Toast the grain for better digestibility and flavor. Toast grains in one of two ways:

Oven toasting: Preheat oven to 350°F. Spread grains on cookie sheet and toast in oven until they give off a nutty aroma (12 to 15 minutes).

Skillet toasting: Place washed grains in large skillet on burner and toast on medium heat, stirring constantly, until grains are dry and give off nutty aroma (about 5 to 8 minutes).

Let toasted grains cool and store them in a sealed container. You can toast a big batch of several different grains at one time and store them in separate jars. This will keep everyone full of wholesome cereal for many moons.

Cooked Cereal

Ground toasted cereal grains
Water
Pinch of sea salt

Grind the amount of cereal you need before cooking. For optimum nutrition, grind the grains in a small electric grinder or food processor just prior to using. Once a grain is ground it begins to lose some nutritional value within 24 to 48 hours.

For a baby-sized portion of cereal, mix together 2 to 3 tablespoons of ground cereal and ½ to ¾ cup water and a pinch of salt in a small pot; bring it to a boil. Reduce heat to low and simmer, covered, for 5 minutes.

For a family-sized portion of cereal (four adult-size servings), use 1 cup ground grains, 3 to 4 cups water, and ½ teaspoon salt. Combine cereal, water, and salt in a pot; bring to a boil. Reduce heat to low and simmer, covered, for 10 to 12 minutes. Stir frequently.

Soaked Whole Grain Baby Porridge

To save time and aid digestibility, soak the toasted grains overnight. As your child gets older, you can use a higher ratio of yogurt to water as long as your child shows no sensitivity to dairy. Be sure to buy high-quality yogurt with active cultures and forgo brands that add nonfat milk solids to thicken the product. Add fresh fruit and toasted nuts to porridge for older children and parents.

Prep time: 8 to 12 hours soaking, 15 minutes to cook cereal
Makes 2 adult portions, numerous baby portions

> **½ cup toasted millet or short-grain brown rice**
> **(see Toasted Whole Grain Baby Cereal for instructions on how to toast grains)**
> **½ to 2 teaspoons plain whole milk yogurt**
> **1 cup water**
> **Pinch of sea salt**

Place grain in a blender. Dilute yogurt in the water. Use the lesser amount of yogurt for babies 6 to 10 months; for older babies you can use a bit more. Cover grain with yogurt-water and let sit in the refrigerator 8 to 12 hours (overnight).

In the morning, blend the grains in a blender until smooth. Add more water if necessary to get a porridgelike consistency. Warm the porridge in a pan over low heat. Add a pinch of salt to bring up the flavor.

Ancient Grain Raisin Cereal

These grains meld to make a creamy cereal with an earthy flavor. I like the recipe because there is no wheat, a grain we tend to overdo. There are several interesting whole grains used here. Amaranth, which was grown by the Aztecs, has a very good nutritional profile—high in protein and calcium. It has a flavor similar to graham crackers without the sweetness. The grain looks like tiny yellow, brown, and black seeds. To find out more about the other grains used in this cereal see Appendix B, "Identifying, Purchasing, and Storing Whole Foods."

Prep time: 15 to 20 minutes for toasting, 15 minutes to cook cereal
Makes 5½ cups dry cereal mix; 1 cup dry mix makes 4 servings cooked cereal

Toasted Cereal Mix
1 cup hulled barley
1 cup millet
½ cup sesame seeds
1 cup whole oats
1 cup polenta
1 cup amaranth

Place barley, millet, sesame seeds, and oats in fine strainer; rinse with water and drain. Combine with polenta and amaranth and toast cereal in one of two ways:

Oven toasting: Preheat oven to 350°F. Spread grains on cookie sheet and toast in oven until they give off a nutty aroma (12 to 15 minutes).

Skillet toasting: Place grains in large skillet on burner and toast on medium heat, stirring constantly, until grains give off nutty aroma (about 5 to 8 minutes). Let toasted grains cool. Store in a sealed container.

Cooked Cereal
1 cup toasted cereal mix
3 cups water
⅓ cup raisins
½ teaspoon sea salt
1 tablespoon butter
Maple syrup, yogurt, nuts, or ground flaxseed, for garnish

Grind toasted grains in a small electric grinder or blender. Combine ground cereal, water, raisins, salt, and butter in a small pan. Stir constantly as you bring to a boil. Turn heat to low, cover, and simmer (10 to 15 minutes). Stir frequently to prevent sticking. Serve with maple syrup, yogurt, nuts, or ground flaxseed on top.

🥄 **For babies 6 months and older:** Toast a cup of millet separately and use the toasted millet to make Toasted Whole Grain Baby Cereal (see page 74).

Five-Grain Morning Cereal

I keep a canister of these five grains mixed together. In the morning, I grind a cup of dry grains, cook the freshly ground grains into this nutritious cereal, and top it with fresh fruit. Wheat berries are whole wheat kernels. To find out more about wheat berries or any of the other grains used in this cereal see Appendix B, "Identifying, Purchasing, and Storing Whole Foods."

Prep time: 5 to 15 minutes for toasting, 15 to 20 minutes to cook cereal
Makes 5 cups dry cereal mix; 1 cup dry mix makes 4 servings cooked cereal

Toasted Cereal Mix
1 cup wheat berries
1 cup millet
1 cup spelt
1 cup brown rice
1 cup quinoa

Place all grains in a fine strainer; rinse and drain. Toast grains in one of two ways:

Oven toasting: Preheat oven to 350°F. Spread grains on cookie sheet and toast in oven until they give off a nutty aroma (12 to 15 minutes).

Skillet toasting: Place grains in large skillet on burner and toast on medium heat, stirring constantly, until grains give off nutty aroma (about 5 to 8 minutes). Let toasted grains cool and store in sealed container.

Cooked Cereal
1 cup toasted cereal mix
3 cups water
½ teaspoon sea salt
1 tablespoon butter
Maple syrup, yogurt, or nuts, for garnish

Grind toasted cereal mix in small electric grinder. Combine ground cereal, water, salt and butter in a small pan. Stir constantly and bring to a boil. Turn heat to low, cover, and simmer 10 to 15 minutes. Stir occasionally to prevent sticking. Serve with maple syrup, yogurt, or nuts on top.

☞ **For babies 6 months and older:** Toast a cup of brown rice or quinoa separately and use the toasted grain to make Toasted Whole Grain Baby Cereal (see page 74).

Steel-Cut Oats with Dates and Cinnamon

Steel-cut oats are whole oats that have been thinly sliced into pieces. They are different than rolled oats, which are oats that have been heated until soft and pressed flat. Steel-cut oats, sometimes called Irish oatmeal, have a heartier flavor and a chewier texture than rolled oats. I like to eat oat cereal with sliced apples, Tamari-Roasted Nuts (page 117), and a dollop of maple yogurt on top.

Prep time: 25 minutes
Makes 4 to 6 servings

> 1 **cup steel-cut oats**
> 3 **cups water**
> 4 **pitted dates, cut into small pieces**
> ½ **teaspoon ground cinnamon**
> ½ **teaspoon sea salt**
> 1 **tablespoon butter**

Place all ingredients in a pan and stir briefly; bring to a boil. Reduce heat to low, cover, and simmer for 20 to 25 minutes.

For a quicker version, soak steel-cut oats in 2-quart pan with water for 8 to 12 hours or overnight. In the morning add remaining ingredients, bring to a boil, reduce heat to low, and simmer, stirring constantly for 5 minutes.

Serve with your favorite toppings.

🥣 **For babies 10 months and older:** Purée cooked cereal briefly before serving.

Homemade Applesauce

There are many excellent brands of jarred applesauce, but there is nothing quite as satisfying as freshly made applesauce from seasonal apples. Perfect for all ages. I like to make this fruit sauce with Italian plums or pears in the fall. Consider removing the skins of the apples if the sauce is intended for children under 1 year.

Prep time: 20 minutes
Makes about 2 cups

> **2 cups sliced apples**
> **⅓ cup apple juice or apple cider**
> **1 cinnamon stick**
> **⅛ teaspoon sea salt**
> **Unrefined cane sugar or brown sugar**

Put apples, juice, cinnamon, and salt in a pot. Bring to a boil, reduce heat, and simmer, covered, until fruit is tender and the liquid has cooked off (about 15 minutes).

Taste the sauce. If you feel it needs to be sweeter, add a teaspoon or two of unrefined cane sugar and reheat, stirring constantly, until it dissolves.

Remove cinnamon stick. Purée the applesauce in a blender, or mash with a potato masher, depending on whether you want a smooth or chunky consistency.

For babies 6 months and older: This is it! Perfect food for baby, mommy, and all. Omit the unrefined cane sugar for these wee ones.

Sunny Millet with Peaches

One summer day for breakfast we added ripe peaches to millet, and the combination became a favorite. As the season of fresh fruit unfolds, try apricots, pears, or plums. Yum!

Prep time: 30 minutes
Makes 4 servings

> **¾ cup millet**
> **1 peach (or other seasonal fruit), sliced**
> **1 cup water**
> **1 cup apple juice**
> **½ teaspoon sea salt**
> **Unsweetened apple butter, for garnish**

Place millet in fine strainer; rinse and drain. Combine millet, peach, water, juice, and salt in a 2-quart saucepan; bring to a boil. Cover and simmer on low for 20 to 25 minutes (until all water is absorbed). Serve in bowls with dollops of apple butter on top.

Orange Millet with Currants

Substitute 1 cup orange juice for 1 cup apple juice and use ¼ cup currants instead of the peach.

🥣 **For babies 6 months and older:** Remove some cooked millet, purée, and serve.

Orange Hazelnut Muesli

Muesli is handy for camping trips and hurried breakfasts. Preparing rolled oats this way gives them a slightly different texture you'll enjoy.

Prep time: 10 minutes (excluding overnight soaking)
Makes 4 servings

**2 cups rolled oats or rolled barley
(or some of both)**
⅓ cup hazelnuts, chopped
⅓ cup raisins
½ teaspoon ground cinnamon
½ teaspoon sea salt
2 cups boiling water
Juice of 2 oranges

Optional toppings
Grated apple
Sliced pear
Dollop of plain or vanilla yogurt

Place oats, hazelnuts, raisins, cinnamon, and sea salt in mixing bowl. Pour boiling water over mixture and stir. Add orange juice to mixture and stir again. Cover bowl with plate or cloth and allow moisture to soften grains 6 to 8 hours or overnight. Serve topped with apple, pear, and/or yogurt.

For babies 6 months and older: Steam some apple or pear slices until soft. Purée and serve.

Variation for children: Some may prefer plainer muesli. Omit hazelnuts and raisins, and they are optional as toppings in the morning.

Maple Butter Nut Granola

Use granola as a topping on hot cereal, fresh fruit, or yogurt. Homemade granola makes a quick snack for children on the move.

Prep time: 70 minutes

Makes 8 cups

> 3½ cups rolled oats
> ½ cup sesame seeds
> ½ cup sunflower seeds
> ½ cup pumpkin seeds
> ½ cup almonds, chopped
> ½ teaspoon ground cinnamon
> ½ teaspoon sea salt
> ½ cup butter
> ½ cup maple syrup
> 1 tablespoon nut butter
> 1 teaspoon vanilla extract
> ¼ teaspoon almond extract

Preheat oven to 325°F.

In a large mixing bowl, combine oats, seeds, almonds, cinnamon, and salt; mix well.

In a small pan melt butter; add maple syrup and nut butter and stir to blend. Remove from heat and add extracts.

Slowly pour wet ingredients over dry ingredients, using a spatula to fold and evenly coat the dry mixture with the wet.

Spread on a cookie sheet or in a shallow pan and bake until granola is dry and golden (45 to 60 minutes), turning granola every 15 or 20 minutes so that it toasts evenly. Store in an airtight jar.

☞ **For babies 10 months and older:** Use some of the rolled oats to make your baby a bowl of warm oatmeal. See page 62 for directions.

Kasha Pilaf with Poached Eggs

Versatile kasha (roasted buckwheat) need not be reserved for dinner. A Ukrainian restaurant on New York's Lower East Side serves kasha and eggs to large breakfast crowds. This hearty breakfast is a favorite of mine during the chilly winter months.

Prep time: 30 minutes
Makes 4 to 6 servings

> 1 tablespoon extra-virgin olive oil
> 1 small onion, chopped
> 1 clove garlic, minced
> ½ teaspoon sea salt
> 1 small potato, diced in ¼-inch cubes
> 1 cup kasha
> 2 cups boiling water
> ½ teaspoon vinegar
> 2 to 4 eggs

Heat oil in a 2-quart pan or a 10-inch skillet. Add onion, garlic, and salt; sauté until onion is soft. Add potato and kasha and stir to coat mixture evenly. Add boiling water, reduce heat to low so that mixture is barely simmering, cover, and cook for 15 to 20 minutes. Remove lid and tip pan to make sure all of the water is absorbed. Let kasha rest for 10 minutes while you poach the eggs.

Fill a 2-quart pan with water and bring to a boil. Add vinegar to boiling water. Break an egg into a small bowl. Lower heat so that water is at a simmer, and swirl the water into a vortex with a wooden spoon. Slide egg into the well formed in the center of the water. The swirling water should collect the egg. Turn the heat off and let the egg stand 3 minutes. Remove with a slotted spoon. Repeat with each egg.

Fluff kasha with a fork and place a scoop on serving plate. Top kasha with a poached egg and serve.

For babies 10 months and older: Purée some of the cooked kasha with a little water and serve.

Jam-Filled Mochi

Mochi is made from sweet brown rice that has been cooked, pounded into a paste, and then compressed into dense bars. When broken into squares and baked, it puffs up like a cream puff and gets gooey inside. Mochi comes plain or in several flavors; cinnamon-raisin mochi is the breakfast favorite at our home. Look for mochi in the refrigerated or frozen section of your natural foods store. Sweet brown rice is an excellent food for nursing moms. Children love this warm, chewy breakfast treat.

Prep time: 15 minutes
Makes 6 mochi squares

1 block mochi
All-fruit jam or preserves (your favorite flavor)

Preheat oven to 400°F. Break mochi into squares. The block is usually scored so that it can be broken easily into 2 x 2-inch squares. Place squares on a lightly oiled cookie sheet and put in the oven. Bake until mochi puffs up (10 to 12 minutes). Remove from oven. Open each square and slip a teaspoon or two of jam inside. Serve immediately.

For babies 6 months and older: Mochi is a little too sticky and chewy for a mouth with few teeth. Make some baby cereal out of sweet brown rice (See Toasted Whole Grain Baby Cereal, page 74) so you can both benefit from this unique type of rice.

Jeff's Potato Pancakes

Jeff Basom has been the chef of Bastyr University's renowned cafeteria for over a decade. I wouldn't know half of what I know about whole foods cooking had it not been for Jeff's tutelage. This recipe comes from a lovely spiral-bound recipe book the school produced called From the Bastyr Kitchen *(Bastyr University Press, 2004), which can be ordered at www.bastyr.edu/bookstore.*

Prep time: 60 minutes
Makes 12 pancakes

> 4 to 6 large potatoes (enough for 4½ cups when grated)
> 1 medium onion, ¼-inch dice
> 3 tablespoons butter and additional for frying
> ⅓ cup unbleached flour
> ¼ teaspoon pepper
> ½ teaspoon salt
> 2 large eggs

Boil potatoes until nearly done (when pierced with a fork the center will still feel slightly undercooked). Cool potatoes. Peel and grate on the largest holes of a grater. Place in a large bowl and set aside.

In a medium pan, sauté onion in butter on low heat until golden. Stir flour slowly into cooked onion. Add pepper and salt. Cook for one minute. Add onion to potatoes. Mix in eggs and form into 12 pancakes.

In a large skillet, on medium-low heat, cook pancakes in butter on both sides until deep golden brown (do not crowd, you may need to cook in batches).

For babies 6 months and older: These pancakes are delightful served with Homemade Applesauce; see page 79 for recipe.

Essene Bread and Fresh Fruit

The Essenes were a sect of monks from early biblical times who prepared a sweet, moist, flourless bread by slow-baking sprouted wheat. The bread is highly digestible. Look for Essene bread or sprouted bread in the refrigerated or frozen food section at your natural foods store.

Prep time: 12 to 15 minutes
Makes 4 servings

> **4 one-inch-thick slices of Essene bread**
> **2 teaspoons butter or nut butter**
> **4 to 6 cups fresh, seasonal fruit (such as blueberries, strawberries, or peaches)**

Heat oven to 300°F. Place bread slices on a cookie sheet and warm in oven for 5 to 10 minutes. Serve warm bread with butter on top next to a bowl of fresh fruit.

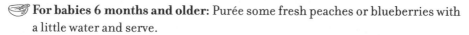 **For babies 6 months and older:** Purée some fresh peaches or blueberries with a little water and serve.

For babies 10 months and older: Serve a few bites of unbuttered bread.

Goldie's Whole Grain Pancake Mix

This basic pancake mix comes from Goldie Caughlan, nutrition educator at Puget Consumers Co-op in Seattle. There are many types of whole grain flours besides wheat that can be used to make baked goods. This recipe utilizes a combination of several. One perk of this mix is that it works equally well for waffles.

Prep time:
Makes 6 cups dry mix

> **2 cups barley or kamut flour**
> **2 cups whole wheat pastry flour**
> **1 cup buckwheat flour**
> **1 cup blue cornmeal**
> **3 tablespoons baking powder**
> **1 teaspoon ground cinnamon**
> **½ teaspoon sea salt**

Combine all ingredients and store in an airtight container.

Gluten-Free Pancake Mix

For a gluten-free pancake mix substitute 2⅓ cups rice flour, 1 cup potato starch, ⅔ cup tapioca flour, and ½ teaspoon xanthan gum for the 2 cups of barley and 2 cups of whole wheat pastry flours.

Buttermilk Banana Pancakes

Buttermilk is a cultured dairy product that is easy to digest. It also adds a rich flavor to baked goods. For a dairy-free version substitute soy, rice, or nut milk with 1 tablespoon lemon juice added to it. You will need to use an expeller-pressed refined oil to hold heat high enough to cook the pancakes without smoking.

Prep time: 25 to 30 minutes
Makes ten 5-inch pancakes

> 1 egg, separated
> 1 ½ cups Goldie's Whole Grain Pancake Mix (page 87) or dry whole grain pancake mix
> 1 cup buttermilk
> ½ cup water
> 1 ripe banana, cut into thin slices
> Oil for griddle

Beat egg white until stiff peaks form. Set aside.

In a large bowl, combine egg yolk, pancake mix, buttermilk, and water. Mix thoroughly with a whisk.

Add egg white and banana to batter and gently fold in.

Heat griddle to medium high and coat surface with small amount of oil. Pour enough batter onto griddle to form a 5-inch-diameter pancake. When pancake has cooked on the bottom (tiny bubbles form on the top), flip with a spatula and cook the other side. Repeat with the rest of the batter. Keep cooked pancakes in a warm oven until ready to serve.

For babies 6 months and older: Reserve some ripe banana. Mash and serve.

Variation for children: Put batter in a squeeze bottle and squeeze batter onto griddle in shapes such as letters, numbers, or animals.

Blueberry Sauce

This topping tastes great on pancakes, waffles, or hot cereal and also makes a beautiful finishing touch for desserts. I have used kudzu as a thickener. Kudzu comes from the dried root of the kudzu plant. It gives thickened liquids a glossy sheen and is thought to be soothing to the digestive tract. You can substitute arrowroot powder for the kudzu.

Prep time: 10 minutes
Makes 2 cups

> **2 tablespoons kudzu**
> **1 cup apple or berry fruit juice**
> **1 cup blueberries (fresh or frozen)**
> **2 to 3 tablespoons maple syrup**
> **1 teaspoon freshly squeezed lemon juice**

Dissolve kudzu in apple juice. Combine kudzu-juice mixture with blueberries and maple syrup in small saucepan. Bring mixture to a simmer, stirring constantly. Cook for about 3 minutes, until mixture turns clear and purple. Remove from heat, stir in lemon juice, and serve immediately.

For babies 6 months and older: Reserve some fresh blueberries, purée with a little water and serve.

Tofu Vegetable Breakfast Burritos

This colorful dish makes a hearty Sunday breakfast. Any vegetables can be substituted for the ones listed; however, this combination is scrumptious. Serve with a fresh fruit salad for brunch.

Prep time: 15 to 20 minutes
Makes 6 servings

1 tablespoon extra-virgin olive oil
½ teaspoon ground cumin
½ teaspoon ground coriander
⅛ teaspoon cayenne
½ medium onion, chopped
2 cloves garlic, minced
¼ red bell pepper, chopped

¼ green bell pepper, chopped
1 pound firm tofu, crumbled
½ teaspoon turmeric
½ to 1 tablespoon tamari or shoyu
¼ cup chopped fresh cilantro
6 whole grain tortillas
Salsa, for garnish

Heat oil in a 10-inch skillet over medium heat. Add cumin, coriander, and cayenne; stir briefly. Add onion and garlic; sauté until soft. Add peppers and sauté until they soften. Add tofu to skillet and stir. Sprinkle in turmeric and mix to add color. Add tamari and cilantro and toss.

Place about ⅓ cup of the tofu mixture in the middle of a tortilla; roll it up. Repeat with other tortillas. Serve warm with salsa on the side.

   For babies 10 months and older: Reserve some of the tofu, cut into cubes, heat briefly in boiling water or a skillet, and serve.

Healthy Home Fries

Just about everybody loves fried spuds. By steaming the potatoes first, you minimize the amount of oil needed. I like to serve these alongside eggs to start out an active day with a stick-with-you breakfast. They are also great for the school lunch box.

Prep time: 25 to 30 minutes
Makes 4 servings

> 6 red potatoes, cut into ¼-inch-thick slices
> 1 tablespoon extra-virgin olive oil
> 1 onion, cut in half-moons
> ½ teaspoon sea salt
> Freshly ground pepper

Place potatoes in a steamer basket and steam 7 to 10 minutes until tender.

Heat oil in a large skillet. Add onion and sauté until soft. Add steamed potatoes, salt, and pepper. Flip potatoes occasionally until browned on both sides. Serve warm.

☞ **For babies 6 months and older:** Reserve plain boiled or baked potatoes and blend or mash with breast milk or water.

Green Eggs (No Ham)

Use eggs from happy hens who have been allowed to dine on bugs and worms. This natural diet increases their anti-inflammatory fat content (omega-3). Remove the heat from the pan just before the eggs are completely set, and they'll be perfect by the time you serve them. This recipe is from my talented colleague Becky Boutch. These eggs can be rolled up in a chapati or tortilla for a different presentation.

Prep time: 10 minutes
Makes 2 to 3 servings

> 4 eggs
> 2 tablespoons water or milk
> ½ teaspoon sea salt
> 1 tablespoon butter
> 1 cup baby spinach leaves
> ¼ cup grated cheese, optional

Whisk together the eggs, water, and salt in a bowl. Heat a 10-inch skillet over medium heat. Add the butter; when it melts, add the eggs.

Using a heatproof rubber scraper or spatula, gently stir the eggs as they cook, lifting the curds from the bottom of the pan. When the eggs are nearly cooked, add the spinach and the cheese, if desired. Cover briefly (less than 1 minute) to wilt the spinach.

Remove from the pan when the eggs appear light and fluffy, but still shiny and wet. Serve immediately.

☞ **For babies 10 months and older:** Remember that egg whites are inappropriate for infants under 1 year of age. Egg yolks, however, are an excellent source of essential fatty acids. Boil an egg for 3 to 4 minutes, peel, discard white, and serve warm yolk with baby's cereal.

Ben's Friday Pancakes

This unique pancake has no flour but uses highly digestible soaked whole grains. It's adapted by Bastyr student Ronit Gourarie from Rebecca Wood's superb cookbook The Splendid Grain *(William Morrow and Company, Inc., 1997). Ronit routinely served these beauties to her son Ben every Friday.*

Prep time: 15 minutes plus 8 hours soaking time
Makes 6 to 8 pancakes

> ⅔ **cup steel-cut oats**
> ⅓ **cup raw buckwheat groats**
> 1¼ **cup milk***
> **1 egg**
> ¼ **teaspoon sea salt**
> **2 tablespoons unrefined cane sugar**
> **1 teaspoon baking powder**
> ½ **teaspoon freshly grated nutmeg**

Combine oats, buckwheat, and milk in blender jar. Cover and let soak overnight or 6 to 8 hours in the refrigerator.

Put blender bowl on base. Add remaining ingredients to grains and blend until smooth.

Preheat an oiled griddle or skillet. Pour about ¼ cup batter onto griddle and cook for about 2 minutes on each side or until golden. Repeat until all batter is used. Keep cooked pancakes warm in the oven while you finish.

🥣 **For babies 10 months and older:** Cut pancakes into small pieces and serve.

---

*   *Any milk—cow, goat, rice, soy, or nut—can be used. I also like using a combination of yogurt and water to soak the grains.*

Tempeh Bacon

Tempeh, originally an Indonesian food, is made from soybeans that have been cooked and split to remove the hull. A culture is added to the cooked beans, which age for several days before forming a solid piece that can be cut and sliced. This high-protein food can be baked, boiled, fried, or steamed. When fried and seasoned, this tasty meatlike substance can be used to accompany pancakes or turned into a vegetarian "TLT" sandwich.

Prep time: 7 to 10 minutes
Makes 4 to 6 servings

> 2 tablespoons coconut oil or ghee, divided
> 1 (8-ounce) package tempeh, cut into ¼-inch strips
> ½ teaspoon dried oregano, divided
> ½ teaspoon thyme, divided
> ½ teaspoon basil, divided
> 1 tablespoon tamari or shoyu

Heat a 10-inch skillet with 1 tablespoon of the oil to medium high. Let the oil get hot, but not smoking. Add half of the tempeh strips and pan fry about 30 seconds on each side. Sprinkle half of the herbs over tempeh as it fries. Remove tempeh and place it on a paper towel. Repeat process with remaining oil, tempeh, and herbs. When finished, sprinkle fried tempeh with tamari and serve.

For babies 6 months and older: Include some fresh melon with this breakfast. For baby, simply give a few chunks of melon a quick whirl in a blender. If the melon is quite ripe, babies with teeth can eat chunks as finger food.

Huevos Rancheros

Many accoutrements are often added to this traditional dish but are not necessary. Fresh eggs from pastured hens have a richer, sweeter flavor. A can of Muir Glen Fire Roasted Diced Tomatoes with Green Chiles is an excellent product to use, and some or all of the chile peppers can be omitted.

Prep time: 20 to 30 minutes
Makes 4 servings

1 tablespoon extra-virgin olive oil
¼ onion, chopped
3 cloves garlic, minced
3 chile peppers—serrano, habanero, or jalapeño
1 (16-ounce) can diced tomatoes
½ teaspoon sea salt
½ teaspoon chili powder
5 teaspoons butter
4 corn tortillas
4 eggs

Toppings and sides
Grated cheese or sour cream
Slices of ripe avocado
Black beans

Heat oil in a medium-size skillet. Add onion, garlic, chiles, tomatoes, salt, and chili powder. Bring sauce to a boil. Reduce heat and let simmer about 10 minutes. Keep warm.

In a second frying pan, heat 3 teaspoons of the butter a little at a time. Fry tortillas for about 30 seconds on each side, and set aside in a warm place.

Heat remaining butter over low heat until it is melted. Crack each egg into a small bowl; gently pour each egg into the skillet. Cook covered for 3 minutes, remove the cover, and cook for a few minutes more, or until the yolk is set, but a little undercooked.

Place each tortilla on a plate with an egg on top. Cover egg with the warm sauce. The sauce will finish cooking the top of the egg. Serve with cheese on top and avocado and beans on the side.

For babies 6 months and older: Some mashed avocado provides healthful fats and vitamins in a delicious, digestible form.

Lively Lunch Boxes

Karen's Sesame Noodles
Dilled Brown Rice and Kidney Beans
Santa Fe Black Bean Salad
Lemon Basil Potato Salad
Aunt Cathy's Crunchy Ramen Coleslaw
Emerald City Salad
Hijiki Pâté
Tempeh Avocado Sushi Rolls
Asian Noodle Salad with Toasted Sesame Dressing
Quick Lemon and Garlic Quinoa Salad
Rice Balls Rolled in Sesame Salt
Tempeh Club Sandwiches
French Lentil Dijon Spread
Hummus
Salmon and Reuben Sandwiches
Apple Miso Almond Butter Sandwiches
Tamari-Roasted Nuts
Sweet Glazed Nuts
Fresh Vegetable Spring Rolls
Savory Lunch Box Roll-Ups

PACKING A WHOLESOME LUNCH BOX

Here are some suggestions for caretakers who pack lunch regularly for children.

▶ Make a lunch box chart (a sample is printed on the following page). If your child is 5 or older, let them help plan and make the chart. Children are more likely to eat the food if they have helped plan the menu. Renew the chart as the seasons change. Post your chart for easy reference.

▶ Include one item in the lunch box that is a "growing food" (a protein source). Choose either a vegetarian protein combination like whole grains with beans or nuts, or include some animal protein.

▶ Always give your child something fresh (fruit or vegetable) in their lunch box. This adds vitamins, minerals, and enzymes!

▶ Though many food companies make convenient, happy-looking foods for lunches, remember to be discerning and read labels. Avoid giving young bodies foods with additives, preservatives, food coloring, cheap oils, and nonnutritious sweeteners (e.g., corn syrup, high-fructose corn syrup, Splenda, or sucralose).

▶ Rather than packing juice, tuck in a small container of fruity herbal tea or sparkling water. This helps prevent children from drinking their meal and discarding the real food their body needs.

▶ For an earth-friendly lunch box, use a bright-colored cloth napkin and silverware instead of wasteful paper and plastic.

▶ On days where you feel like adding something extra, add a fresh flower, a poem, a neat rock or crystal, a jingle bell, a cartoon, a finger puppet, or a note from you instead of candy.

▶ If your child's school is open to the idea, consider having "Hot Soup Fridays," where parents bring in enough hot soup and bread for the whole class on a rotating basis. This is especially nice on cold days where warm food can be so satisfying.

You and your child can use the chart on the next page to plan some favorite combinations. Post your chart for easy reference.

Lunch box	GROWING FOOD	VEGETABLE	SEASONAL FRUIT
MONDAY			
TUESDAY			
WEDNESDAY			
THURSDAY			
FRIDAY			

SAMPLE LUNCH BOXES

The following are a handful of lunch box combinations I have used. The foods in **bold** are recipes that can be found in this book.

GROWING FOOD	VEGETABLE	SEASONAL FRUIT
Burrito (whole wheat tortilla, mashed pinto beans, salsa, grated cheese)	Cucumber slices	Red grapes and **Lemon Raspberry Thumbprint Cookies**
Tofu slices sautéed in butter and tamari with brown rice	Nori (cut in shapes)	Satsuma
Karen's Sesame Noodles and **Tempeh Bacon**	Baked sweet potato	Plum
Turkey sandwich on sprouted whole grain bread	Corn	Apple slices
Rice Balls Rolled in Sesame Salt	Snap peas	Nectarine slices
Baked or grilled chicken slices	Sweet squash, corn muffin	Kiwi slices
Apple Miso Almond Butter Sandwich	Steamed green beans	Melon slices
Whole wheat pita bread and **Hummus**	Celery sticks	Dates and **Tamari Roasted Nuts**
Smoked salmon chunks	Roasted potatoes and carrots	Pear
Black beans and corn chips	Carrot sticks	Strawberries
Avocado, cheese, cucumber, and sprouts sandwich	Blanched broccoli	Fresh pineapple chunks

Karen's Sesame Noodles

My daughter's godmother, Karen Brown, always made these for our potlucks in New York, and they were the first entrée to disappear. Udon or soba noodles work well in this dish. Tahini is a creamy paste made of crushed, hulled sesame seeds. Different nut and seed butters can be interchanged in this recipe to vary the flavor.

Prep time: 15 minutes
Makes 4 servings

> **8 ounces udon or soba noodles**
> **3 tablespoons tahini**
> **1 tablespoon almond or cashew butter**
> **1 teaspoon maple syrup**
> **2 tablespoons brown rice vinegar**
> **2 tablespoons tamari or shoyu**
> **1 teaspoon toasted sesame oil**
> **½ teaspoon ground coriander**

Cook noodles in plenty of boiling water according to directions on package.

While noodles cook, make the sauce. Put the remaining ingredients in small bowl and blend. Add enough warm water to create a creamy texture.

Rinse and drain cooked noodles. Pour sauce over noodles and toss well.

For babies 10 months and older: Omit sauce. Cut plain noodles into bite-size pieces and serve.

Variation for children: Try serving the sauce on the side and letting children dip the noodles in the sauce.

Dilled Brown Rice and Kidney Beans

This is a wonderful summer salad that can be used for picnics, potlucks, or a cold supper. Dill and red onion give the grain-and-bean combination a genuine zip. Umeboshi plum vinegar, the leftover juice from the umeboshi plum–pickling process, gives a unique salty-sour taste to food.

Prep time: 10 minutes if rice is already cooked
Makes 4 servings

Salad

2 cups cooked brown rice
1½ cups cooked kidney beans
½ cup red onion, chopped

Dressing

3 tablespoons extra-virgin olive oil
3 tablespoons brown rice vinegar
1 tablespoon umeboshi plum vinegar
2 tablespoons snipped fresh dill or
2 teaspoons dried

Put rice, beans, and onion in a large bowl. Mix oil, vinegars, and dill in a separate bowl with whisk or shake in a small jar. Pour dressing over rice mixture; toss gently. If possible, let set an hour or two, as flavors will mellow with time.

For babies 6 months and older: Reserve some of the cooked brown rice and blend with water or breast milk.

For babies 10 months and older: Reserve some plain, cooked kidney beans and plain rice and blend to desired consistency; add water if necessary.

Santa Fe Black Bean Salad

A delicious combination of Southwestern flavors, perfect for a potluck, lunch box entrée, or a summer meal. Serve with corn tortillas or Polenta (page 63). Frozen corn can be thawed and used if fresh corn is unavailable.

Prep time: 20 minutes
Makes 6 servings

Salad

1 red pepper
2 cups cooked black beans
½ cup fresh corn, cut off the cob
⅓ cup chopped cilantro

Dressing

2 to 3 cloves garlic
½ teaspoon sea salt
2 tablespoons extra-virgin olive oil
2 tablespoons lime juice
¼ teaspoon cayenne

Roast the red pepper.

To roast the pepper on a gas stove, place pepper directly on the low flame of a gas burner, letting skin char. Keep turning pepper until skin is charred on all sides. Let cool and remove black char under cool running water. Cut pepper open and remove seeds and stem. Cut into small strips.

To roast the pepper on an electric range, place pepper in shallow pan and put in oven under the broiler. Let the skin char. Turn pepper every few minutes until the skin is completely charred. Remove pepper from oven and place in brown paper bag. Close bag and let pepper sweat for 15 to 30 minutes. Remove pepper and peel off charred skin under cool running water. Cut pepper open and remove seeds and stem. Cut into small strips.

To make the salad, combine strips of roasted red pepper, beans, corn, and cilantro in medium-size mixing bowl; set aside. Place garlic and salt on a cutting board; chop to a pastelike consistency. In a separate small bowl, mix together garlic paste, oil, lime juice, and cayenne. Pour dressing over beans and vegetables; toss gently.

✎ **For babies 10 months and older:** Reserve some plain, cooked black beans and corn and purée together.

Lemon Basil Potato Salad

Fresh basil makes an impressive contribution to the flavor of soups, vegetables, noodles, beans, and fish. Try growing basil in your yard or in your kitchen window. This is a not-just-for-lunch kind of salad. Try serving it with Orange-Glazed Salmon Kebobs with Yogurt Garlic Dip (page 167) for your next summer dinner party.

Prep time: 20 minutes
Makes 6 servings

Salad

6 to 8 cups red potatoes washed, scrubbed, and cut in chunks

Dressing

3 to 4 cloves garlic
⅓ cup tightly packed fresh basil
½ teaspoon sea salt
1 teaspoon lemon zest
¼ cup extra-virgin olive oil
¼ cup freshly squeezed lemon juice

Place potatoes in large pot of boiling water. Cook 10 to 12 minutes, or until tender.

While potatoes are cooking, place garlic, basil, salt, and lemon zest on cutting board. Chop together to a pastelike consistency. Combine garlic paste with oil and lemon juice; set aside.

Drain potatoes and let cool. Pour dressing over slightly warm potatoes; toss gently. Serve immediately or chill to serve later.

For babies 6 months and older: Reserve some boiled potatoes and mash with water or breast milk.

Aunt Cathy's Crunchy Ramen Coleslaw

Ramen is a small block of curly noodles that can be prepared in just minutes. It is made from a variety of flours and usually comes packaged with a packet of dry seasonings to be used in cooking. Look for ramen made from whole grain flours. This coleslaw uses the noodles dry to create a wonderful texture and taste.

Prep time: 10 to 15 minutes
Makes 6 servings

Salad
3 to 4 tablespoons sunflower seeds
3 cups shredded cabbage
3 scallions, finely sliced
½ cup grated carrot
½ package (single serving)
   brown rice ramen

Dressing
4 tablespoons extra-virgin olive oil
3 tablespoons balsamic vinegar
½ teaspoon sea salt
Freshly ground pepper

Toast sunflower seeds by placing them in a dry skillet on medium heat. Stir or shake constantly until seeds begin to emit a nutty aroma (about 5 minutes).

Combine cabbage, scallions, carrot, and sunflower seeds in large mixing bowl. Place ramen noodles on a cutting board. Using a rolling pin, roll over uncooked noodles to break into small pieces; add to salad. Toss salad with oil and vinegar; add salt and pepper to taste.

🥣 **For babies 10 months and older:** Cook unused half of ramen noodles according to package directions. Cut into small pieces and serve plain.

Emerald City Salad

This colorful salad was inspired by the beautiful deli salad at Puget Consumers Co-op, Seattle's beloved chain of natural foods grocery stores. It is so popular that I have filled many classes with the mere mention that I would be demonstrating how to make this salad.

Prep time: 1 hour and 15 minutes
Makes 6 to 8 servings

2½ cups water or vegetable
  or chicken stock
1 tablespoon butter
1 teaspoon sea salt, divided
1 cup wild rice (black, ½-inch long)
¼ cup lemon juice
¼ cup olive oil
1 clove garlic, minced
½ cup chopped fennel bulb,
  core removed

½ red or yellow pepper, diced
½ cup chopped red cabbage
½ cup chopped Italian parsley
2 cups very finely chopped dark, leafy greens
  (6 to 7 leaves of chard, kale, or collards)
Salt and lemon to taste
Pecorino or Gorgonzola cheese, for
  garnish (optional)

Bring water to a boil. Add butter, ½ teaspoon of the salt, and rice. Bring to a boil again, cover, lower heat, and simmer 60 to 65 minutes. Make sure all of the water is absorbed by tipping the pan to one side to check for pooled liquid.

Combine lemon juice, olive oil, garlic, and remaining ½ teaspoon of salt in a large serving bowl. Add fennel, red pepper, cabbage, parsley, and greens and toss thoroughly.

Once the rice is fully cooked, cool until it ceases steaming but is still warm, then place it on top of the dressed vegetables. When the rice cools to room temperature, toss it with the vegetables. Taste the salad and adjust seasonings; some extra salt and/or lemon may be required. Garnish with cheese, if desired.

For babies 6 months and older: Add a teaspoon of fresh chopped parsley to baby's cereal.

For babies 10 months and older: Offer some simple plain, cooked wild rice. Though the flavor is strong, you may be surprised by your child's reaction.

Hijiki Pâté

Hijiki is the richest in calcium of all the sea vegetables. Its thick, black strands look striking with other colors. As with other sea vegetables, it is purchased dried and reconstituted before using. The strong "sea" taste can be moderated by cooking hijiki in apple juice. Mim Collins and her teacher, Roberta Lewis, came up with this scrumptious way to use hijiki. I have seen 2-year-olds, as well as adults, gobble it up with glee.

Prep time: 30 to 40 minutes
Makes 2½ to 3 cups

> **1 cup hijiki*, dry**
> **1 to 1½ cups water or apple juice**
> **1 tablespoon tamari or shoyu**
> **¼ cup sesame seeds**
> **½ pound firm tofu, crumbled with a fork**
> **2 tablespoons white or mellow miso**
> **½ bunch parsley, finely chopped**
> **2 scallions, thinly sliced**

Soak hijiki in water for 5 minutes and chop fine. Put hijiki in a medium-size pan and add water to cover; bring to a simmer. Cover pan and cook until water is absorbed, about 20 minutes. Toward the end of the cooking time, season hijiki with tamari.

While hijiki is cooking, prepare other ingredients. Toast sesame seeds in a skillet on the stove for 5 to 8 minutes, then grind them in a coffee or spice grinder. Gently mix tofu, sesame seeds, miso, parsley, and scallions together in a bowl.

Let the hijiki cool and then add to the tofu mixture. For a more puréed texture put mixture in food processor and pulse a few times. Serve with whole grain crackers or bread, or as a side dish. Dish will keep 3 days in the refrigerator.

For babies 10 months and older: Serve cubes of blanched (quickly dropped in boiling water) tofu.

---

*   *There has been some recent information warning against consumption of hijiki because of its arsenic content. The sources I have looked into claim that it is of little risk unless hijiki is consumed on a daily basis. I feel the benefits of occasional consumption outweigh the risks.*

Tempeh Avocado Sushi Rolls

Sushi rolls can contain a variety of fillings. Nori and daikon (Japanese white radish) are available at natural foods stores and Asian markets. You can find a bamboo rolling mat at most Asian markets. These rolls make wonderful, nutritious food for traveling or picnics.

Prep time: 30 minutes, if rice is precooked
Makes 24 pieces

4 cups cooked short-grain rice
2 tablespoons mirin
2 tablespoons brown rice syrup
2 tablespoons brown rice vinegar
4 ounces tempeh
2 tablespoons coconut oil
1 ripe avocado
1 carrot
4 sheets toasted nori

Dipping sauce

¼ cup tamari
1 tablespoon grated daikon
2 tablespoons water

Place rice in a large bowl. Heat mirin, syrup, and vinegar in a small pan until pourable. Add warm mixture to the rice and toss together. It is best to season the rice while it is still warm.

Cut tempeh into long thin strips. Heat oil in a skillet. Add tempeh, turning strips until brown on all sides. Remove and place on a paper towel.

Cut the avocado into thin slices (you may use only half the avocado). Cut the carrot lengthwise into long thin strips.

Lay nori shiny side down on a bamboo mat. Spread rice mixture onto the nori, leaving ½ inch open on the top and bottom. Place strips of filling lengthwise in the middle of the rice. Lift bamboo rolling mat from edge nearest you and begin to roll, tucking firmly into the center while bending the mat up, taking care not to catch it in the roll. Gently squeeze the roll to make it even. Set the roll aside and repeat the procedure with the remaining nori.

Using a wet, sharp knife, cut the roll into equal pieces using a back-and-forth sawing motion.

Put all ingredients for dipping sauce together in a small attractive bowl. These rolls will hold well for several hours placed in a sealed container or wrapped in plastic wrap.

For babies 6 months and older: Reserve some rice before dressing it. Purée rice and a few bits of nori together with water or breast milk and serve. Mashed avocado is also an option.

Asian Noodle Salad with Toasted Sesame Dressing

I have taught a class called "Whole Foods Salads" many times, and Asian Noodle Salad is often the favorite dish. You can create a most impressive summer meal by serving this with Nori-Wrapped Wasabi Salmon (page 168). Nutritionally impressive, too!

Prep time: 20 to 25 minutes
Makes 4 to 6 servings

Salad

1 (8-ounce) package soba noodles
¼ cup sesame seeds
¼ cup chopped cilantro leaves

Optional Additions

Chives
Chopped red cabbage
Finely sliced radishes
Sliced scallions

Dressing

2 tablespoons toasted sesame oil
3 tablespoons tamari or shoyu
3 tablespoons balsamic vinegar
1 tablespoon maple syrup
1 tablespoon hot pepper oil

Cook soba noodles according to package directions. Drain and rinse in colander.

Toast sesame seeds by placing in a dry skillet over medium heat. Keep seeds moving until they give off aroma, pop, and begin to change color. Remove and set aside.

Combine dressing ingredients in small bowl; whisk together.

Place drained noodles in a large bowl. Add dressing, sesame seeds, and cilantro; toss gently. Add chopped vegetables, if desired, and toss again.

For babies 10 months and older: Reserve some plain noodles and cut up into small pieces.

Variation for children: Omit hot pepper oil in dressing. Some children may prefer plain noodles without any dressing and cut-up vegetables on the side.

Quick Lemon and Garlic Quinoa Salad

Quinoa has an excellent nutritional profile (10.5 grams of protein per cup). This unique whole grain, which was a staple food of the Incas, is also rich in calcium and iron. I find myself getting very hungry for this salad.

Prep time: 15 to 20 minutes
Makes 4 to 6 servings

Salad

1 cup dry quinoa
½ teaspoon sea salt
1¾ cups water
½ cup chopped carrots
⅓ cup minced parsley
¼ cup sunflower seeds

Dressing

3 to 4 cloves garlic, minced
¼ cup freshly squeezed lemon juice
¼ cup extra-virgin olive oil
1 to 2 tablespoons tamari or shoyu

I added dressing per portion
I also cooked carrots & sunfl. seeds —

Rinse quinoa and drain. Place rinsed quinoa, salt, and water in a 2-quart pot. Bring to a boil, reduce heat to low, cover, and let simmer 15 to 20 minutes, until all the water is absorbed. Tip pan to the side to make sure all the water has been absorbed. Let stand for 5 to 10 minutes uncovered, then fluff with a fork.

Place cooked quinoa in a large bowl. Add carrots, parsley, and sunflower seeds to quinoa. Mix thoroughly. Combine dressing ingredients; pour over quinoa and toss well. Serve at room temperature or chilled.

For babies 6 months and older: Reserve some plain, cooked quinoa. Purée quinoa with water or breast milk.

Rice Balls Rolled in Sesame Salt

I did a cooking project with elementary school children on brown rice and its various uses. To my surprise, they literally licked the bowls when we prepared this simple snack. Rice balls travel well in a lunch box or backpack, and they give children the nutritional boost they need to stay on the go. A suribachi is a serrated ceramic mortar that is available at many Asian markets.

Prep time: 20 minutes if rice is already cooked
Makes 12 to 15 rice balls and 1 cup sesame salt

Rice
¾ cup brown rice
¼ cup sweet brown rice
½ teaspoon sea salt
1½ cups water

Sesame Salt
1 cup brown sesame seeds
1 teaspoon sea salt

To make the rice: It is best to pressure-cook the rice for rice balls. Boiled rice will not hold together to form balls. Rinse and drain brown and sweet brown rice. Place rice, salt, and water in the pressure cooker. Lock cooker. Place on high heat and bring up to pressure. When pressure gauge rises and is firm, you will hear a gentle, steady hissing sound. Lower heat and cook for 35 to 40 minutes. Remove from heat and allow pressure to come down naturally or by running cold water over the top. Allow rice to cool to room temperature before making rice balls (this can be speeded up by setting the cooker in a sink full of cold water).

To make the sesame salt: Rinse sesame seeds and drain through a fine strainer. Put seeds in a dry skillet (preferably cast iron) on medium heat. Toast seeds, stirring constantly, until seeds begin to pop, change color slightly, and give off a toasty aroma. Put toasted seeds and salt in a suribachi and grind with a pestle, or grind seeds and salt together in a blender or food processor. This condiment can be stored in a sealed container and used to flavor many foods, such as popcorn.

To make the rice balls: Spread about ⅓ cup of the sesame salt on a plate or a shallow baking pan. Moisten hands with water and gather a small handful of cooked rice in your hand. Press your hands around the rice, packing it into a small ball about the size of a Ping-Pong ball. Roll the ball in the sesame salt, covering all sides. Repeat until rice is used up or desired amount is obtained. Rice balls will keep for 5 days in a covered container in the refrigerator.

For added flavor make a tamari-ginger sauce for dipping: add 1 teaspoon grated ginger to ¼ cup tamari and ¼ cup water.

For babies 6 months and older: Reserve some of the cooked brown rice and blend with water or breast milk to make cereal.

Tempeh Club Sandwiches

Marinated tempeh is very versatile. I especially like this hearty and tasty sandwich with pickles on it. Serve with a simple vegetable soup for an easy-to-prepare meal. To learn more about tempeh or mirin see Appendix B, "Identifying, Purchasing, and Storing Whole Foods."

Prep time: 5 minutes to make marinade, 5 minutes to make sandwiches
Makes 4 sandwiches

3 cloves garlic, sliced
4 to 5 slices (⅛-inch thick)
   of fresh ginger
½ cup water
1 tablespoon brown rice vinegar
1 tablespoon mirin
1 tablespoon tamari
1 (8-ounce) package of tempeh
2 tablespoons coconut oil or ghee
8 slices sprouted whole grain bread

Optional garnishes
Lettuce
Pickle slices
Sprouts
Avocado slices
Tomato slices
Mustard
Mayonnaise
Ketchup

In the morning, combine garlic, ginger, water, vinegar, mirin, and tamari in a glass container that has a lid that seals. Slice the tempeh block in half. Take each half and bisect it through the middle to make four thin slabs of tempeh, each slightly smaller than a piece of bread. Put tempeh in the marinade and seal container. Refrigerate for a minimum of 4 hours.

Heat oil in a skillet over medium high heat. Remove tempeh pieces from marinade, pat with a paper towel, and put in skillet. Brown for a minute or so on each side. Serve on bread with your favorite garnishes.

For babies 6 months and older: Mash or blend some ripe avocado and serve.

OK (I forgot to put tempeh in skillet)
try w/ lettuce as wrap next time

French Lentil Dijon Spread

French lentils are those tiny black lentils that are so tasty. This sandwich spread tastes scrumptious on whole wheat toast with lettuce, tomato, and mayonnaise, or wrapped snugly in a whole wheat chapati. Works well as a party dip for crackers and vegetables, too. For basic lentil cooking instructions see page 65.

Prep time: 10 minutes
Makes 1-plus cups

pretty good

2 tablespoons walnuts
1 cup cooked French lentils
2 mushrooms, sliced
1 scallion, sliced
1 clove garlic
1 tablespoon whole grain mustard
1 tablespoon tamari
½ teaspoon pepper
Water

Finely grind walnuts in a blender or coffee grinder, or chop well with a knife on a cutting board. Place nuts, lentils, mushrooms, scallion, garlic, mustard, tamari and pepper in a food processor and blend until smooth. Add a little water if desired to get the consistency you desire. This spread will keep in the refrigerator for several days.

For babies 10 months and older: Reserve plain, cooked lentils and purée with a little water. Add cooked brown rice or baked sweet potato to purée for a swell combination.

Hummus

Hummus is a traditional Middle Eastern dish excellent for vegetarian sandwiches. The combination of chickpeas and tahini creates a high-protein spread. Tahini is a creamy paste made of crushed, hulled sesame seeds. Serve this delicious spread with warm pita bread and fresh vegetables.

Prep time: 10 minutes
Makes 2¾ to 3 cups

> 2 cups cooked chickpeas
> 5 tablespoons tahini
> 1 teaspoon sea salt
> ⅓ cup freshly squeezed lemon juice (juice of 1½ to 2 lemons)
> 2 to 3 cloves garlic
> 3 tablespoons extra-virgin olive oil
> ¼ cup water or cooking liquid
> Chopped parsley, for garnish
> Paprika, for garnish

Place chickpeas in a food processor or blender with tahini, salt, lemon juice, garlic, and olive oil. Blend until smooth. Add water or cooking liquid from beans a little at a time to get desired consistency. Garnish with chopped parsley or paprika, if desired. Stores well refrigerated for at least a week.

For babies 10 months and older: Reserve some plain, cooked chickpeas and mash. Some babies may enjoy picking up and eating plain, cooked chickpeas; be sure they are cooked well.

Variation for children: Hummus may be too spicy; try reducing lemon juice and garlic by half.

Salmon and Reuben Sandwiches

I had something like this in a restaurant for lunch and thought it was heavenly. When my colleague Jennifer Adler introduced me to Bubbies Sauerkraut, which contains just cabbage and salt and is found in the refrigerated section, I started making these. When sauerkraut is fermented naturally it is full of beneficial enzymes and has a very fresh taste. For a nondairy version use avocado slices instead of cheese.

Prep time: 10 to 15 minutes
Makes 2 sandwiches

½ **pound smoked salmon**
4 **slices rye bread** *(millet)*
2 **slices Swiss cheese** *(rice cheese)*
¾ **cup sauerkraut**
2 **teaspoons butter** *(earth balance)*

Optional condiments
Avocado slices
Ketchup
Mayonnaise
Mustard ✓

Cut salmon into thin pieces. Spread preferred condiments on each side of the bread. Place cheese on one side, salmon on the other. Place half of the sauerkraut on top of the salmon. Put sandwiches together.

Heat butter in a large skillet over medium heat. Place sandwiches in the skillet, salmon side down, and brown the bread. Turn, cover skillet with a lid, and heat sandwiches until cheese melts. Cut in half and serve.

For babies 6 months and older: Use avocado on the sandwich and mash up a few slices for baby.

For babies 10 months and older: Use real rye bread, where the only ingredients are rye flour, water, and salt, and serve a few pieces of toasted bread.

great for a splurge

Can use collards instead of bread
doesn't need cheese

pan steamd chard w/ wild sockeye salmon, sauerkraut avocado, mustard — yum!

Apple Miso Almond Butter Sandwiches

Try this sweet and nutty combo for a new twist on the usual peanut butter and jelly. It's quick to make, and I think you'll be surprised by the delicious and satisfying taste.

Prep time: 5 minutes
Makes 4 to 5 sandwiches

> ⅓ **cup unsweetened apple butter**
> **1 to 2 teaspoons white or mellow miso**
> ¼ **cup smooth almond butter**
> **Whole grain bread**

Place apple butter in a small bowl and stir miso into it. Spread bread with a light layer of almond butter on one side and apple miso butter on the other. Put bread together.

🥄 **For babies 6 months and older:** Stir ½ teaspoon of apple butter into baby's whole grain cereal for a new flavor.

For babies 10 months and older: Stir ½ teaspoon of almond butter into baby's warm whole grain cereal for added calories and other nutrients.

Tamari-Roasted Nuts

Tamari-roasted nuts make a crunchy addition to any lunch box. Sprinkle a few on salads or grains to liven up flavor and texture. A jar of these nuts makes a welcome Christmas gift as well. For more information about tamari and shoyu, see Appendix B, "Identifying, Purchasing, and Storing Whole Foods."

Prep time: 15 minutes
Makes 2 cups

> **1 cup whole raw almonds**
> **1 cup whole raw cashews**
> **1 to 2 tablespoons tamari or shoyu**
> ½ **teaspoon ground cumin**
> ½ **teaspoon ground coriander**
> **Pinch cayenne (optional)**

Preheat oven to 300°F. Place nuts on a cookie sheet. Toast in oven until they begin to turn golden and give off a nutty aroma (10 to 12 minutes).

Mix tamari and spices together. Sprinkle over toasted nuts; stir and return to oven to dry out (2 to 3 minutes). For a more even coating, put tamari in a spray bottle and mist roasted nuts, then stir in spices and dry in oven. Store in a sealed jar.

🥄 **For babies 10 months and older:** Remove a few of the toasted nuts before sprinkling with tamari and spices. Grind to a fine meal and stir tiny amounts into baby's cereal or vegetables for added calories and new flavor.

Variation for children: For picky children, tamari-roast just one kind of nut instead of mixing several.

Sweet Glazed Nuts

These are delicious on hot cereal, in a fresh green salad, or as an excellent snack. They satisfy the need for sweets and fats in a very nutritious way.

Prep time: 20 minutes
Makes ⅔ cup

> **2 tablespoons plus ½ teaspoon extra-virgin olive oil**
> **2 tablespoons maple syrup**
> **¼ teaspoon ground cinnamon**
> **Pinch of sea salt**
> **Tiny pinch of cayenne**
> **⅔ cup whole pecans or walnuts**

Preheat oven to 300°F. Lightly coat a cake pan or 8 x 8-inch ovenproof dish with ½ teaspoon of oil.

Combine remaining 2 tablespoons oil, maple syrup, cinnamon, salt, and cayenne in a bowl, add nuts and toss to coat. Spread nut mixture in cake pan.

Bake until nuts are golden and maple syrup bubbles—about 15 minutes. Stir occasionally to break up clumps. Remove from oven and cool slightly; remove from pan with a spatula while slightly warm.

🥄 **For babies 10 months and older:** Make Soaked Whole Grain Baby Porridge (page 75) for baby. Toast one or two walnuts with the grain before soaking and cooking.

BREAD FOR SANDWICHES

Finding good bread is important for making a great sandwich. When closely inspected, many whole grain breads have undesirable ingredients. A good loaf of bread should actually be quite simple, with a short list of ingredients on the label. Flour, salt, water, yeast, and a little sweetener to make the yeast grow is really all you need.

Some 100 percent whole wheat breads can be a bit heavy and hard to digest, especially for young children. What's a nutrition-conscious sandwich-maker to do? There are actually many excellent choices. Check out some of these for your next sliced masterpiece.

▶ **Whole grain bread:** Regardless of what the title of the bread is, read the label. Terms like "wheat flour" or "multi-grain" are ambiguous. If you are going for whole grains in your bread, the label needs to say "whole wheat flour," "whole wheat," "stoneground whole wheat," or "whole grain [name of grain]." Look for the word "whole." Avoid buying breads with refined sweeteners and additives.

▶ **Sprouted grain bread:** Sprouted grain bread involves soaking the grain and allowing it to sprout. The sprouted seedlings are then mashed together and baked. Sprouting allows the enzymes in the grain to convert some of the carbohydrates and fats to vitamins, minerals, and amino acids. These flourless whole grain breads are light and very digestible—a nice choice for young children.

▶ **Sourdough bread:** The live cultures created by the sourdough culture allow the bread to rise without using yeast or a sweetener. The culture also aids in the digestibility of the bread. There are whole grain sourdough breads that are 100 percent whole wheat and some that use a combination of whole wheat and white flour. The combination of flours works well to make light but very tasty bread for children.

▶ **Artisan breads:** Many metropolitan areas have bakeries where fresh bread can be purchased or who deliver fresh bread to local grocery stores. They usually offer a whole grain choice and are happy to reveal the ingredients used. Breads that combine whole grain flour and white flour can be a good compromise if you don't want the heavy texture, but want the nutritional benefits of whole grain. Artisan breads tend to be a bit pricey, but their fresh flavor and simple ingredients make them worth the cost.

▶ **Wheat-free breads:** Most natural foods grocery stores and some bakeries carry breads made from spelt or kamut. Both grains are very nutritious and contain enough gluten for easy bread making. Another option is sourdough rye bread, which should have very few ingredients (rye flour, water, salt, starter).

▶ **Gluten-free breads:** These are sometimes more difficult to find but essential for those who suffer from severe gluten intolerances. The breads are usually made from potato, rice, soy, amaranth, quinoa, buckwheat, or bean flour (or some combination of these) instead of wheat flour.

Fresh Vegetable Spring Rolls

As with roll-ups (page 121), there are endless variations in creating fresh spring rolls. Many combinations are awfully yummy served with Coconut Peanut Sauce (page 228) as a dipping sauce. Rice wrappers are available in most Asian grocery stores. Many thanks to my former students Teresa Dowling and Carlie Bockelman for sharing their love of spring rolls and their recipes with me.

Prep time: 30 minutes
Makes 10 rolls

1 medium carrot	**Optional additions**
1 medium zucchini	**Fried tofu**
2 lettuce leaves	**Grilled chicken**
1 medium ripe avocado	**Cooked shrimp**
10 rice wrappers	**Fresh basil, mint, or cilantro leaves**
Juice of 1 medium lime	

Julienne or coarsely shred the carrot and zucchini. Cut the lettuce leaves by rolling them up and cutting them into very thin strips. Halve the avocado and remove the pit. Score thin slices on one avocado half and remove, repeat for the other half.

Fill a large round pie plate or cake pan with warm water. Soak rice wrappers, one at a time, for about 15 seconds on each side until soft but still firm to the touch. Remove the soft skin from the water and lay it flat on a hard surface; plastic or metal works best.

Place a couple of avocado slices on the top third of the skin. Top that with some of the grated carrot, zucchini, lettuce, and any other additional ingredients. The key here is not to add too many vegetables to overstuff the roll. Next, squeeze a ¼ teaspoon of the lime juice over the vegetables.

Working quickly, fold the edge closest to you over the filling and pull the filling in. Fold the sides toward the center and then roll closed. Rolls will be about 4 inches long and 1½ inches wide. Repeat procedure until you have made 10 rolls. Place them in a dish, cover, and refrigerate until ready to serve.

For babies 10 months and older: Any of the finely cut up vegetables can be blended into baby's cereal or served as a finger food.

Savory Lunch Box Roll-Ups

Roll-ups can be filled with your favorite foods. Use the suggestions on the following page or create your own. They are scrumptious served with a dipping sauce like Lemon Tahini Sauce (page 231) or Mango Salsa (page 235). Sprouted whole wheat tortillas make a nice option for these roll-ups.

Prep time: 5 minutes
Makes 4 roll-ups

4 whole wheat tortillas or chapatis
2 cups filling (your choice of grain-
    protein-vegetable combinations;
    see "Suggestions for Roll-Up
    Fillings," page 121)

Optional spreads and garnishes

Avocado slices
Grated carrots
Grated zucchini
Shredded lettuce or cabbage
Pickles
Sprouts
Tomatoes

Place tortilla flat on your working surface. Spread the filling in a fat line down the middle. Put whatever other garnishes you want on top.

Fold in the left and right edges to form a rectangle. Wrap the edge closest to you around the filling, press in tight, fold up the sides and finish by wrapping the rest up like a rug.

🥄 **For babies 10 months and older:** Leftover cooked beans not only make great roll-ups, they can be mashed or puréed to make food for baby. Well-cooked whole beans can be used for finger food once your baby has a few teeth.

SUGGESTIONS FOR ROLL-UP FILLINGS

- Black beans and brown rice with scallions and cilantro
- Cooked shrimp, shredded lettuce, and a vinaigrette
- Dilled Brown Rice and Kidney Beans (page 102)
- French Lentil Dijon Spread (page 113)
- Grilled chicken and avocado
- Grilled Vegetable Salad with Sweet Poppy Seed Dressing (page 205)
- Hijiki Pâté (page 107)
- Hummus (page 114) with sprouts and tomato
- Indian Rice and Lentils with Caramelized Onions (page 156)
- Orange-Glazed Salmon Kebobs with Yogurt Garlic Dip (page 167) and cooked rice
- Pan-Fried Tofu and Greens with Almond Ginger Drizzle (page 152) and shredded cabbage
- Mexican Brown Rice with Pinto Beans (page 149)

- Quick Lemon and Garlic Quinoa Salad (page 110)
- Santa Fe Black Bean Salad (page 103)
- Sliced turkey, Havarti cheese, and lettuce
- Sloppeh Joes (page 165)
- Thai Steak Salad Over Soba (page 174)
- Tofu Vegetable Breakfast Burritos (page 90)

Soothing Soups

Cynthia's Hearty Vegetable Miso Soup
Cream of Asparagus Soup with Dill
Red Lentil Soup with East Indian Spices
Split Pea Soup with Fresh Peas and Potatoes
Rosemary Red Soup
Golden Mushroom Basil Soup
Thick Potato, Cauliflower, and Dulse Soup
Tomato Basil Soup
White Bean and Kale Minestrone
Nina's Famous Spring Beet Soup
Chipotle Navy Bean Soup
French Lentil and Potato Stew
Thai Coconut Chicken Soup
Simple Chicken Stock
Easy Vegetarian Stock

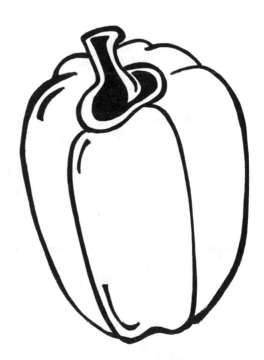

Cynthia's Hearty Vegetable Miso Soup

Wakame is a green, leafy sea vegetable high in calcium and other minerals. Sea vegetables like wakame are purchased dried in packages and reconstituted in water. This hearty soup is excellent when a family member is fatigued or feeling ill. Don't let the vegetables and tofu overwhelm the broth—this should be a very light soup. To learn more about miso, see Appendix B, "Identifying, Purchasing, and Storing Whole Foods."

Prep time: 25 minutes
Makes 4 servings

> 3-inch piece wakame
> 4 cups water
> 1 very small potato, cut into ½-inch dice
> 1 small carrot, chopped
> ½ cup chopped bok choy
> ¼ pound firm tofu, cut into small cubes
> 4 tablespoons light or mellow unpasteurized miso, divided
> 2 scallions, thinly sliced, for garnish

Soak wakame in a small bowl of cold water for 5 minutes to rehydrate.

Put water, potato, and carrot in a 4-quart pot; bring to a boil.

Remove wakame from bowl and tear into pieces, removing the spine. Add wakame to soup. Lower heat, cover pot, and let soup simmer 15 to 20 minutes, until vegetables are tender.

Near the end of cooking time, add bok choy and tofu cubes and let them simmer 2 or 3 minutes.

Ladle about ¼ cup of broth from the soup into each of 4 soup bowls. Dissolve 1 tablespoon of miso in the broth in each bowl. Add more broth with plenty of vegetables to each bowl and stir gently. Garnish each bowl with scallions.

For babies 6 months and older: Remove boiled potatoes or carrots from soup after it simmers and mash with fork. Baby will benefit from the nutritious broth made by the seaweed.

For babies 10 months and older: Those that can handle soft things to chew can enjoy some pieces of cooked vegetables and tofu cubes from the soup.

Cream of Asparagus Soup with Dill

Rolled oats add extra whole grain nutrition to this soup and help create the creamy texture. Use this simple recipe to make a tasty soup out of any seasonal vegetable. Serve this soup with Quick Lemon and Garlic Quinoa Salad (page 110) and Black-Eyed Peas and Arame with Cilantro (page 163) or Caribbean Lime Halibut (page 169) for a nutritious springtime meal.

Prep time: 25 minutes
Makes 6 servings

2 tablespoons extra-virgin olive oil or butter
1 onion, chopped
1 rib celery, chopped
1 teaspoon ground cumin
1 tablespoon fresh snipped dill or 1 teaspoon dried
1 bunch asparagus, washed, trimmed, and cut into 2-inch pieces

2 cups vegetable or chicken stock
2 to 3 cups water
1 bay leaf
½ cup rolled oats
1 teaspoon sea salt
Freshly squeezed lemon juice
¼ cup sour cream, for garnish (optional)

Heat oil in a 4-quart pot. Add onion, celery, cumin, and dill and sauté until vegetables are soft. Add asparagus and sauté a few more minutes. Add stock, water, bay leaf, oats, and salt. Bring to a boil. Simmer 15 minutes.

Let cool. Transfer to a blender and purée in small batches or use an immersion blender to purée.

Reheat if necessary. Add some fresh lemon juice to taste. Top each serving of soup with a dollop of sour cream before serving, if desired. This soup can also be served cold in warm weather.

For babies 10 months and older: Use some of the rolled oats to make your baby a bowl of warm oatmeal. See page 62 for directions.

Red Lentil Soup with East Indian Spices

Red lentils are a small, flat, orange-colored legume. They are different than the normal gray-green lentil in flavor and appearance. A lovely Indian vegetarian restaurant in Seattle called Silence-Heart-Nest serves this very flavorful and satisfying soup, called masoor dal in India. I have adapted it to a family-size portion. Ghee is clarified butter, which is used frequently in Indian cooking. To learn more about ghee, see Appendix B, "Identifying, Purchasing, and Storing Whole Foods."

Prep time: 1 hour
Makes 4 servings

1 tablespoon plus 1 teaspoon ghee or butter	1 cup chopped tomatoes
1 onion, chopped	1 cup dried red lentils, washed and drained
1 to 2 tablespoons minced garlic	4 cups water or vegetable or chicken stock
1 teaspoon turmeric	1 teaspoon sea salt
1 teaspoon ground cumin	1 teaspoon cumin seeds
⅛ teaspoon cayenne	1 teaspoon mustard seeds
	¼ cup chopped cilantro

Heat 1 tablespoon of the ghee in a 4-quart pot. Sauté onion and garlic in ghee until brown. Add spices and stir for 2 to 3 minutes. Add tomatoes and cook until they break down, if using fresh tomatoes; if using canned, simply proceed. Add lentils and water to pot. Let simmer for 45 minutes, stirring often, until creamy. Stir in salt.

Heat the remaining 1 teaspoon ghee in a small skillet and fry cumin and mustard seeds until they pop. Stir fried seeds and cilantro into finished soup.

For babies 10 months and older: Use ¼ cup red lentils and simmer in a separate small pan with 1 cup water to make a simpler soup for baby.

Split Pea Soup with Fresh Peas and Potatoes

My daughter's second-grade class had a hot lunch program where parents took turns bringing hot soup and bread to school for the children's lunch. This soup, created by Lee Carrillo, was one of their favorites. It is fine to leave out the bone to make this a vegetarian soup. The vinegar is added to pull minerals from the bone into the broth.

Prep time: 50 minutes in pressure-cooker; 1 hour 45 minutes in soup pot
Makes 4 servings

1 cup green split peas
1 tablespoon butter or
    extra-virgin olive oil
1 onion, chopped
1 to 2 teaspoons sea salt
1 rib celery, chopped
1 carrot, chopped
2 small red potatoes, cubed
1 teaspoon ground cumin

Freshly ground pepper
4 cups water or vegetable stock
1 large bay leaf
1 small ham bone (optional)
2 teaspoons apple cider vinegar
½ cup fresh or frozen peas
1 tablespoon snipped fresh dill or
    1 teaspoon dried

Soak split peas 4 to 6 hours in 4 cups of water. This will help digestibility, quicken cooking time, and improve the texture of the soup. Discard soaking water.

Heat butter in a pressure cooker or 4-quart pot. Add onion and salt and sauté until onion begins to soften. Add celery, carrot, potatoes, cumin, and pepper to taste; sauté 3 to 4 minutes more. Add split peas, water, and bay leaf. Add ham bone, if using, and vinegar.

If pressure-cooking: Bring up to pressure on high heat, then lower heat and cook 40 minutes.

If using a soup pot: Bring to a boil, lower heat, and simmer 60 to 90 minutes.

Once split peas have softened and the soup has become creamy, remove the ham bone. Cut off any meat, discard skin and bone, dice meat into small pieces, and add to soup with peas and dill. Check seasonings; add more salt and pepper if needed. Continue cooking a few minutes more until peas are tender.

For babies 6 months and older: Reserve some fresh peas. Steam them until tender. Mash and serve.

Rosemary Red Soup

This soup is a gorgeous red color with a deep, satisfying taste to match. Because of the combination of legumes and vegetables, all you need is some whole grain bread and salad to make this into a beautifully balanced meal. Try it with Sweet Squash Corn Muffins (page 218) and Romaine Chop Salad with Basil Dressing (page 195).

Prep time: 50 minutes
Makes 6 to 8 servings

> 3 medium carrots
> 1 large beet
> 1 tablespoon extra-virgin olive oil
> 1 large onion, diced
> 1 3-inch sprig of fresh rosemary or 1 teaspoon dried
> 1 tablespoon fresh oregano or 1 teaspoon dried
> 1 cup dried red lentils, washed and drained
> 2 bay leaves
> 6 cups water or vegetable or chicken stock
> 2 to 3 tablespoons light miso

Scrub and chop carrots and beet. Remove beet greens, if present. No need to peel unless vegetables are not organic. Heat oil in a 4-quart pot; add onion and sauté until soft. Add carrots and beet; sauté a few minutes more.

Finely chop rosemary and oregano leaves, if using fresh herbs. Add herbs, lentils, bay leaves, and water to sautéed vegetables; bring to a boil. Lower heat and simmer 40 minutes.

Remove bay leaves. Let soup cool and purée in small batches in blender or use an immersion blender. Dissolve miso in ½ cup water and stir into puréed soup. Gently reheat before serving.

🥣 **For babies 6 months and older:** Steam a few extra carrot slices and purée with some water.

Variation for children: Make a face in the bowl with crackers!

Golden Mushroom Basil Soup

This soup and Thick Potato, Cauliflower, and Dulse Soup (page 130) are variations of Jeff Basom's sensuous nondairy soups served at the Bastyr University cafeteria. Jeff's inventive use of vegetables with a touch of cashew butter creates a satisfying taste everyone loves. Serve this soup with Nori-Wrapped Wasabi Salmon (page 168) and Susan's Succulent Supper Salad (page 203) for an impressive, well-balanced meal.

Prep time: 45 minutes
Makes 6 servings

> 3 teaspoons extra-virgin olive oil, divided
> 4 cups chopped onions (about 2 large or 3 medium onions)
> 1 teaspoon sea salt
> 2 cups diced potatoes (about 2 medium potatoes)
> ½ cup chopped celery (about 2 ribs)
> 1 large carrot, diced
> 3½ to 4 cups water or vegetable or chicken stock
> 2 tablespoons cashew butter
> 2 tablespoons tamari or shoyu
> ¾ pound mushrooms, sliced
> ½ cup fresh basil, finely chopped
> Sea salt and freshly ground pepper, to taste

Heat 1 teaspoon of the oil in a 4-quart pot over medium heat. Add onions and salt. Cover the pot and simmer on low heat, stirring occasionally, until onions cook down to a nice mush (15 to 20 minutes). Add potatoes, celery, carrot and water to the mixture; cover and simmer 15 to 20 minutes until potatoes are soft.

Let soup cool then put into blender in small batches with cashew butter and tamari; blend until smooth. Return soup to pot.

Heat the remaining 2 teaspoons oil in a small skillet. Add mushrooms and sauté until soft. Stir sautéed mushrooms and basil into finished soup. Add salt and pepper to taste and serve.

For babies 6 months and older: Remove some of the cooked potato from the soup and purée.

For babies 10 months and older: Blend a portion of soup before adding tamari.

Thick Potato, Cauliflower, and Dulse Soup

This soup is great for nursing moms and babies who have iron-deficiency issues. Dulse is a dark red sea vegetable extremely high in absorbable iron (14 mg per ¼ cup) and other minerals. Like other sea vegetables it is purchased dried. The dried leaves can be soaked for 5 minutes and added to soups or salads. Iron-rich dulse marries well with the simple flavors of potatoes and cauliflower.

Prep time: 45 minutes
Makes 6 servings

> 1 tablespoon extra-virgin olive oil or butter
> 4 cups chopped onions (about 2 large or 3 medium onions)
> ½ teaspoon sea salt
> 3 cups diced potatoes (about 2 medium potatoes), divided
> ½ cup chopped celery (about 2 ribs)
> 1 large carrot, diced
> 3 cups of bite-size cauliflower pieces, divided
> 3½ to 4 cups water
> 2 tablespoons cashew butter
> 2 tablespoons tamari or shoyu
> ⅓ cup dry dulse
> Sea salt and freshly ground pepper

Heat oil in a 4-quart pot over medium heat. Add onions and salt. Cover the pot and simmer on low heat, stirring occasionally, until onions cook down to a nice mush (15 to 20 minutes). Add 2 cups of the potatoes, celery, carrot, 1 cup of the cauliflower pieces, and water to the mixture, cover, and simmer until potatoes and cauliflower are soft (15 to 20 minutes). Let cool. Put cooled soup into blender in small batches with cashew butter and tamari and blend until smooth.

Place the remaining 1 cup potatoes and 2 cups cauliflower pieces in a pot of boiling water and cook until tender (10 to 12 minutes).

Prepare dulse by washing in cold water and gently tearing into bite-size pieces.

Drain the cooked potato and cauliflower. Stir cooked vegetables and dulse into the finished soup. Season with salt and pepper and serve.

For babies 6 months and older: Steam some extra cauliflower pieces until very soft (20 minutes). Purée with a pinch of dulse and serve.

Tomato Basil Soup

When I was a child, tomato soup was one of my main comfort foods. It is simple to make. The nightshade plants, such as tomatoes, are thought by some to affect calcium stores negatively. Perhaps that is why they are traditionally paired with calcium-rich dairy. The food company Muir Glen makes a "fire-roasted" canned tomato that is yummy to use in this recipe.

Prep time: 25 to 30 minutes
Makes 4 servings

> 2 tablespoons extra-virgin olive oil
> 1 tablespoon butter
> 1 onion, chopped
> 2 to 3 cloves garlic, minced
> 1 teaspoon sea salt
> 2 cups vegetable or chicken stock
> 1 (14.5-ounce) can chopped tomatoes
> 1 tablespoon honey
> ¼ cup sour cream
> ¼ cup finely chopped fresh basil
> Freshly ground pepper

Heat oil and butter in a 4-quart pot over medium heat. Add onion, garlic, and salt and sauté until onions are soft and translucent. Add stock, tomatoes, and honey and simmer for about 10 to 15 minutes to marry flavors.

Let soup cool slightly and put half of it into blender with sour cream. Blend until smooth. Transfer to another pot. Blend the other half of the soup and add. Reheat blended soup. Add basil and pepper to taste before serving.

For babies 6 months and older: Serve this soup with steamed broccoli on the side. Purée part of the steamed broccoli with water for baby.

White Bean and Kale Minestrone

This recipe was inspired from a recipe in one of my favorite cookbooks, Sundays at Moosewood Restaurant *by The Moosewood Collective (Fireside, 1990). The kale adds energy-boosting vitamins and minerals, while the beans provide a simple protein base.*

Prep time: 30 minutes
Makes 3 to 4 servings

> **5 to 6 leaves of kale**
> **1 tablespoon extra-virgin olive oil**
> **2 large cloves of garlic**
> **3 cups cooked white beans, divided**
> **2½ cups vegetable or chicken stock, divided**
> **1 tablespoon tomato paste**
> **4 fresh sage leaves**
> **1 teaspoon sea salt**
> **Freshly ground pepper**
> **1 tablespoon freshly lemon juice**
> **Freshly grated pecorino cheese**

— try cashew "cheese"!

Wash kale and remove the stems from the leaves. Roll up kale leaves and cut into thin ribbons. Set aside.

In a 4-quart pot, heat oil and sauté the garlic briefly over medium heat. Add about half of the cooked beans and half of the stock.

Purée the rest of the beans and stock in a blender along with the tomato paste and sage. Stir the puréed beans into the soup. Add salt and pepper to taste.

Mix the kale into the soup and simmer until it has wilted (about 10 minutes). Add the lemon juice and enough water to make the soup a desirable thick consistency. Taste and adjust seasonings. Serve the soup topped with pecorino cheese.

For babies 10 months and older: This soup makes lovely baby food for the baby used to eating beans. Just purée a small amount before adding lemon juice and cheese.

Nina's Famous Spring Beet Soup

Do you ever get the urge to clean in the spring? Here is a delicious, cleansing soup for your body that my friend Nina invented. It's bursting with nutrients and flavor. The fresher the beets, the better the soup. Serve with Szechwan Tempeh (page 164) over quinoa for a beautiful and satisfying meal.

Prep time: 30 minutes
Makes 4 servings

> 1 tablespoon extra-virgin olive oil or butter
> 1 medium onion, cut into thin crescents
> 1 clove garlic, minced
> 1 teaspoon sea salt
> 3 to 4 cups water
> 1 bunch spring beets, cut into large matchsticks (save the beet greens)
> 1 carrot, cut into large matchsticks
> ¼ head green cabbage, shredded
> 2 tablespoons freshly squeezed lemon juice
> 1 tablespoon tamari or shoyu
> 1 tablespoon snipped fresh dill or 1 teaspoon dried, for garnish
> ¼ cup sour cream, for garnish

Heat oil in a 4-quart pot. Add onion, garlic, and salt; sauté until soft. Add water, beets, carrot, and cabbage and bring to a boil. Lower heat and simmer, covered, for 10 to 15 minutes, until vegetables are tender.

Meanwhile, wash beet greens, remove tough stems, and cut greens into short, thin strips. Add beet greens, lemon juice, and tamari to soup; simmer another 3 to 5 minutes. Serve at once, garnished with dill and sour cream.

🥣 **For babies 10 months and older:** Remove some cooked beet and carrot pieces from the soup and purée or serve whole as finger foods. Go easy on beets for babies (only a teaspoon or less at a time) as they have a strong cleansing effect on the bowels.

Chipotle Navy Bean Soup

Chipotle chiles are smoked, dried jalapeño peppers that richly enhance humble beans. The smoky flavor is similar to that of cooking beans with ham. Lima beans or pinto beans work equally well. Try this soup with Luscious Beet Salad with Toasted Pumpkin Seeds (page 196) and Quinoa Garlic Herb Bread (page 215) for a flavorful, well-balanced meal.

Prep time: 1 hour, 15 minutes in soup pot; 60 minutes in pressure cooker
Makes 6 servings

> 1½ cups dried navy beans, soaked for 6 to 8 hours
> 1 tablespoon extra-virgin olive oil or butter
> 1 onion, chopped
> 2 chipotle chiles, soaked 10 to 15 minutes in cold water
> 4 cups water or vegetable or chicken stock
> 2 teaspoons sea salt
> 1 to 2 teaspoons brown rice vinegar
> Freshly ground pepper

Drain soaking water off beans. Heat oil in a 4-quart pot or pressure cooker over medium heat. Add onion and sauté until soft. Add drained beans, chiles, and water. Bring heat up to high to either establish a simmer or, if using a pressure cooker, bring up to pressure. Lower heat and cook for 1 hour in soup pot or 45 minutes in pressure cooker, until beans are creamy.

Remove chiles. For added creaminess, purée part of the soup in a blender, then add back to the pot. Stir in salt, vinegar, and pepper to taste and serve.

🥄 **For babies 6 months and older:** Chipotle chiles make this soup a bit too spicy for babies. This soup is wonderful served with Mediterranean Quinoa (page 143). Remove some of the plain quinoa before dressing the salad, purée, and serve as cereal to baby.

French Lentil and Potato Stew

This simple, hearty stew is my favorite standby for a one-dish meal. It is economical in preparation time as well as food dollars. The tiny French lentils are wonderful, but if you can't find them, substitute regular brown lentils. Ghee, or clarified butter, gives a buttery taste, but it can also hold a higher temperature than butter without burning. You can substitute 1 tablespoon of Homemade Curry Paste (page 238) for the ginger and spices if you like.

Prep time: 1 hour, 10 minutes in soup pot; 50 minutes in pressure cooker
Makes 6 servings

1 tablespoon ghee or extra-virgin
   olive oil
1 onion, chopped
1 teaspoon ground cumin
1 teaspoon ground coriander
1 teaspoon freshly grated ginger
¼ teaspoon cayenne
¼ teaspoon ground cinnamon
1 teaspoon turmeric
⅛ teaspoon pepper

¼ teaspoon allspice
2 red potatoes, cubed
1 parsnip, sliced
1 stalk celery, diced
1 carrot, chopped
1 cup French lentils
4 cups water or vegetable or chicken stock
1 teaspoon sea salt
Plain whole milk yogurt or sour cream,
   for garnish

Melt ghee in a 4-quart pot on medium heat. Add onion and sauté until soft. Add all spices and sauté a few more minutes.

Add potatoes, parsnip, celery, carrot, lentils, and water. Bring soup to a boil. Reduce heat and simmer, covered, for 50 to 60 minutes. If using a pressure cooker, bring up to pressure over high heat, then lower heat and cook 40 minutes. When lentils are creamy, stir in salt. Serve stew garnished with a dollop of yogurt.

☞ **For babies 10 months and older:** A small portion of this puréed soup is fine for baby to eat.

TAKE STOCK

Stock is the secret elixir that can change soup from a humble lunch to fine dining, from a meal to medicine. When you slowly simmer the bones of poultry, lamb, or beef in water with salt and something acidic (like vinegar), the calcium, magnesium, phosphorus, silicon, and other trace minerals leech into the water creating a bio-available, mineral-rich broth. The bones also release gelatin, which contains amino acids and aids in maintaining cartilage, tendons, and ligaments. Similarly, the nutrients that reside in garlic cloves, carrot peelings, celery ribs, and other vegetables used will be pulled into the salted water surrounding them in a simmering pot.

Stock does not have to be anything fancy. In fact, it should be a utilitarian task. Unused raw chicken parts, an onion, a bay leaf, and a few vegetable scraps are really all you need. Alternately, you can begin with the carcass of your Thanksgiving turkey or the bone from the Easter ham. Cooked bones yield a stronger flavor and darker color than raw bones. Stock isn't on a schedule. So if you forget about it while you change a diaper and a nap or two later it is still simmering, don't worry. It's still good.

Concerned about babies and children getting enough vegetables in their diet? Make soup, baby cereal, rice, sandwich spreads, or beans for tacos with homemade stock and skip the vitamin pills. Anything you cook that requires water can be replaced with stock!

There are many brands of organic stock you can buy in the store. They won't give you all the love and nutrients that a homemade stock will, but they definitely enhance flavor. Note that some prepackaged stocks, especially vegetarian ones, are quite thick. Better to use half stock and half water in this case so that the stock doesn't overwhelm the other flavors of the soup.

Thai Coconut Chicken Soup

Otherwise known as tom ka gai, this traditional Thai soup uses coconut milk, lemongrass, and fish sauce to form a flavorful base. For a vegetarian version, use tofu cubes instead of chicken and omit fish sauce (you will need to add additional salt to compensate for this).

Prep time: 1 hour
Makes 4 servings

2 tablespoons olive oil	1 6- to 8-inch stalk lemongrass
1 onion, thinly sliced into half-moons	½ pound boneless, skinless chicken breast
2 to 3 cloves garlic, minced	2 to 3 cups water
1 teaspoon sea salt	1 (14-ounce) can coconut milk
2 tablespoons grated ginger	3 to 4 tablespoons fish sauce
½ teaspoon crushed red pepper	1 large baby bok choy, sliced thin
1 teaspoon ground coriander	¼ cup chopped fresh cilantro
1 teaspoon ground cumin	

Heat oil in a 4-quart pot over medium heat. Stir in onion, garlic, and salt and sauté until onion is translucent. Add ginger, red pepper, coriander, and cumin and cook until fragrant, 2 minutes.

Bisect the lemongrass stalk lengthwise. You will see a small core at the bottom. Cut out the core and chop ½ inch or so of the stalk where it is tender. Add the chopped lemongrass to the other spices and reserve the rest of the stalk.

Tenderize chicken breast with a meat pounder on both sides, and then cut it diagonally into thin strips. Add chicken to onion and spices and cook, stirring, until chicken is white on the outside.

Stir in water, coconut milk, fish sauce, and the lemongrass stalk and simmer until chicken is thoroughly cooked and flavors are well blended, about 10 minutes. Add bok choy and cilantro and simmer another 5 minutes. Remove stalk before serving.

☞ **For babies 10 months and older:** Remove some of the broth and serve with some plain brown rice cereal.

Simple Chicken Stock

This nutritious stock can be used to cook rice, simmer vegetables, thin sauces, and make super soups. By adding vinegar to the stock, the calcium in the bones is extracted into the broth.

Prep time: 1 hour
Makes 1 quart

> 1 tablespoon olive oil
> 1 onion, chopped
> 2 teaspoons sea salt
> 4 cups water
> 2 bay leaves
> ½ pound chicken parts with bones
> 1 tablespoon rice vinegar

Heat oil in a 4-quart pot. Add onion and salt and sauté until soft. Add water, bay leaves, chicken, and vinegar and bring to a low boil. Lower heat and simmer for 30 to 45 minutes or longer. Stock flavors deepen with more time. Taste it after 30 minutes to see if you are satisfied or want it to simmer longer.

Allow to cool, remove chicken, strain stock into glass jars, and store in the refrigerator until needed. Any meat from the cooked chicken can be removed, sliced, and used in soups, pasta, or rice dishes. Stock will keep refrigerated at least a week.

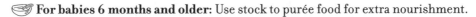 **For babies 6 months and older:** Use stock to purée food for extra nourishment.

Variation for children: Make a gentle and nourishing broth by stirring some cooked noodles into a cup of this stock.

Easy Vegetarian Stock

Worth the effort for making soups more flavorful and nourishing, this broth is excellent and can be used instead of water to purée food for babies. Kombu is a sea vegetable. It is used here to impart extra nutrients to the broth. For more about kombu see Appendix B, "Identifying, Purchasing, and Storing Whole Foods."

Prep time: 25 minutes
Makes 1 quart

1 tablespoon extra-virgin olive oil
1 onion, chopped
1 carrot, cut into large chunks
1 rib of celery, cut into chunks
1 scallion or leek, cut into pieces
Skin of 1 yellow onion
1 3-inch piece of kombu

1 bay leaf
1 teaspoon dried marjoram
1 teaspoon dried thyme
1 quart water
1 teaspoon sea salt
⅛ teaspoon pepper

Heat oil in a 4-quart pot. Add onion and sauté until soft. Add carrot, celery, scallion, onion skin, kombu, herbs, and water; bring to a boil. Lower heat and simmer 15 to 20 minutes.

Add salt and pepper. Taste and adjust seasoning. Let cool.

Strain liquid into an empty quart jar (a rinsed-out juice bottle works well). Stores well in the refrigerator while awaiting its debut in your next soup. Stock will keep refrigerated at least a week.

For babies 6 months and older: Use stock to purée food for extra nourishment.

Variation for children: Make a gentle and nourishing broth by stirring a teaspoon of light miso into a cup of this stock.

Substantial Suppers

Golden Spice Rice with Chickpeas
Mediterranean Quinoa
Deep-Fried Millet Croquettes
Peasant Kasha, Potatoes, and Mushrooms
Sweet Rice Timbales
Polenta Pizza
Mexican Brown Rice with Pinto Beans
Bok Choy and Buckwheat Noodles in Seasoned
    Broth (Yakisoba)
Red Bean and Quinoa Chili
Pan-Fried Tofu and Greens with Almond
    Ginger Drizzle (Bathing Rama)
Mexican Bean and Corn Casserole
Nut Burgers
Indian Rice and Lentils with Caramelized
    Onions (Mojadra)
Three Sisters Stew
Curried Lentils and Cauliflower
Tempeh Tacos
Middle Eastern Falafel
Black Bean Tostados

Tofu Kale Supper Pie
Black-Eyed Peas and Arame with Cilantro
Szechwan Tempeh
Sloppeh Joes
Dr. Bruce's Awesome Grilled Salmon
Orange-Glazed Salmon Kebobs with Yogurt
    Garlic Dip
Nori-Wrapped Wasabi Salmon
Caribbean Lime Halibut
Rainbow Trout Poached in Herbs
Sweet Potato and Shrimp Tempura
Thea's Greek Shrimp Stew
Spice Island Beef Stew
Cay's Mini Pot Roast with Many Vegetables
Thai Steak Salad Over Soba
Squash- and Raisin-Stuffed Chicken Breasts
Lemon- and Herb-Roasted Chicken
Baked Chicken with Mushrooms and
    Rosemary
Spinach Feta Quiche

Golden Spice Rice with Chickpeas

Sautéing the rice before cooking it makes the finished grain fluffier and less sticky. By adding a few simple spices, you add fragrance and a lovely golden color to the rice. Adding cooked chickpeas balances the dish by combing the whole grain with a legume.

Prep time: 55 minutes
Makes 4 servings

> 2 tablespoons butter, ghee, or olive oil, divided
> 1 cup brown basmati rice, rinsed and drained
> ¼ teaspoon turmeric
> 1¾ to 2 cups water
> 2 green cardamom pods
> ½ teaspoon sea salt
> 1 cup cooked chickpeas
> ½ cup frozen green peas
> ¼ cup currants

Heat 2 teaspoons of the butter in a 2-quart pan over low to medium heat. Add rice and sauté until well coated. Add turmeric and stir again. Add water, cardamom, and salt. Bring to a boil. Turn heat to low, keeping a light simmer. Cover the pan and let the rice simmer for 45 to 50 minutes, or until all the water is absorbed. Don't stir the rice while it is cooking. Check rice for doneness by tipping the pan. If any water remains, continue cooking until all water is absorbed.

Heat remaining butter in a large skillet over low to medium heat. Add chickpeas, green peas, and currants and stir. Fold cooked rice into skillet a little at a time. Serve while warm.

For babies 10 months and older: Either puréed golden rice or mashed cooked chickpeas are an easy offering from this dish.

Mediterranean Quinoa

Inspired by a recipe from a student named David St. Martin, this whole grain salad has it all. Amino acid–rich quinoa combines with pine nuts and feta to provide protein. The raw herbs add the digestive element to the dish. This makes a stupendous meal coupled with Middle Eastern Falafel (page 160) or Caribbean Lime Halibut (page 169). Cooked millet, rice, or other grain can be substituted for quinoa.

Prep time: 30 minutes
Makes 4 servings

1 cup quinoa
1 ¾ cups water
½ teaspoon sea salt
¼ cup toasted pine nuts
¼ cup olive oil
¼ cup lemon juice
3 tablespoons chopped fresh mint
3 tablespoons chopped fresh Italian parsley
2 scallions
¼ cup currants
⅓ cup crumbled feta cheese

Wash, rinse, and drain quinoa. Place in a 2-quart pot, add water and salt, bring to a boil, lower heat, and simmer with lid on until all water is absorbed (15 to 20 minutes). Don't stir the grain while it is cooking. Test for doneness by tilting the pan to one side, making sure all of the water has been absorbed. Remove lid and let rest 5 to 10 minutes.

Dry-toast pine nuts in skillet or 300°F oven until they begin to change color and give off aroma, about 10 minutes.

Combine olive oil, lemon juice, mint, and parsley in a large bowl. Add scallions, currants, feta cheese, and toasted pine nuts and toss. Add cooked warm quinoa a little at a time. Toss well. Serve at room temperature.

☞ **For babies 6 months and older:** Reserve a small amount of plain quinoa and purée for baby.

Deep-Fried Millet Croquettes

Properly done, deep-frying is actually very low in calories. Cooking with oil at the correct temperature is the key. Compare the amount of oil you're using before and after cooking—only a few teaspoons should be missing! Millet is a small, round, yellow whole grain with a sweet earthy flavor. Serve Millet Croquettes with White Bean and Kale Minestrone (page 132) to provide the grain and bean combination needed for a well-balanced meal.

Prep time: 45 minutes
Makes 8 to 10 croquettes, 1 cup sauce

Millet

1 cup millet
2½ cups water
½ teaspoon sea salt

Croquette

1 carrot
2 scallions
cooked millet
1 quart expeller-pressed safflower oil
   (the pan you use to deep-fry should be ⅔ full)

Sauce

1 to 2 tablespoons kudzu
1 cup water
1 teaspoon grated ginger
3 tablespoons shoyu or tamari

Garnish

Lemon wedges

To make the millet, rinse and drain millet 2 or 3 times. Put millet, water, and salt in a 2-quart pot and bring to a boil. Reduce heat to low, cover, and let simmer 25 to 30 minutes, until all water is absorbed. Remove from heat.

To make the croquettes, grate carrot and chop scallions very fine or pulse in a food processor. Add chopped vegetables to cooked and cooled millet. Mix in well. With moist hands, form mixture into croquettes about the size of a golf ball, packing tightly.

Heat oil in a deep, stainless steel pot or wok to 375°F. Use a deep-fry thermometer to make sure the temperature is correct. Too high a temperature will burn the outside and leave the inside raw. If the temperature is too low, it will result in soggy croquettes. When the temperature is correct, there will be dancing ripples on the bottom of the pan.

Lower 3 or 4 croquettes (depending on the size of your pan) into oil with tongs or chopsticks. Croquettes should drop to the bottom, and then quickly rise to the top. When croquettes are golden on the outside, remove with a slotted spoon and place on a piece of brown paper bag to drain.

To make the sauce, dissolve kudzu in water. Put in a small pan. Add ginger. Bring mixture to simmer, stirring constantly. When mixture becomes clear and thick (5 minutes), turn heat off. Stir in shoyu. Serve immediately over the croquettes.

Garnish each plate with a lemon wedge. A squeeze of lemon is tasty on the croquettes.

For babies 6 months and older: Reserve some cooked millet and purée with water or breast milk and serve.

For babies 10 months and older: Serve some cooked millet and purée with an extra carrot that has been sliced and steamed.

Peasant Kasha, Potatoes, and Mushrooms

Whole grains and vegetables have been the chief food of common people for centuries. Kasha and potatoes combine here for a rib-sticking dish. I would recommend serving this dish with Rosemary Red Soup (page 128) or Nori-Wrapped Wasabi Salmon (page 168) to give the grain a complementary protein.

Prep time: 25 to 30 minutes
Makes 6 servings

> 1 tablespoon butter or extra-virgin olive oil
> 1 small onion, chopped
> 2 cloves garlic, minced
> 1 teaspoon sea salt
> 1 small red potato, cut into ¼-inch dice
> 3 to 4 mushrooms, sliced
> 1 cup kasha
> 2 cups boiling water
> Freshly ground pepper

Heat the butter in a 2-quart pot. Add onion, garlic, and salt; sauté until the onion is soft. Add potatoes and mushrooms to onions; cook 2 to 3 minutes more, covered, until nice and juicy. Add kasha to mixture and stir, coating kasha. Pour in boiling water. Turn heat to low. Cover pot and simmer 15 minutes on low until all water is absorbed. Remove lid and allow kasha to rest for a few minutes. Fluff up and serve garnished with pepper to taste. Add more salt if needed.

☞ **For babies 10 months and older:** Remove a baby-size portion, mash potato bits with a fork, and slice mushrooms into tiny pieces and serve.

Kasha Salad

Turn leftover kasha and potatoes into a salad for lunch. Add fresh chopped vegetables, such as parsley, cabbage, red pepper, and scallions, and a tablespoon of your favorite vinaigrette.

Sweet Rice Timbales

This elegant-looking mounded rice looks like you spent hours when you didn't. Lovely served next to grilled fish or Szechwan Tempeh (page 164) and Sweet Apple Walnut Kale (page 193). This recipe uses fantastic flavors to achieve nutritional balance!

Prep time: 55 minutes
Makes 6 to 8 timbales

> 1 ½ **cups brown rice**
> ½ **cup sweet brown rice**
> ½ **teaspoon sea salt**
> 3 **cups water**
> 2 **tablespoons mirin**
> 2 **tablespoons brown rice syrup**
> 2 **tablespoons brown rice vinegar**
> 2 **teaspoons brown or black sesame seeds**

Rinse and drain rice. Place brown rice, sweet brown rice, salt, and water in the pressure cooker. Lock cooker. Place on high heat and bring up to pressure. When pressure gauge rises and is firm, you will hear a gentle, steady hissing sound. Lower heat and time for 35 to 40 minutes. Remove from heat and allow pressure to come down naturally or by drizzling cold water over the top. Allow rice to cool slightly, until just warm.

While rice is cooking, combine mirin, syrup, and vinegar in a small saucepan and heat until flavors marry and mixture is warm. Pour over warm rice and stir to combine.

Place sesame seeds in a dry skillet over medium heat and stir constantly until they begin to pop and change color. Set aside.

Oil a small ramekin or cup. Pack rice into the cup until it is as dense as possible and the top is level. Invert and place on a plate. Garnish the top with toasted seeds. Repeat with remaining rice.

☞ **For babies 6 months and older:** Blend some of the cooked sweet brown rice and brown rice with some breast milk or formula. Fresh rice cereal for baby!

Polenta Pizza

A fun, healthful way to enjoy pizza with whole grains and lots of vegetables.

Prep time: 1 hour
Makes 8 slices

1 tablespoon plus 1 teaspoon butter
   or extra-virgin olive oil, divided
1 onion, chopped
1 teaspoon sea salt, divided
2 cloves garlic, minced
1 tablespoon fresh oregano
   or 1 teaspoon dried
1 tablespoon fresh basil
   or 1 teaspoon dried
½ medium zucchini, cut into ½-inch cubes

½ eggplant, cut into ½-inch cubes
1 patty-pan squash, cut into ½-inch cubes
½ green pepper, cut into ½-inch cubes
1½ cups chunky tomato sauce
3 cups boiling water
1 cup polenta
¼ cup Parmesan cheese
8 tablespoons grated Monterey Jack cheese,
   for garnish (optional)

Preheat oven to 350°F. Heat 1 tablespoon of the butter in a skillet. Sauté onion and ½ teaspoon of the salt until soft. Add garlic and herbs; sauté a few minutes more. Put zucchini, eggplant, squash, green pepper, onion mixture, and tomato sauce into a lightly oiled 8 x 8-inch pan. Cover and bake for 1 hour.

While the vegetables bake, prepare the polenta. Bring water to rapid boil. Add the remaining ½ teaspoon salt and 1 teaspoon butter or oil. Slowly add polenta, stirring continuously with a whisk. Lower heat and continue stirring for 10 to 15 minutes until mixture thickens. Stir in Parmesan cheese. Lightly oil a 10-inch pie plate or 8 x 8-inch pan. Pour polenta into pan and smooth the top. Bake for 30 minutes.

Remove both dishes from oven. Spoon tomato vegetable mixture on top of the baked polenta. Cut into slices and serve with grated cheese on top, if desired.

For babies 6 months and older: Reserve some of the zucchini, steam it, and purée.

Variation for children: Some children may prefer a slice of the plain baked polenta.

Mexican Brown Rice with Pinto Beans

Here is another easy way to give rice an exciting flavor. See page 69 for instructions on how to prepare basic beans. Try cooking the pintos with a chipotle chile for a deep smoky flavor. A side dish of Santa Fe Black Bean Salad (page 103) can be used instead of pintos.

Prep time: 50 minutes
Makes 4 servings

- 1 tablespoon extra-virgin olive oil or butter
- 1 teaspoon ground cumin
- 1 teaspoon chili powder
- ½ onion, diced fine
- ½ teaspoon sea salt
- 1 cup long-grain brown rice, rinsed and drained
- 1¾ to 2 cups water
- 1 tablespoon tomato paste or sauce
- 3 cups cooked pinto beans

Heat oil in a 2-quart pot. Add cumin and chili powder and sauté for a few seconds. Add onion and salt and continue cooking until onion is soft. Add rice and stir well to coat. Now add water and tomato paste and bring to a boil. Lower heat and simmer, covered, until all of the water is absorbed (about 40 minutes).

Serve alongside pinto beans.

☞ **For babies 6 months and older:** Serve this rice with mashed avocado slices on top.

Bok Choy and Buckwheat Noodles in Seasoned Broth (Yakisoba)

This traditional Japanese dish is one of my favorites. My daughter has loved yakisoba from kindergarten to college. I like to pan-fry the tofu cubes before adding them, but the dish is equally good if the tofu is added raw. Soba is a hearty noodle made from buckwheat and wheat flour that can be found in natural foods stores and Asian markets.

Prep time: 30 minutes
Makes 4 servings

1 (8-ounce) package soba noodles
2 tablespoons toasted sesame oil
1 onion, cut into thin half-moons
2 to 3 cloves garlic, minced
1 carrot, cut into matchsticks
5 shiitake mushrooms, cut into bite-size pieces
4 cups water
⅓ cup tamari or shoyu
½ pound firm tofu, cut into ½-inch cubes
1 tablespoon freshly grated ginger
2 cups chopped bok choy
2 scallions, cut into thin slices, for garnish

Prepare soba noodles according to package directions. Drain and set aside.

Heat oil in a 4-quart pot. Add onion and garlic; sauté over medium heat until onion begins to soften. Add carrot and mushroom pieces; sauté a few minutes more. Add water, tamari, tofu and ginger. Bring heat up until mixture begins to simmer. Cover and let simmer for 10 minutes. Add bok choy and simmer until leaves are bright green.

Serve this dish by placing a handful of noodles in each serving dish. Ladle broth and vegetables over the noodles. Garnish with scallions.

For babies 6 months and older: Reserve some carrots and bok choy. Steam until tender, purée with some of the broth, and serve.

For babies 10 months and older: Serve plain slices of tofu and/or cooked soba noodles cut into small pieces.

Red Bean and Quinoa Chili

I often serve this vegetarian chili to guests, and they love it. By precooking the kidney beans, you will have a one-dish meal in 45 minutes. Because whole grains and beans are combined in the chili, a vegetable or salad is all you need to make a nutritionally complete meal.

Prep time: 1 hour 15 minutes; 30 minutes if beans are precooked
Makes 6 to 8 servings

1 cup dried kidney beans, soaked
   and drained
3 cups water, divided
2 teaspoons ground cumin, divided
1 tablespoon extra-virgin olive oil
1 medium onion, chopped
2 teaspoons sea salt, divided
2 cloves garlic, minced
1 large green pepper, chopped

1 teaspoon dried oregano
¼ teaspoon ground cinnamon
⅛ teaspoon cayenne
⅔ cup quinoa, rinsed in warm water
   and drained
1 cup fresh or frozen corn
1 to 2 cups organic tomato sauce
Grated cheese, for garnish (optional)

Place beans in a large pot with 2 cups of the water and 1 teaspoon of the cumin; bring to a boil. Simmer over low heat, covered, until tender (50 to 60 minutes), or pressure-cook (45 minutes).

Heat oil in 4-quart pot on medium heat. Add onion, 1 teaspoon of the salt, garlic, green pepper, the remaining 1 teaspoon of cumin, and the rest of the spices and sauté for 5 to 10 minutes. Add quinoa and stir in. Add corn, tomato sauce, and the remaining 1 cup of water to onion/quinoa mixture. Simmer for 20 minutes. Add cooked beans and second teaspoon of salt; simmer another 10 minutes. Top each bowl with grated cheese, if desired.

☔ **For babies 10 months and older:** Serve plain, cooked, mashed beans or purée some extra cooked corn with water.

Pan-Fried Tofu and Greens with Almond Ginger Drizzle (Bathing Rama)

The traditional way to make Bathing Rama is to serve tofu on a bed of cooked spinach, covered with a spicy peanut sauce. For a new twist on this classic, I have used collards instead of spinach and soba noodles instead of white rice. The sauce is made with almond butter, but cashew butter works nicely too; another variation of this sauce, Coconut Peanut Sauce, can be found on page 228. This is a superb one-dish meal.

Prep time: Overnight for marinade; 30 minutes to make dish
Makes 4 servings and 1 cup of sauce

Marinated Tofu

3 cloves garlic, sliced
4 to 5 slices (⅛-inch thick) ginger
1 cup water
1 tablespoon brown rice vinegar
1 tablespoon toasted sesame oil
⅓ cup tamari or shoyu
1 pound firm tofu
2 tablespoons unrefined coconut oil, divided

Greens

1 large bunch collard greens, rinsed and stemmed
2½ quarts water
½ teaspoon sea salt

Noodles

2½ quarts water
8 ounces soba noodles

Sauce

¼ cup creamy almond butter
2 teaspoons maple syrup
2 tablespoons tamari or shoyu
1 tablespoon brown rice vinegar
1 tablespoon grated ginger
1 to 2 teaspoons hot pepper oil
⅓ cup water

To make the marinated tofu, in the morning, combine garlic, ginger, water, vinegar, oil, and tamari for the marinade. Cut tofu into ½-inch slabs, and then cut slabs into triangles. Put marinade and tofu in a glass storage container with a tight-fitting lid for 30 minutes to 8 hours. The longer it sits, the stronger the flavor in the tofu.

To pan-fry the tofu, heat 1 tablespoon of the coconut oil in a skillet until very hot, but not smoking. Remove tofu from marinade and pat dry with a paper towel. This will protect you from splattering oil. Place half of the tofu pieces in oil and brown on both sides. Repeat with the remaining oil and tofu pieces.

To make the greens, bring water and sea salt to boil. Submerge greens. Boil for 5 to 8 minutes. Pour cooked greens into a colander in the sink. Let cool. Squeeze out excess water with your hands. Chop into bite-size pieces. Set aside.

To make the noodles, bring a large pot of water to boil and cook noodles according to package directions. While noodles are cooking, prepare sauce.

To make the sauce, put all ingredients in a small pan on low heat. Using a whisk, mix ingredients until smooth and warm. Add extra water for desired consistency. Serve noodles with cooked greens and browned tofu on top. Drizzle sauce over all.

For babies 10 months and older: Reserve some unmarinated tofu, cut up into cubes, and serve with bite-size pieces of cooked noodles

Variation for children: Separate foods. Serve plain noodles, fried tofu, a small pile of greens, and a little bowl of the sauce for dipping.

Mexican Bean and Corn Casserole

Black beans and coarsely ground corn (polenta) make this dish delicious and nutritious vegetarian fare. This recipe is very popular in my classes that focus on beans. It is also a favorite of several of my neighbors.

Prep time: 60 minutes for beans, 40 minutes for casserole
Makes 8 servings

Beans
**1 cup dried black beans,
    soaked and drained**
1 garlic clove
1 teaspoon cumin seeds
3 cups water
1 teaspoon sea salt

Vegetables
1 teaspoon extra-virgin olive oil
1 onion, chopped
1 garlic clove, minced
½ teaspoon sea salt
½ red or green pepper, chopped
**1 cup chopped zucchini or
    shredded green cabbage**
2 teaspoons ground cumin
1 teaspoon dried oregano
½ cup organic tomato sauce
¼ cup water

Polenta
3 cups water
½ teaspoon salt
1 tablespoon oil
1 cup polenta
¼ cup grated Parmesan cheese

To make the beans, place them in a large pot with the garlic clove, cumin seeds, and water. Bring to a boil, then simmer over low heat, covered, until tender (50 to 60 minutes) or pressure-cook with 2 cups of water (45 minutes). Add salt after beans are cooked.

To make the vegetables, heat the oil in a large skillet. Add onion, minced garlic, and salt; sauté until soft. Add pepper, zucchini, ground cumin, and oregano; sauté 5 more minutes. Add cooked beans to the vegetables with tomato sauce and water. Check taste and add salt if necessary.

To make the polenta, in a separate pot, bring the water to boil. Add salt and oil. Slowly add polenta, stirring continuously. Lower heat and continue stirring for 10 to 5 minutes until mixture is quite thick.

To assemble the casserole, preheat oven to 350°F. In a lightly oiled casserole dish, spread the bean and vegetable mixture across the bottom. Spread the polenta on top. Sprinkle top with Parmesan cheese. Bake, covered, for 25 minutes at 350°F; remove cover and bake 5 minutes more at 400°F.

☞ **For babies 6 months and older:** Reserve some of the zucchini; steam it and purée.

Variation for children: Serve the bean-vegetable part of the casserole in a bowl and cut some strips of polenta to use as dippers.

Nut Burgers

This delicious burger recipe will give you an opportunity to pile up a bun with mustard, pickle, tomato or whatever and chow down without bothering a single cow. The nut and grain combination makes a complete protein; all you need is a vegetable soup or salad to make the meal complete.

Prep time: 15 to 20 minutes (without refrigeration time)
Makes 4 burgers

> ¾ cup sunflower seeds
> ¾ cup walnuts
> 1 teaspoon ground cumin
> 1 teaspoon dried oregano
> ⅛ teaspoon cayenne
> 2 cloves garlic, finely chopped
> 1 small carrot (or half of a large one), grated finely
> ½ teaspoon sea salt
> 1½ cups cooked brown rice
> 2 tablespoons tomato sauce
> 1 to 2 teaspoons ghee or butter
> 4 sprouted whole grain buns

Grind sunflower seeds and walnuts to a fine meal in a small grinder or food processor. Place in a bowl and add cumin, oregano, cayenne, garlic, carrot, and salt; mix well. Fold in cooked brown rice. Add tomato sauce a little at a time until you get a stiff, but workable, texture.

Form mixture into patties with moist hands. Refrigerate patties for a few hours if possible. Lightly coat a skillet with ghee or butter and brown patties on both sides. Serve on whole grain buns with your favorite fixin's.

☞ **For babies 6 months and older:** Purée extra cooked brown rice with a little breast milk or water.

Indian Rice and Lentils with Caramelized Onions (Mojadra)

Mojadra is an economical and flavorful dish. Use it as standby for hurried days. Cook the rice and lentils in the morning; just 10 minutes' evening preparation and you have a fast homemade meal. Serve this dish with Spinach Salad with Balsamic Vinaigrette (page 200) for a well-balanced meal. For ghee recipe, see page 239.

Prep time: 50 minutes
Makes 6 servings

2 tablespoons ghee or extra-virgin olive oil, divided
1 cup short-grain brown rice, rinsed and drained
1 cup dried brown or green lentils, rinsed and drained
1 bay leaf
3¾ cups water
2 teaspoons sea salt, divided
2 large onions, sliced in thin rounds
2 cloves garlic, minced
1½ teaspoons ground coriander
1 teaspoon ground cumin
⅛ teaspoon cayenne
1 cup plain yogurt with 1 teaspoon snipped fresh dill mixed in, for garnish

Heat 1 tablespoon of the ghee in a 4-quart pot and add rice and lentils. Sauté until nicely coated. Add bay leaf, water, and 1 teaspoon of salt and bring to a boil. Lower heat and simmer 45 minutes, covered. To pressure-cook, use 2¾ cups water and cook at pressure 35 to 40 minutes.

Meanwhile, heat remaining ghee in a skillet on medium to low heat. Add onions and 1 teaspoon salt and sauté. When onions begin to soften, add garlic and spices. Cook until onions are golden and have begun to caramelize.

When all water is absorbed from rice and lentils, remove from heat and take out bay leaf. Serve rice and lentils topped with caramelized onions and a dollop of dilled yogurt.

For babies 10 months and older: Purée some of the lentil-rice mixture before adding onions and spices.

Three Sisters Stew

Author Jackie Williams shared this incredible stew with me. Native Americans grew corn and planted the beans at the base. The corn stalks served as a bean pole. The ground space between the stalks was used to grow squash. The three sisters (corn, beans, and squash) lived harmoniously. This is an excellent dish for the holidays and the chilly nights of winter. If you choose delicata squash, the skin is thin enough that there's no need to peel.

Prep time: 1 hour and 10 minutes
Makes 6 to 8 servings

1 cup dried Christmas lima beans*,
    soaked 6 to 8 hours and drained
4 cups vegetable or chicken stock
    or water, divided
2 teaspoons ground cumin, divided
1 tablespoon extra-virgin
    olive oil or ghee
2 teaspoons dried oregano
½ teaspoon ground cinnamon
1 medium onion, chopped

2 teaspoons sea salt
3 cloves garlic, minced
2 to 3 cups winter squash,
    peeled and cut in chunks
1 (14-ounce) can chopped tomatoes
1 teaspoon chili powder
1½ cups fresh or frozen corn
½ cup grated cheese, for
    garnish (optional)

Place beans, 2 cups of stock and 1 teaspoon of the cumin in a pot; bring to a boil. Cover and simmer until beans are tender (50 to 60 minutes) or pressure-cook (45 minutes).

Heat a 4-quart pot to medium, add oil and sauté the remaining cumin, oregano, and cinnamon for about 30 seconds. Add onion, salt, and garlic; sauté until onion is soft (5 minutes). Add squash, tomatoes, and chili powder, bring to a simmer and cook until squash is soft (about 20 minutes). Add ½ to 1 cup stock if mixture is dry. Add cooked beans and corn; simmer until corn is tender. Adjust seasoning to your taste. Serve hot with grated cheese for garnish, if desired.

For babies 6 months and older: Reserve some peeled squash cubes, steam well, and purée.

For babies 10 months and older: Reserve some cooked Christmas limas before adding to stew and purée with steamed squash cubes. Serve beans in small amounts to babies.

---

* *Kidney, pinto, black, or Swedish brown beans can be substituted. More information about Christmas limas and other interesting heritage beans can be found at www.purcellmountainfarms.com or www.ranchogordo.com.*

Curried Lentils and Cauliflower

My dear friend Joy Taylor made this dish for me many years ago. I jotted down the recipe and adapted it over time. Try serving it over brown basmati rice, which is prepared the same way as Boiled Brown Rice (page 59), with Yogurt Cucumber Topping (page 230) on top. A tablespoon of Homemade Curry Paste (page 238) can be substituted for the spices.

Prep time: 30 to 35 minutes
Makes 4 servings

1 cup dried lentils, washed and drained	1 teaspoon ground cumin
1 bay leaf	1 teaspoon turmeric
2¾ cups water, divided	½ teaspoon ground cinnamon
2 teaspoons ghee or extra-virgin olive oil	1 small head cauliflower, cut into small flowerets
1 onion, chopped	
1 clove garlic, minced	1 cup tomato sauce
2 teaspoons sea salt	1 teaspoon freshly grated ginger
1 teaspoon ground coriander	½ cup roasted cashews, for garnish

Place lentils in pot with bay leaf and 2 cups of the water; bring to a boil. Lower heat, cover, and let simmer 25 to 30 minutes, until lentils are soft and all of the water is absorbed.

Heat ghee in a 4-quart pot or pressure cooker. Add onion, garlic, and salt; sauté until onion is soft. Add coriander, cumin, turmeric, and cinnamon. Add cauliflower, tomato sauce, ginger, and ¾ cup of the water; stir well. Cover and let simmer until cauliflower is tender (about 15 to 20 minutes) or bring up to pressure and cook for 5 to 7 minutes.

Stir cooked lentils into cauliflower mixture, discarding the bay leaf. Serve over whole grains and garnish with roasted cashews, if desired.

☙ **For babies 10 months and older:** Set aside some of the plain cooked lentils and purée, or steam a bit of extra cauliflower and purée it with some water.

Tempeh Tacos

One of my students at Bastyr University, Jeff Johnson, who now works for the Kashi company, presented this dish as part of his final project, and I thought it was not only very tasty but so easy to make! I served it to my family and got rave reviews. Jeff, of course, got an A.

Prep time: 30 minutes to marinate, 15 minutes to make tacos
Makes 6 to 8 servings

1 pound (two 8-ounce packages) tempeh
2 tablespoons extra-virgin olive oil, divided
2 teaspoons sea salt
¼ cup lime juice
1 tablespoon chili powder or Mexican seasoning
1 onion, chopped
¼ cup chopped fresh cilantro
12 taco shells

Optional taco fixings
Avocado slices
Grated cheese
Salsa
Shredded lettuce

Crumble or chop tempeh into small pieces and place in large a mixing bowl. Combine 1 tablespoon of the olive oil, salt, lime juice and chili powder in small bowl and pour this marinade over the tempeh. Let stand 10 to 30 minutes; the longer time allows more absorption of the flavor.

Heat the remaining oil in a large skillet. Add onion and sauté until soft. Add marinated tempeh and keep mixture moving in the pan until tempeh turns golden brown. Add cilantro just prior to serving. Warm taco shells according to directions on package. Fill shells with tempeh mixture and your favorite fixin's.

For babies 6 months and older: Serve tacos with ripe avocado slices and reserve some of the avocado for baby. Purée or mash well and serve.

Middle Eastern Falafel

Small croquettes made of spiced, ground chickpeas are fried crisp and served inside pita bread along with salad and a yogurt- or tahini-based sauce. Adapted from an original recipe by Birgitte Antonsen, a fellow teacher in the PCC Cooks program.

Prep time: 1 hour
Makes 12 to 18 patties

¾ cups dried chickpeas, soaked
   10 to 12 hours and drained
2 tablespoons lemon juice
1 tablespoon extra-virgin olive oil
1 small or half large yellow
   onion, finely chopped
1 teaspoon sea salt
2 cloves garlic, minced
2 teaspoons ground coriander
2 teaspoons ground cumin

½ teaspoon pepper
1 teaspoon baking soda
¼ teaspoon hot sauce or chili powder
¼ bunch parsley, finely chopped
Coconut oil for frying
Romaine lettuce, shredded, for garnish
Sliced tomatoes, for garnish
Lemon Tahini Sauce (page 231) or
   Yogurt Garlic Dip (page 167), for garnish
Whole grain pita bread

Place chickpeas in food processor. Process until broken into small pieces, scraping sides as necessary. Add lemon juice and continue blending until very finely ground, but not paste.

In a medium skillet over medium heat add olive oil. Add onion, salt, garlic, coriander, and cumin and sauté for 7 to 10 minutes. Set aside.

Combine ground chickpeas, sautéed onion mixture, pepper, baking soda, hot sauce, and parsley in a separate mixing bowl; mix well.

Using your hands, firmly squeeze mixture into balls and then slightly flatten into small patties. Heat 2 to 3 tablespoons coconut oil in a frying pan until hot but not smoking. Place half of the patties in oil. They should sizzle and brown quickly. Turn each one over, adding extra oil if needed, and fry for another 30 to 60 seconds so the patties are brown on both sides. If the patties fall apart, the oil is not hot enough. Remove and place on paper towels until all of the patties have been fried.

Serve falafel warm in a whole grain pita bread with lettuce, tomatoes, and Lemon Tahini Sauce.

🥄 **For babies 10 months and older:** A great dressing for falafel is plain yogurt. Stir a teaspoon into baby's cereal for a probiotic booster.

Black Bean Tostados

We often set out black beans, Mexican Brown Rice (page 149), salsa, guacamole, and other favorite toppings and let guests create their own tostados or burritos or whatever. It's a crowd pleaser. Make extra beans and recycle them into soup, spreads, dips, or casseroles later in the week.

Prep time: 1 to 2 hours, 20 minutes if beans are precooked
Makes 6 to 7 cups of beans or 12 to 14 tostados

1 teaspoon extra-virgin olive oil
1 onion, chopped
4 cloves garlic, minced
1 teaspoon ground cumin
2 cups dried black beans, soaked
   and drained
1 dried chipotle chile
4 cups water
2 teaspoons sea salt
¼ cup chopped fresh cilantro
½ cup chopped tomatoes
12 to 14 flat corn tortillas

Optional garnishes
Avocado slices
Black olives
Grated cheese
Grated zucchini
Leaf lettuce, thinly sliced
Sour cream
Salsa
Sprouts

Heat oil in a 4-quart pot or pressure cooker. Sauté onion, garlic, and cumin in oil until onions are soft. Add beans, chile, and water to onions and spices; bring to a boil. Turn down to simmer and cook, covered, until beans are tender (50 to 55 minutes), or use pressure cooker and bring up to pressure for 40 to 45 minutes. When beans are tender and have absorbed the water, stir in salt, cilantro, and tomatoes.

Bake or heat tortillas (read the instructions on the package). Serve tortillas, beans, and garnishes in separate bowls. Let diners create their own tostados.

  For babies 10 months and older: Reserve some cooked black beans before adding tomatoes and cilantro, mash well, and serve. Serve beans in small amounts to babies. I have a picture of my daughter at age 1 with black beans smeared all over her face and hands. I guess she liked them.

Tofu Kale Supper Pie

This recipe is an adaptation of the wonderful tofu quiche found in Annemarie Colbin's book The Natural Gourmet *(Ballantine Books, 1989). This version utilizes supernutritious kale and carrots. Kale is a big-leafed, dark green plant that is rich in vitamin A, vitamin C, and calcium. Umeboshi vinegar, the leftover liquid from making umeboshi plums, gives a sour-salty zip to the filling. This dish is a perfect combination of grains, beans, and vegetables. Serve with a fresh salad for a well-balanced meal.*

Prep time: 55 minutes
Makes 8 slices

Crust

- 1 cup whole wheat pastry flour
- ½ teaspoon sea salt
- 4 tablespoons cold, unsalted butter
- 2 tablespoons coconut oil
- 2 tablespoons ice-cold water

Filling

- 2 teaspoons plus 1 tablespoon extra-virgin olive oil
- 1 onion, chopped
- Pinch of sea salt
- 2 carrots, thinly sliced into half-moons
- 1 bunch kale, stems removed and cut into bite-size pieces
- ¼ cup water
- 1 pound firm tofu
- 1 tablespoon umeboshi vinegar
- 1 tablespoon mustard
- 2 teaspoons tamari or shoyu
- 1½ teaspoons snipped fresh dill or ½ teaspoon dried

To make the crust, preheat oven to 350°F. Put flour and salt in a large mixing bowl. Cut butter and oil into flour with a pastry cutter or two knives until crumbly. Slowly dribble water into flour, blending with a fork. Alternately, butter and oil can be incorporated into flour in a food processor, then water added slowly while pulsing to make dough. Gather dough into a ball; it should be moist and pliable. Roll out into a crust on a floured surface or a piece of wax paper. Transfer to an 8- or 9-inch pie pan. Trim edges. Prebake for 10 minutes in the oven.

To make the filling, heat 2 teaspoons of the oil in a large skillet. Add onion, salt, and carrots; sauté until onion is soft. Add kale, stirring several times until kale begins to wilt. Add water to skillet and cover. Blend the remaining 1 tablespoon of oil, tofu, vinegar, mustard, tamari, and dill in a blender or food processor until smooth. You may need to add a little water.

To assemble the pie, put the vegetables in the bottom of the prebaked crust. Pour the tofu mixture over the top, covering the vegetables. Bake 30 minutes, or until the top of the pie begins to turn golden at the edges. Cut and serve.

For babies 6 months and older: Steam some extra carrot slices and purée.

For babies 10 months and older: Reserve some cubes of tofu and serve with carrot purée.

Black-Eyed Peas and Arame with Cilantro

Arame is a sea vegetable that has been finely shredded, cooked, and then naturally sun dried. When reconstituted, it looks like small, black threads. Its mild flavor makes it a useful introductory sea vegetable. This dish, created by my talented friend Minx Boren, delights the taste buds with its unique combination of flavors. Combines well with Sweet Squash Corn Muffins (page 218) and any green vegetable.

Prep time: 45 to 50 minutes
Makes 6 to 8 servings

> 2 cups dried black-eyed peas
> 4 cups water
> 1 cup arame, soaked in cold water and drained
> 2 tablespoons tamari or shoyu
> 2 tablespoons brown rice syrup or maple syrup
> ½ tablespoon grated ginger
> 1 teaspoon brown rice vinegar
> ⅓ cup chopped cilantro, for garnish

Put peas and water in a pot; bring to a boil. Lower heat and simmer until tender (30 to 35 minutes). Add arame, tamari, rice syrup, and ginger. Gently stir, and simmer mixture 10 more minutes. Add vinegar just before serving. Garnish with cilantro.

For babies 10 months and older: Remove some black-eyed peas when tender and purée with a little water.

Szechwan Tempeh

Tempeh can be stored in the refrigerator for a week or it can be stored in the freezer for 6 months. Allow an hour or two for frozen tempeh to thaw before using. This is a favorite dish of mine that I use frequently to introduce my students to tempeh. We usually have it with Quick Lemon and Garlic Quinoa Salad (page 110) and Mango Salsa (page 235), and it gets rave reviews. Szechwan Tempeh is also excellent served over udon noodles.

Prep time: 15 minutes
Makes 3 servings

¼ cup coconut oil, divided
1 (8-ounce) package tempeh, cut into ¼-inch strips
2 tablespoons white miso
¼ to ⅓ cup water
2 tablespoons tamari or shoyu
2 tablespoons mirin
2 tablespoons balsamic vinegar
2 tablespoons brown rice syrup
2 teaspoons toasted sesame oil or hot pepper oil
1 scallion, thinly sliced, for garnish

Heat 2 tablespoons of the coconut oil over high heat in a 10-inch skillet. Place half of the tempeh strips in the skillet and let them quick-fry, turning them so that both sides brown. Remove fried tempeh onto a paper towel, and repeat the process with the other half of the oil and tempeh strips. Let skillet cool.

In a small bowl, mix miso and water with a whisk until miso is dissolved. Add tamari, mirin, vinegar, rice syrup, and sesame oil to miso and whisk again.

Place fried tempeh back in the skillet and turn heat to medium low. Pour sauce over the tempeh and bring to a low simmer. Sauce will begin to reduce and thicken. Once sauce becomes thick and glistening, garnish with scallion and serve immediately.

For babies 6 months and older: Serve this dish over cooked long-grain brown rice. Reserve some of the cooked grain and purée with water or breast milk to make cereal.

Variation for children: Reserve some of the crispy fried tempeh before adding the sauce and serve with a sprinkle of tamari.

Sloppeh Joes

Can you tell I was raised in the '50s and '60s? The vegetarian version of the familiar classic was styled from one of my mother's recipes. I guess it goes without saying that the same flavorings can be added to cooked ground beef instead of tempeh, which was how I ate it as a child. Serve with corn on the cob and Creamy Coleslaw (page 202).

Prep time: 20 minutes
Makes 4 servings

> 2 teaspoons extra-virgin olive oil
> 1 onion, chopped
> 1 green pepper, chopped
> 1 clove garlic, minced
> ½ teaspoon sea salt
> 1 (8-ounce) package tempeh, crumbled
> ⅔ cup fruit-sweetened, organic ketchup
> 2 teaspoons whole grain mustard
> 1 tablespoon brown rice vinegar
> ½ teaspoon ground cloves
> 4 sprouted whole grain hamburger buns

Heat oil in a 10-inch skillet. Add onion, pepper, garlic, and salt; sauté until soft. Add tempeh to onion mixture. Let the tempeh brown. Mix ketchup, mustard, vinegar, and cloves together in a small bowl. Add to tempeh mixture, mixing well. Warm buns in oven if desired. Spoon tempeh mixture onto buns and serve with your favorite garnish.

For babies 6 months and older: Try some steamed zucchini with Sloppeh Joes. Reserve some of the zucchini and purée.

For babies 10 months and older: Serve a warmed bun spread with a little apple butter or squash butter.

Dr. Bruce's Awesome Grilled Salmon

Dr. Bruce Gardner, a family practitioner, prepared this mouthwatering delicacy for us one summer and I have never forgotten it. The ginger lime marinade makes this dish awesome. Be sure to purchase wild salmon, not Atlantic or farm-raised. Serve the salmon with Lemon Basil Potato Salad (page 104) and Spinach Salad with Balsamic Vinaigrette (page 200) for your next family gathering.

Prep time: 1 hour for marinating, 10 to 15 minutes for grilling
Makes eight to ten, 4-ounce servings

> ⅓ cup tamari or shoyu
> 2 teaspoons toasted sesame oil
> 2 tablespoons grated ginger
> Juice of 1 large lime
> 4 cloves garlic, minced
> 4 scallions, finely chopped
> 2 to 3 pounds salmon fillet
> 2 red peppers, cut into big slices, for garnish

Put tamari, oil, ginger, lime juice, garlic, and scallions in a small mixing bowl; whisk together. Place salmon in a shallow pan and pour marinade over the top. Allow to marinate one hour in the refrigerator. Prepare grill.

When your grill is hot, remove salmon from pan and place on the grill, skin side down. Brush the top of the salmon with marinade and grill for about 5 minutes. The rule of thumb for cooking fish is 10 minutes of cooking time per inch of thickness. Turn the salmon over. Remove the skin: it should come off easily. Brush the top with marinade again and grill for 4 to 7 minutes more, until the salmon is tender at the thickest part. Flip it over and serve grilled side up. Roast chunks of red pepper on the grill while cooking salmon and serve alongside as a garnish.

🥄 **For babies 6 months and older:** This grilled salmon is delightful served with Lemon Basil Potato Salad (page 104). Reserve some of the boiled potatoes and mash with water or breast milk.

For babies 10 months and older: A few bites of cooked salmon combined with one of baby's regular foods are fine. Check salmon and remove any tiny bones before serving.

Orange-Glazed Salmon Kebobs with Yogurt Garlic Dip

Instead of salmon chunks, you can try chicken breast, beef, or tofu. Directions are for broiling, but these are yummy grilled, too. For fun, use rosemary stems instead of wooden skewers.

Prep time: 20 minutes, 1 hour for marinating
Makes 4 to 6 kebobs

6 wooden skewers
1 to 1 ½ pounds salmon fillet

Marinade
¼ cup thawed orange juice concentrate
4 cloves garlic, minced
2 tablespoons honey
2 tablespoons balsamic vinegar
2 tablespoons tamari
2 teaspoons toasted sesame oil

Yogurt Garlic Dip
1 small or ½ large cucumber, peeled, seeded, and grated
1 teaspoon sea salt
1 cup plain whole milk yogurt
1 clove garlic, minced
2 teaspoons lemon juice
2 tablespoons chopped parsley

Soak skewers in water. Cut salmon into 1-inch strips. Remove skin from each strip and then cut into 1-inch cubes. Place in a shallow dish.

Mix all ingredients for the marinade in a small saucepan. Warm just enough to incorporate honey. Pour over salmon pieces. Let salmon marinate about an hour, turning occasionally.

Place cucumber in a small bowl with salt and set aside. In a separate bowl combine yogurt, garlic, lemon juice, and parsley; set aside.

When salmon is well marinated, preheat oven to broil. Put four chunks on each skewer. Place in baking dish in oven. Broil about 3 to 4 minutes, turn skewers, and pour some of the marinade over the salmon. Broil another 3 to 4 minutes. Alternately, the remaining marinade can be reduced on the stove and used as a sauce for grains or vegetables served with the kebobs.

Squeeze grated cucumber to discard excess water and blend into yogurt mix. Place some dip in a small bowl for each diner. Serve salmon kabobs with dip.

🥄 **For babies 10 months and older:** These kabobs are delicious served with Rosemary- and Garlic-Roasted Potatoes (page 207). Mash some of the potatoes with a teaspoon of plain yogurt.

Nori-Wrapped Wasabi Salmon

This recipe is a compilation of one by Mary Shaw and one published in the Fall 2001 Desert Dining Guide from the En Fuego restaurant in Arizona, with a few twists of my own. By wrapping the salmon before baking, it stays very moist and tender. The nori adds unusual flavor and bonus minerals.

Prep time: 15 minutes
Makes 4 small or 2 regular servings

> 1 tablespoon olive oil
> 1 tablespoon finely chopped herbs: any combination of thyme, basil,
>   garlic, parsley, and mint
> Salt and pepper
> 2 (8-ounce) salmon fillets
> 1 tablespoon Dijon mustard
> ¼ teaspoon wasabi powder
> 2 sheets nori

Preheat oven to 450°F. Mix oil, herbs, and salt and pepper to taste. Rub salmon with mixture.

Mix mustard and wasabi together. Spread on nori.

Place salmon face down in the middle of the nori sheet and wrap like a package so that fish is fully covered. The nori will stick to itself and the salmon.

Place wrapped salmon in a lightly oiled baking dish. The general rule for fish is to cook it 10 minutes for each inch of thickness. The nori will lightly flavor the salmon and seal in the juices.

🥣 **For babies 6 months and older:** This dish is lovely served with Sweet Rice Timbales (page 147). Reserve some of the cooked rice and purée with water to make cereal.

Caribbean Lime Halibut

This is a very easy way to prepare fish. The pan-frying to start seals the juices in. Serve this fish with Emerald City Salad (page 106) or Quick Lemon and Garlic Quinoa Salad (page 110).

Prep time: 30 minutes to 1 hour for marinating, 10 to 15 minutes for cooking
Makes four, 4-ounce servings

1 tablespoon tamari or shoyu
3 tablespoons extra-virgin olive oil, divided
1 tablespoon grated ginger
3 tablespoons lime juice
1 teaspoon agave nectar or sugar
3 to 4 cloves garlic, minced
1 pound halibut fillet — *no halibut - fishman suggested substituting chilean sea bass*

delicious

To marinate the halibut, put tamari, 2 tablespoons of the oil, ginger, lime juice, agave, and garlic in a small mixing bowl; whisk together. Place fish in a shallow pan and pour marinade over the top. Allow to marinate 30 minutes to 1 hour in the refrigerator.

Preheat oven to 400°F. Heat the remaining olive oil in an ovenproof skillet; cast iron is good. Remove halibut from marinade; set marinade aside. Place halibut in the pan, skin side up, and sear for 1 minute; turn and sear second side for 1 minute.

Leave fish in the skillet and place in oven. Bake until fish is almost cooked through, about 7 to 10 minutes.

Remove skillet from oven and place on stove. Add reserved marinade and deglaze the pan, letting the liquid reduce some before serving.

For babies 6 months and older: This dish is lovely served with a quinoa dish. Reserve some of the cooked quinoa and purée with water to make cereal for baby.

Rainbow Trout Poached in Herbs

When I was growing up, my family went to southern Colorado in the summer. My dad fished the Conejos River and caught fresh rainbow trout. This fish has long been a favorite of mine. I like this recipe because the family shares the whole fish together. Most trout available in stores is farm-raised, but the methods for most trout farming are sustainable and healthy for the fish. Serve with a grain salad like Mediterranean Quinoa (page 143).

Prep time: 20 to 25 minutes
Makes 3 to 4 small servings

> 2 teaspoons extra-virgin olive oil
> 1 onion, chopped
> 1 teaspoon sea salt
> 2 quarts water
> 1 cup white wine
> 2 bay leaves
> 4 to 5 sprigs fresh thyme
> 4 to 5 sprigs fresh parsley
> 1 whole, fresh rainbow trout
> ½ lemon
> 2 to 3 feet of cheesecloth

Heat oil in an 8-quart pot. Add onion and salt and sauté until soft. Add water, wine, and herbs. Bring mixture to a gentle simmer and let it cook 10 to 12 minutes.

While poaching liquid is simmering, prepare fish. Gently rinse the whole fish. Cut lemon into thin slices. Place lemon slices in body of fish, then wrap the whole fish in cheesecloth, leaving long ends of cloth at the head and tail.

Lower the fish into the poaching water, leaving the two long ends of the cheesecloth draped over the edge of the pan. Let fish cook in simmering poaching liquid for 10 minutes.

Lift fish out by the dry ends of the cheesecloth. Remove fish from cheesecloth. Open down the middle and remove head, spine and tail. Gently lift out the meat of the fish and serve immediately.

🥣 **For babies 6 months and older:** This dish is lovely served with long-grain brown rice. Reserve some of the cooked rice and purée with water to make cereal.

For babies 10 months and older: If your baby has some incisors and molars, it might be time to introduce fish. This fish is very tender and mild tasting. Be extremely careful about removing all tiny bones before serving to baby.

Sweet Potato and Shrimp Tempura

Tempura is a delicious, deep-fried dish. Care should be taken to prepare the dish carefully so that it is light and delicate. The frying oil needs to be 350°F to 400°F, the batter needs to be cold and the sweet potato slices should not be too thick or too thin.

Prep time: 20 minutes
Makes 4 appetizer servings

1 sweet potato or red garnet yam,
   cut into ⅛-inch-thich slices
6 to 12 prawns
1-quart high-heat safflower oil

Batter
½ cup whole wheat pastry flour
½ cup rice flour
1 cup ice-cold sparkling water

Dipping Sauce
½ cup vegetable or chicken stock
2 tablespoons tamari
1 tablespoon ginger, peeled and grated

Bring a few inches of water to boil with a steamer basket in a pot. Place sliced sweet potatoes in the basket. Cover and steam 2 to 3 minutes. Remove and let cool. Pat dry with a paper towel.

Remove outer shell from shrimp but not tail. Devein shrimp.

Heat oil in a wok on high. Use direct-read thermometer to tell when oil has reached the right temperature, 350°F to 400°F.

To make batter, put whole wheat and rice flours in a bowl. Add ice-cold sparkling water and gently mix until blended and frothy. Use a minimum of strokes—be sure not to overmix.

Prepare a plate or cookie sheet with paper towels or a brown paper bag for draining the finished tempura pieces.

Take each sweet potato or shrimp piece, dip in the batter, and shake off excess. Gently drop into hot oil. Pieces should drop to the bottom, and then quickly rise to the top. Turn pieces so that both sides are gold and crispy. Remove and place on paper towel. You can fry 3 to 4 pieces at a time. Keep adjusting oil so it stays hot.

Tempura should be served and eaten right away. Whisk ingredients for dipping sauce together and give each diner a small bowl.

For babies 6 months and older: Reserve some of the steamed sweet potato and purée with water.

Thea's Greek Shrimp Stew

We serve this rich, scrumptious stew to company. The recipe is really fast and easy to make. Serve it with warm whole grain bread and Susan's Succulent Supper Salad (page 203) for a simple feast.

Prep time: 30 minutes
Makes 6 servings

> 1 tablespoon extra-virgin olive oil
> 2 onions, chopped
> 1 teaspoon sea salt
> 4 cloves garlic, minced
> 3 cups organic chopped or diced tomatoes
> 1 cup organic tomato sauce
> 2 teaspoons Dijon mustard
> 3 tablespoons snipped fresh dill or 1 tablespoon dried
> 1 teaspoon honey
> 1 pound cooked shrimp
> ¼ to ½ pound feta cheese, crumbled
> 1 cup chopped parsley

In a large soup pot heat oil, and then add onions, salt, and garlic. Sauté until onions are soft. Add tomatoes, tomato sauce, mustard, dill, and honey; simmer for 20 minutes. Five minutes before serving, add shrimp, feta, and parsley. Stir well and serve.

 For babies 6 months and older: This stew is wonderful served with warm whole grain bread like the Whole Wheat and Rice Bread on page 214. Take part of the leftover cooked brown rice used for making the bread and purée it with water to make cereal for baby.

Spice Island Beef Stew

One excellent brand of beef is Country Natural Beef, which is a cooperative of ranches run by Doc and Connie Hatfield (www.oregoncountrybeef.com). Chuck is perfect for stews, as it is inexpensive, flavorful, and ideal for long cooking. This is an original recipe by my talented colleague Becky Boutch.

Prep time: 10 minutes to prepare stew, 1½ to 2½ hours cooking time, depending on whether you are using a pressure cooker or stew pot
Makes 4 to 6 servings

3 tablespoons extra-virgin
   olive oil, divided
1 pound beef chuck, trimmed
   and cut into 1-inch cubes
1 large onion, coarsely chopped
2 cloves garlic, minced
¼ habanero pepper, seeds
   removed, minced
½ teaspoon dried thyme
½ teaspoon allspice
¼ cup brown rice flour

1 bay leaf
Zest of 1 orange
Juice of 1 orange plus water, wine,
   and/or stock to equal 1½ cups
1 (14-ounce) can diced tomatoes
2 teaspoons sea salt
1 green bell pepper, diced
1 medium zucchini, diced
1 cup cooked red beans
¼ cup pimento-stuffed olives,
   coarsely chopped (optional)

Heat a large stew pot or pressure cooker over medium-high heat. Add 2 tablespoons of the oil and meat. Brown meat on all sides, about 5 minutes. Remove meat and set aside on plate.

Add remaining oil to pot along with onion. Sauté briefly, until onion begins to turn translucent. Add garlic, habanero, thyme, and allspice. Cook for 30 seconds, until garlic and spices are fragrant.

Return meat to pot. Sprinkle flour over sautéed mixture and stir to coat meat and vegetables. Cook 1 to 2 minutes, then add bay leaf, orange zest and juice, liquid, tomatoes, and salt.

To pressure-cook, lock lid of cooker in place. Bring to high pressure. Lower heat and continue to cook at high pressure 30 minutes. Reduce pressure and open cooker. Meat should begin to tenderize. Continue as follows.

To cook in a stew pot, bring to a boil. Turn heat to low, cover, and simmer 1½ hours, or until meat begins to tenderize. Continue as follows.

Add bell pepper and zucchini. Return to a simmer and cook, covered, 20 minutes, or until vegetables are nearly tender. If you are using a pressure cooker, you can return the cooker to high pressure after adding vegetables and cook for no more than 5 minutes.

Add beans and olives, if desired. Simmer 10 minutes more, until flavors have blended and meat can be shredded with a spoon. Discard bay leaf, adjust seasonings if necessary, and serve.

For babies 10 months and older: Purée some of the cooked red beans with a little water and serve.

Gay's Mini Pot Roast with Many Vegetables

My daughter Grace will drop anything she is doing to rush over to her good friend Emi's house for some of her mom Gay's pot roast. Her two radiant daughters reflect Gay's devotion to fine home cooking.

Prep time: 3-plus hours
Makes 6 servings

1½ pounds chuck roast
Salt and pepper
3 to 4 tablespoons extra-virgin
   olive oil, divided
1 large onion
2 stalks celery, diced
1 tablespoon fresh thyme
1 tablespoon fresh marjoram

1 tablespoon fresh rosemary
2 cups beef broth
2 cups red wine
2 large carrots, cut into chunks
3 to 4 small potatoes, cut into chunks
1 to 2 parsnips, cut into chunks
10 to 12 brussels sprouts

Preheat oven to 350°F. Season pot roast liberally with salt and pepper. Add 1 to 2 tablespoons of olive oil to a heavy 4-quart pot. When hot, add the roast and brown on all sides. Remove from pot and set aside.

Cut onion in half. Chop one half and cut the other into large chunks.

Add the remaining oil to the pot, then the chopped onion and the celery. Sauté until onion is caramelized then add thyme, marjoram, and rosemary.

Return the roast to the pot, and cover with the broth and wine. Bring to a boil, then cover pot, remove from stove, and put in oven for 2 hours.

When the roast is quite tender, add the onion chunks along with the carrots, potatoes, and parsnips. Salt the vegetables. Continue roasting for another 30 minutes until vegetables are tender. Add the brussels sprouts and roast for about 10 minutes longer, until the sprouts are tender.

For babies 6 months and older: Mash up some of those tender roasted parsnips—yum.

Thai Steak Salad Over Soba

Choosing beef from healthfully raised cows is important nutritionally, ecologically, and politically. If you can't find grass-fed or humanely raised beef from a local farmer, ask questions at your food co-op or grocery store to find beef from cows that were not given antibiotics or hormones. Grass-fed beef requires a shorter cooking time because the beef is less fatty.

Prep time: 1 to 12 hours for marinade, then 20 minutes
Makes 4 servings

⅓ cup lime juice
⅓ cup olive oil
¼ cup packed fresh
  cilantro, chopped
1 to 2 cloves garlic, minced
¼ teaspoon hot pepper oil
  or hot pepper sauce
3 teaspoons honey or sugar
1 teaspoon sea salt

Freshly ground pepper
1 pound sirloin or flank
  steak, 1-inch thick
1 (8-ounce) package soba noodles
3 to 4 cups salad greens, washed, dried,
  and torn into bite-size pieces
½ small red onion, cut into half-moons
½ cucumber, peeled, seeded,
  and cut into half-moons

Combine lime juice, oil, cilantro, garlic, hot pepper oil, honey, salt, and pepper to taste in a small bowl. Whisk together and set aside.

Place sirloin between two sheets of plastic wrap and pound on both sides to tenderize. Remove wrap and place sirloin in a shallow pan. Pour half of the marinade over the meat. Cover and marinate in the refrigerator for at least 1 hour or up to 12 hours.

Preheat oven to 400°F. Heat a cast iron or oven-safe skillet with a teaspoon or so of oil. Place marinated steak in skillet and brown for a few minutes on each side. This is a good time to salt and pepper the meat. Transfer steak to the oven for 7 to 10 minutes. Check center for doneness (red for medium rare, pink for medium) and remove from oven when it is redder than you desire; the meat will continue to cook once it is out of the oven.

While meat is cooking, prepare noodles according to package directions.

Transfer meat to a carving board and let rest 10 minutes before slicing into thin slices on a diagonal against the grain of the meat. To assemble, place a small bed of noodles on each plate. Toss the greens, onion, and cucumber with almost all of the remaining marinade and divide among four plates. Top each plate of noodles and salad with an equal portion of steak slices and a drizzle of dressing.

For babies 10 months and older: Some soba noodles with fresh cilantro and a few drops of dressing are perfectly fine to serve.

Variation for children: Instead of arranging this dish like a salad, keep meat, noodles, and vegetables separate and serve with a few tablespoons of dressing for dipping.

Squash- and Raisin-Stuffed Chicken Breasts

I've always been a little intimidated by stuffed entrées, but they are really fun and easy. These are amazing topped with a savory/sweet sauce. A traditional cranberry sauce, fruit chutney, and thinned savory jam (like pepper jam) work well. Or simply plop some Sweet Pepper Relish (page 229) on top to add zip as well as color. Fit for company with a green salad on the side!

Prep time: 45 minutes
Makes 4 servings

> ½ to ¾ cup baked winter squash, diced
> 1 pound boneless, skinless chicken breasts
> ¼ cup raisins
> 2 to 3 tablespoons walnuts, chopped
> 1 teaspoon Sucanat or brown sugar
> ½ teaspoon thyme
> Salt and pepper
> 1 egg
> ½ cup bread crumbs

Preheat oven to 375°F. If you do not have some leftover baked squash, prepare squash by cutting in half, scooping out seeds, and placing face down on a buttered baking dish. Bake 45 to 60 minutes (depending on the size of the squash).

Slice chicken breasts through the middle, creating 4 to 6 flat pieces of similar size. Cover with plastic wrap and pound breast with a meat pounder on both sides, until about ½-inch thick.

Place squash in a small bowl with raisins, walnuts, Sucanat, thyme, salt and pepper. Stir gently.

Place 2 to 3 tablespoons of squash mixture on a piece of chicken and firmly roll it up, starting at the widest end. Repeat with remaining chicken and squash.

Beat egg in a shallow bowl. Place bread crumbs in a separate shallow bowl. Dip each rolled breast in the egg, and then roll in the bread crumbs. Repeat.

Place coated rolls in a greased baking dish and bake at 375°F for 25 to 30 minutes, until tender.

🥣 **For babies 6 months and older:** Some of that baked squash is perfect for baby!

Lemon- and Herb-Roasted Chicken

Using the whole chicken is more economical than buying parts and creates less waste. This simple recipe produces a moist, flavorful dish that can be used as a side accompaniment or as the main dish. In class we prepare this dish with Emerald City Salad (page 106), though it is also quite good with mashed sweet potatoes.

Prep time: 1 hour and 20 minutes
Makes 4 main dishes or 8 side dishes

> 1 whole free-range chicken (about 4 to 5 pounds)
> 2 tablespoons fresh rosemary
> 3 to 4 tablespoons fresh oregano or marjoram
> 4 to 6 cloves garlic
> 2 teaspoons sea salt
> Freshly ground pepper
> Zest of 1 lemon
> 2 tablespoons lemon juice

Preheat oven to 450°F. Cut chicken into eight parts, first removing legs and thighs, then the wings, and finally the breast, which is divided in half. Discard back, neck, and organs, or use back and neck to make stock for later use. Place chicken pieces in a 9 x 13 baking dish.

Remove leaves from rosemary and oregano and place with garlic and salt on a wooden cutting board. Chop together until herbs are finely minced, and put into a small bowl. Add pepper to taste and zest to bowl with herbs and mix. Coat both sides of each chicken piece with herb mixture, using a brush or rubbing it on. Make sure the breasts are bone side up.

Put pan into oven and immediately lower temperature to 400°F. Let chicken roast, uncovered, for 1 hour, or until meat is tender and skin has browned nicely. Remove from oven and sprinkle lemon juice over the meat before serving.

🥄 **For babies 6 months and older:** To balance the meal you will need a grain or starchy vegetable and something green. Steamed, puréed broccoli will work for baby, as will some mashed sweet potato.

Baked Chicken with Mushrooms and Rosemary

This is a simple way to make a very tasty dish. The liquids and juices form a yummy gravy in the bottom of the baking dish that is fabulous over mashed potatoes.

Prep time: 65 to 70 minutes
Makes 4 small servings

> 8 to 10 whole mushrooms
> ½ cup white wine or mirin
> 2 tablespoons tamari or shoyu
> 1 pound whole bone-in chicken breasts
> 1 3-inch sprig of fresh rosemary

Preheat oven to 350°F. Wipe mushrooms clean with a damp towel or rag. Put wine and tamari in an 8-inch baking dish. Place chicken breasts and cleaned mushrooms in the dish. Remove leaves from rosemary sprig, chop them, and sprinkle on top of the chicken. Cover the dish and bake for one hour. Remove cover and broil for a minute or two before serving, if desired.

☞ **For babies 6 months and older:** Serve dish with brown basmati rice. Reserve a portion of cooked rice, purée with a little water, and serve as cereal to baby. For older babies, use a little of the juice from the chicken and mushrooms to purée rice.

Spinach Feta Quiche

If you can locate eggs from chickens that have been allowed to eat their natural diet (bugs, worms, greens), their yolks will be rich in omega-3 fatty acids. It is tricky to create a whole grain pie crust that is flaky and tasty. I have found the best combination of fats for texture and flavor is two parts unsalted organic butter and one part unrefined coconut oil or lard.

Prep time: 15 minutes, 40 for baking
Makes 8 slices

Crust

1 cup whole wheat pastry flour
½ teaspoon sea salt
4 tablespoons cold, unsalted butter
2 tablespoons coconut oil
2 tablespoons ice-cold water

Filling

1½ cups milk or half-and-half
4 eggs
½ teaspoon sea salt
2 cups baby spinach leaves
1 cup crumbled feta cheese
½ ripe tomato, cut into thin slices

Preheat oven to 375°F.

To make the crust, put flour and salt in a large mixing bowl. Cut butter and oil into flour with a pastry cutter or two knives until crumbly. Slowly dribble water into flour, blending with a fork. Alternately, butter and oil can be incorporated into flour in a food processor, then water added slowly while pulsing to make dough. Gather dough into a ball; it should be moist and pliable. Roll out into a crust on a floured surface or a piece of wax paper. Transfer to an 8- or 9-inch pie pan. Trim edges.

To make the filling, first scald the milk to hasten baking time. Let milk cool, then whisk with eggs and salt. Sprinkle spinach and feta in the bottom of the crust and pour egg mixture over the top. Decorate the top with tomato slices in a pleasing arrangement. Bake 35 to 40 minutes, or until the top is golden and a knife inserted into the center of the quiche comes out clean. Let pie cool slightly before serving.

For babies 10 months and older: Remember that egg whites are inappropriate for infants under 1 year of age. Egg yolks, however, are an excellent source of essential fatty acids. Boil an egg for 3 to 4 minutes, peel, discard white, and serve warm yolk with baby's cereal.

Got Color?

One-Trick Vegetables
Quick Boiled Greens
Sesame Greens
Greens in Cashew Curry Sauce
Dark Greens Salad with Creamy Ginger Garlic
    Dressing
Garlic-Sautéed Greens
Becky's Braised Greens
Sweet Apple Walnut Kale
Massaged Kale and Currant Salad
Romaine Chop Salad with Basil Dressing
Luscious Beet Salad with Toasted Pumpkin Seeds
Mustard Greens Salad with Tofu Dill Dressing
Watercress Salad with Creamy Ginger Dressing
Greek Salad
Spinach Salad with Balsamic Vinaigrette
Triple "A" Salad (Avocado, Arame, and Almonds)
Creamy Coleslaw
Susan's Succulent Supper Salad
Lime Cabbage Slaw
Grilled Vegetable Salad with Sweet Poppy Seed
    Dressing
Dulse Salad with Lemon Tahini Dressing
Rosemary- and Garlic-Roasted Potatoes
Potato Gratin
Pressure-Cooked Garlic Mashed Potatoes

Got Greens? Identifying Dark Leafy Greens

Many people think that steaming greens is the only way to eat them. Others only imagine greens in salads, raw. The sturdier dark, leafy greens actually get more bitter if you steam them, but they let go of some of that bitter flavor given enough heat and water.

There are a variety of greens and just as many ways to prepare them. Most green vegetables are rich in vitamins A and C, folic acid, calcium, and iron. The darker the color, the more nutrients present. Remember that nutrients like vitamin A and calcium are better absorbed if there is fat present, so don't be shy about using butter or olive oil in any greens dish!

▶ **Arugula** is also known as "rocket." This leaf has a peppery flavor and is very popular in "wild greens" mixes. Buy fresh-looking leaves. Arugula adds a spicy dimension to salads.

▶ **Beet greens** are the tops of the beet plant. Often you can purchase beets with the tops still attached. Only use them if the leaves are full and vibrant; discard wilted tops.

▶ **Bok choy** is a beautiful-looking plant with an edible juicy white part that melds into dark green leaves. You can chop up the whole plant and use it, however the white part will require a bit more cooking time than the leaves. I love this vegetable sautéed in butter and garlic with a tiny splash of vinegar.

▶ **Broccoli**, as Mollie Katzen let us all know in her classic vegetarian cookbook *The Enchanted Broccoli Forest*, is unique. The beautiful treelike structure of the plant is appealing to children. Blanching it and giving it a sauce or a dip is one easy way of preparing broccoli.

▶ **Chinese cabbage (napa)** looks like green cabbage with a perm. It has a wavy texture to its leaves. It has a slightly more delicate taste than common cabbage and can be used in place of green cabbage in any recipe. Savoy cabbage looks and tastes similarly.

▶ **Collard greens** are big, broad, oval-shaped, dark green leaves that need some heat to bring out their goodness. They are easy to grow and overwinter nicely in temperate climates. My favorite cooking method for collards is braising.

▶ **Dandelion greens** are the most bitter of all the greens (at least to my taste buds). Some folks really yearn for that strong bitter flavor. It gets all the juices in their mouths in full swing. And yes, they are the leaves of those tight, yellow-flowered plants that have no trouble growing anywhere.

▶ **Endive's** most commonly seen variety is Belgian endive, which is a delicate, small cream to pale green, cigar-shaped plant. It only needs a brief whisper of heat, or it can be served raw in salad.

▶ **Escarole** is a type of endive with a milder flavor. It is most often used as a leafy green in salads but can be cooked briefly or added to soups.

▶ **Green cabbage**, also known as "common cabbage," is really not common at all. Slice a head in half and stare at that pattern! The way the leaves are tightly woven is amazing. Cabbage is wonderful lightly cooked, raw in slaws, or used as a wrapper.

▶ **Kale**, a member of the cabbage family, comes in a number of shapes, sizes, and types. There is curly leafed kale, red kale, dinosaur kale, and more. All kales have a pretty assertive flavor and benefit from some cooking. Kale is very dense in nutrients.

- **Mustard greens** are another member of the kale family. These leaves have a peppery flavor. Mizuna is a type of mustard green that is milder than some.

- **Swiss chard** has big, majestic-looking leaves with white, yellow, pink, or red stems—a beautiful-looking plant. Cook it as you would collards or kale but with much less cooking time.

- **Watercress** likes to grow near running water. It has small, round leaves and a bright, sharp taste. Use it like a fresh herb to finish soup, grain, or bean dishes or add to salads for a spark.

There are more not listed here. Please forgive. Many of our favorite fresh herbs—basil, oregano, sage, cilantro, and parsley—are nutrition-packed, dark, leafy greens, too. Let's graze!

Got Orange? Identifying Winter Squashes and Sweet Potatoes

Just about everyone loves the taste of sweet vegetables. I returned home to Kansas one Thanksgiving and prepared baked winter squash and sweet potatoes mashed together for the family gathering. Several relatives praised me for the offering and asked for the recipe. I repeated many times that it was simply baked buttercup squash and sweet potatoes. My grandmother was sure I was wrong. She insisted that there must be brown sugar, pineapples, marshmallows, or all three in the dish.

The autumn harvest brings pumpkins and a wide variety of winter squashes, each with its own unique and unbelievably sweet flavor. These vegetables not only score high on taste, but they are also rich in vitamin A, vitamin C, fiber, and trace minerals. Here is a description of some of the varieties to shop for:

- **Acorn squash** is shaped like a large acorn with prominent ridges; comes in dark green, yellow or orange; has sweet, light flesh.

- **Buttercup squash** is shaped like a pumpkin but smaller; has green or gold skin; meat is dark orange, moist, and creamy.

- **Butternut squash** is gourd-shaped with a neck, a bulbous base, and buff-colored skin; flesh is orange and firm.

- **Delicata squash** is a small, oblong-shaped squash; has yellow skin with green stripes; particularly sweet, golden-colored flesh.

- **Golden turbans** are like a double-decker pumpkin; have a distinctive turban shape; come in hues of green, gold, orange, and red; mild, pleasant flavor.

- **Hubbard squash** is a large, smooth-skinned squash with a gray-green color and classic flavor.

- **Kabocha squash** is pumpkin-shaped and dark green with gray-brown nubs on the outside; dark orange flesh inside.

- **Spaghetti squash** is a large, oval-shaped squash with yellow skin; insides become long thin golden strands when cooked.

- **Sugar pie pumpkins** are small, dark orange pumpkins; perfect for pie making.

- **Sweet potatoes** (sometimes called red garnet yams) have beige or brown skins and are shaped like a potato with pointed ends. The meat is gold or dark orange.

One-Trick Vegetables

Blanched Broccoli

Keep a variety of blanched vegetables in your refrigerator and pull them out for a quick snack. Dip them in Coconut Peanut Sauce (page 228), Lemon Tahini Sauce (page 231), or Tofu Dill Dressing (page 197). Cauliflower, asparagus, carrots, and green beans are all bright, crispy, sweet, and tender when blanched!

Prep time: 10 minutes
Makes 4 to 6 servings

1 bunch broccoli
Lemon juice (optional)

Bring a large pot of water to boil. Cut florets off broccoli into uniform pieces. If you wish to use the thick stem, you will need to peel it and then cut it at an angle into bite-size pieces. Prepare a large bowl or sink full of ice-cold water.

Drop broccoli into boiling water. Let boil until bright green and tender (less than a minute!). Drain off water and immediately plunge vegetables into cold water until they are cool.

Remove from cold water. Toss with a splash of lemon juice, if desired.

Roasted Carrots

Sounds plain-Jane but it's not, especially if you have purchased really fresh carrots. Look for moist, fresh ones with tops, and pass on by the bagged ones that are brownish on the ends.

Prep time: 20 minutes
Makes 4 servings

3 to 4 small carrots
Olive oil
Sea salt

Preheat oven to 450°F. Cut carrots in long angled chunks if big, leave whole if small or if baby carrots are used. Place carrots in a baking dish and brush each one with oil and sprinkle with salt. Roast coated carrots until tender when pierced with a fork (about 10 to 15 minutes, depending on size).

Pressure-Cooked Beets

Beets are velvety when you pressure-cook them. Countless times students tell me they don't like beets but they like these. Hmmmm.

Prep time: 30 minutes
Makes 4 servings

> **3 to 4 large beets**
> **Butter or olive oil (optional)**
> **Balsamic vinegar (optional)**

Remove leafy tops of beets if present and scrub beets. Do not peel or remove roots. Place beets in pressure cooker with enough water to cover the bottom half of the beets. Secure lid. Bring heat to high. When cooker has reached pressure, lower heat to medium low and cook 20 to 25 minutes.

Remove from heat and let pressure come down naturally. Beets should be quite tender when pierced with a fork. When cool enough to handle, slip skins off under cool running water. Trim ends if needed. Slice beets, dress with a bit of butter and vinegar if desired, and serve.

Sautéed Green Beans

Of course, almost any vegetable is nice just lightly sautéed in butter. No question. Asparagus, carrots, zucchini, red peppers—they all respond well. Sauté literally means "to jump," so make sure you keep your vegetables moving! If you want them light and crispy, wait to add any type of salt until after they are complete.

Prep time: 10 minutes
Makes 4 to 6 servings

> **½ pound green beans**
> **2 teaspoons butter or ghee**
> **Sea salt**
> **Lemon (optional)**

Trim ends of green beans. Wash and drain. Heat skillet over medium heat. Then add butter—don't let it burn. Add green beans—they should sizzle. Keep them moving until they turn bright green. Remove from heat and sprinkle with a little salt before you serve them. They are also nice with a squeeze of lemon.

Baked Winter Squash

Soothes the soul. Wonderful served with black beans and collard greens—a beautiful balance of colors and nutrients. See page 183 for a description of the many varieties of winter squash to choose from. This simple dish becomes even more magical when baked with a little cinnamon, cumin, and/or maple syrup.

Prep time: Depends on size of squash; see directions
2½ pounds of winter squash makes 4 servings

> **1 winter squash**
> **Butter**
> **Sea salt**

Preheat oven to 350°F. Cut squash in half. Be sure to use a strong, sharp knife. Scoop out the pith and seeds. Rub butter on the face of the squash, sprinkle with a few grains of salt and lay flat on a lightly oiled baking dish. Bake until tender.

Test by inserting a fork; it should slide in easily and the flesh should feel soft. Small squashes, such as delicata, will only take 35 to 45 minutes to bake, while a squash weighing 3 pounds may take up to 90 minutes.

🥣 **For babies 10 months and older:** These simple "One-Trick Vegetables" are the perfect food for babies. Just keep beet servings to a minimum because they are real bowel scrubbers, which most babies don't need.

Quick Boiled Greens

Assertive hearty greens can be bitter and tough. They need heat and water to become tame and sweet. Vitamin A, vitamin C, folic acid, calcium, iron, and even protein are a part of most dark, leafy greens. These powerful vegetables should be a daily part of the diet, especially for nursing mothers.

Prep time: 10 minutes
Makes 4 servings

> **1 large bunch of collards, kale, chard, bok choy, or dandelion greens**
> **Lemon juice**
> **Brown rice vinegar or umeboshi plum vinegar**

For greens with tough stems, such as collards, kale, or chard, cut or pull away the leaves from the stem before washing. Wash greens carefully. An easy way is to fill your sink with cold water and submerge the greens. If the water has sediment, drain the sink and repeat.

Bring 2 quarts of water to boil in a large pot. Submerge the whole leaves of the greens. Boil tender young greens (such as chard) for about 10 to 20 seconds. Tougher leaves (such as mature collards or kale) need to be cooked for 3 to 4 minutes. Timing is everything. If you remove the greens too soon, they will be bitter. If you let them cook too long, they will lose nutrients and have a flat taste. Remove a piece and test every 30 seconds or so. You are looking for a slightly wilted leaf that still has a bright green color and (most important) a succulent, sweet flavor.

Pour cooked greens into a colander in the sink or a bowl to catch the cooking water. Let cool. Squeeze out excess water with your hands. Chop into bite-size pieces. Serve with a few drops of lemon juice or vinegar. Reserve cooking water to water your plants.

  For babies 10 months and older: Take a teaspoon or two of plain, cooked greens and purée it with whatever grains or vegetables baby is eating tonight. For example, blend the greens with rice cereal, quinoa cereal, or peas.

Sesame Greens

Sesame greens make a tasty and impressive side dish for any meal. Try these greens with Szechwan Tempeh (page 164) over quinoa or as a side dish with Dr. Bruce's Awesome Grilled Salmon (page 166).

Prep time: 15 minutes
Makes 4 servings

> **1 teaspoon brown rice syrup**
> **1 to 2 teaspoons brown rice vinegar**
> **1 teaspoon toasted sesame oil**
> **1 teaspoon hot pepper oil**
> **2 cups Quick Boiled Greens (page 187)**
> **2 tablespoons toasted sesame seeds**

Mix syrup, vinegar and oils together in a small pan and warm over low heat until flavors meld. Pour dressing over greens; add sesame seeds and toss well. Serve warm, cold, or at room temperature.

> **For babies 10 months and older:** Take a teaspoon or two of plain, cooked greens and purée it with whatever grains or vegetables baby is eating tonight. For example, blend the greens with cooked rice or quinoa.

Greens in Cashew Curry Sauce

This sauce is a mouthwatering treat served over cooked rice or quinoa. For texture, top with a few whole, roasted cashews. Serve this dish over grain with Rosemary Red Soup (page 128) for a very colorful grain, bean, and vegetable combination.

Prep time: 15 minutes
Makes 4 servings

> ¼ cup cashew butter
> 1 tablespoon Homemade Curry Paste (page 238)
> 1 tablespoon tamari or shoyu
> ¾ cup water
> 2 cups Quick Boiled Greens (page 187)

Blend cashew butter, curry paste, tamari, and water in a blender until creamy. Combine greens and blended sauce in a pan. Gently heat before serving.

For babies 10 months and older: Stir ½ teaspoon of cashew butter into baby's warm whole grain cereal for added calories and other nutrients.

Dark Greens Salad with Creamy Ginger Garlic Dressing

This is a delicious way to add dark greens to your diet—just plop them into your favorite salad. The dressing is not only good on salads; it also makes an excellent sauce for cooked grains.

Prep time: 15 minutes
Makes 4 servings, more than 1 cup dressing

Salad

½ head red leaf lettuce
1 bunch watercress, tough stems removed
2 cups Quick Boiled Greens (page 187)
½ cucumber, peeled and thinly sliced

Dressing

½ pound tofu
1 teaspoon grated ginger
2 cloves garlic, minced
3 tablespoons extra-virgin olive oil
2 tablespoons freshly squeezed lime juice
2 teaspoons tamari or shoyu
⅓ cup water, to desired consistency

Wash lettuce and watercress by placing leaves in a sink full of cold water. Drain and repeat. Spin or pat dry. Tear greens into bite-size pieces. Place lettuce and watercress in a large salad bowl. Add greens and cucumber and toss together. Set aside.

Place all dressing ingredients in a blender. Blend until smooth. Serve salad with about 2 tablespoons of dressing per serving. Leftover dressing will keep in the refrigerator for about a week.

🥣 **For babies 10 months and older:** Reserve some of the tofu. Cut up into cubes and steam. Serve in cubes or mashed.

Garlic-Sautéed Greens

Consider this recipe as part of a New Year's Day meal of black-eyed peas, cornbread, and collard greens designed to bring good luck and fortune: peas for the silver, yellow corn for the gold, and a helping of collard greens symbolizing greenbacks.

Prep time: 15 minutes
Makes 4 servings

> **1 bunch sturdy greens such as collards, kale, or bok choy**
> **1 to 2 tablespoons extra-virgin olive oil or ghee**
> **1 tablespoon minced garlic**
> **1 teaspoon brown rice vinegar**
> **½ teaspoon tamari**

For greens with tough stems, cut or pull off the leaves from the stem before washing. Wash greens carefully. An easy way is to fill your sink with cold water and submerge the greens. If the water has a lot of sediment, drain the sink and repeat. Shake off excess water, pile leaves one on top of the other, and chop into thin strips.

Heat oil in a 10-inch skillet. Add garlic and sauté a minute or so. Make sure the heat is low enough that the garlic doesn't burn. Add greens and keep them moving in the skillet. Turn frequently so that all greens reach the heat. Remove a piece and test every minute or so. You are looking for a slightly wilted leaf that still has a bright green color and (most important) a succulent, sweet flavor. When all greens have turned bright green and begun to wilt, remove from heat. Sprinkle vinegar and tamari over the top. Toss gently and serve.

For babies 10 months and older: Serve these greens with Black-Eyed Peas (page 65). Reserve some unseasoned peas for baby; mash well or purée and serve.

Becky's Braised Greens

Braising is a wonderful cooking method for greens, as it gently tenderizes and adds flavor. My friend and colleague at Bastyr University, Becky Boutch, makes simple foods taste divine.

Prep time: 15 to 20 minutes
Makes 4 servings

> 10 leaves (1 bunch) sturdy greens, such as kale, collards, or chard
> 2 to 3 tablespoons olive oil
> ½ onion, cut into crescents
> 1 tablespoon tamari
> 1 tablespoon mirin or sherry vinegar
> 2 tablespoons water

Wash greens carefully and remove stems. Chop leaves into bite-size pieces. Chard stems may be kept and chopped separately. Discard stems of other greens.

Heat a large skillet over medium heat. Add oil and onion. Sauté onion over slow heat, stirring occasionally, until translucent and soft. Add chard stems, if using, and sauté briefly. Add greens and toss to coat with oil. Sauté over medium heat until leaves begin to turn brilliant green and wilt down.

Mix together tamari, mirin, and water. Pour into pan. Cover pan tightly. Cook until leaves are tender, 5 to 8 minutes, adding 1 to 2 tablespoons of water if pan becomes dry. Taste to check for doneness: greens should be tasty, not bitter; still green, not gray.

For babies 10 months and older: Blend a teaspoon or two of cooked leaves with cereal or sweet potato.

Sweet Apple Walnut Kale

Using Becky's braising method, a variety of tastes can be created by simply changing the braising liquid. Here the hearty taste of kale is nicely balanced with sweet flavors, and the toasted walnuts give texture to the cooked greens.

Prep time: 15 to 20 minutes
Makes 4 servings

> 1 **bunch kale**
> 2 **to 3 tablespoons butter**
> ½ **apple, very thinly sliced**
> ½ **cup walnuts, coarsely chopped**
> 1 **tablespoon unrefined cane sugar or brown sugar**
> 2 **to 3 tablespoons apple juice or cider**
> 1 **tablespoon tamari**
> 2 **teaspoons unfiltered apple cider vinegar**

Pull away the kale leaves from the stems before washing. Wash carefully by filling your sink with cold water and submerging the greens. If the water has sediment, drain the sink and repeat. Tear leaves into bite-size pieces.

Melt butter in a large skillet over medium-low heat. Add apple and walnuts, and sauté for a few minutes. Sprinkle cane sugar over the apple and walnuts and stir so that they are evenly coated. When apple is softened, add kale leaves and sauté over medium heat until leaves begin to turn brilliant green.

In a small bowl combine juice and tamari. Pour into skillet. Cover tightly. Cook until leaves are tender, 5 to 7 minutes. Taste to check for doneness: greens should be tasty, not bitter; still green, not gray. Dress with vinegar before serving.

For babies 10 months and older: Remove some of the soft-cooked apple slices before adding unrefined cane sugar and serve on baby's cereal.

Massaged Kale and Currant Salad

Bastyr adjunct faculty member Jennifer Adler, M.S., C.N., contributed this recipe. I love to watch Jennifer work with food because she loves to use her hands. She touches and loves food into magnificent flavor and tenderness. Jennifer likes to make a bunch of this salad at once to ensure she has dark, leafy greens ready when busy days are ahead. It tastes better as the days go by.

Prep time: 15 minutes
Makes 6 servings

> **1 bunch kale**
> **1 teaspoon sea salt**
> **¼ cup diced red onion**
> **⅓ cup currants**
> **¾ cup diced apple (about ½ apple)**
> **⅓ cup sunflower seeds, toasted**
> **¼ cup olive oil**
> **2 tablespoons unfiltered apple cider vinegar**
> **⅓ cup Gorgonzola cheese, crumbled**

Destem kale by pulling leaves away from the stems. Wash leaves. Spin or pat dry. Stack leaves, roll up, and cut into thin ribbons. Put kale in a large mixing bowl. Add salt, and massage it into the kale with your hands for 2 minutes.

Stir onion, currants, apple, and sunflower seeds into kale. Dress with oil and vinegar. Taste for salt and vinegar, adding more if necessary. When at desired flavor, toss in cheese. This salad will keep for several days and still be great!

🥣 **For babies 10 months and older:** Try blending just a teaspoon or two of the massaged kale with some cooked brown rice.

Romaine Chop Salad with Basil Dressing

This is a fun main dish sort of salad because of its egg, cheese, and chickpeas. Chopping ingredients to a similar size gives the salad an even look and integrated flavor. A fine summer lunch served with whole grain bread and butter.

Prep time: 15 minutes
Makes 4 servings

Dressing

- 2 cloves garlic
- 1 teaspoon Dijon mustard
- 1 teaspoon honey
- 3 tablespoons brown rice vinegar
- ¼ cup extra-virgin olive oil
- ⅓ cup fresh basil

Salad

- 1 egg
- ½ head romaine lettuce
- ½ cucumber, diced
- 1 large or 2 small ripe tomatoes, diced
- ½ cup cooked chickpeas
- ⅓ cup crumbled blue cheese

Place garlic, mustard, honey, and vinegar in a blender and blend well. With the blender running, slowly pour in olive oil. Once the oil is incorporated, add basil and pulse a few times to blend.

Place egg in a 1-quart pan filled with cold water. Bring to a boil. As soon as it is boiling rapidly, turn off the heat, cover, and set timer for 10 minutes. When the timer goes off, drain water from pan and refill with cold water repeatedly until egg is cool. Peel egg and cut into small pieces.

Break apart lettuce leaves and wash in a sink of cold water. Stack leaves on top of each other. Bisect the stack with a knife then begin chopping into 1-inch squares. Place chopped lettuce in a salad spinner and spin dry. Put lettuce in a salad bowl. Add cucumber, onion, tomato, egg, chickpeas, and blue cheese. Pour dressing over the salad and toss well. Serve immediately.

For babies 10 months and older: Mash some of the cooked chickpeas with a leaf or two of chopped basil or blend in a blender with a little water.

Luscious Beet Salad with Toasted Pumpkin Seeds

This recipe was inspired by Jeff Basom and his friend Tara. I love it because it uses the whole beet. Adds beautiful color and a bounty of vitamins to a simple rice and fish meal. If beet greens are unavailable or if the greens are wilted, use raw spinach, watercress, or arugula leaves.

Prep time: 1 hour to cook beets, 15 to 20 minutes to assemble salad
Makes 6 servings

Dressing	Salad
3 tablespoons extra-virgin olive oil	4 large beets with greens
2 tablespoons balsamic vinegar	¼ cup pumpkin seeds
¾ teaspoon Dijon mustard	2 scallions, finely chopped
¼ teaspoon freshly ground pepper	¼ pound feta cheese
1 tablespoon finely chopped fresh basil	

Place all dressing ingredients in a jar and shake well. Set aside.

Remove greens from beets. Wash beets and place in a large pot covered with water; bring to a boil. Lower heat and simmer until beets are tender (about an hour). You can hasten this step by pressure-cooking beets (see page 185). Set aside to cool.

Toast pumpkin seeds by placing seeds in a dry skillet over medium heat. Move the skillet back and forth over the heat with one hand; stir the seeds using a wooden spoon with the other hand. This will toast the seeds evenly and prevent burning. When seeds begin to puff up and give off a nutty aroma they are ready. Remove seeds from skillet and set aside.

To prepare beet greens, follow directions for Quick Boiled Greens on page 187. Squeeze excess water out of the cooked beet greens and chop. If the greens on your beets are wilted or puny, skip this step and use fresh spinach, watercress, or arugula instead.

Peel beets by holding under a trickle of cold water and pushing the skins off with your fingers. Cut into small cubes. Put cubed beets, greens, pumpkin seeds, and scallions in a salad bowl. Pour dressing over salad and toss gently. Crumble feta cheese on top. Serve at room temperature or chilled.

🥄 **For babies 10 months and older:** Reserve a teaspoon of the toasted pumpkin seeds, grind them to a fine powder, and stir into baby's cereal or puréed vegetables for extra calories and other nutrients.

Variation for children: Cook the beets in apple juice instead of water and serve plain, cut-up cooked beets.

Mustard Greens Salad with Tofu Dill Dressing

The sharp taste of calcium-rich mustard greens works well with an easygoing tofu dressing. Buy mizuna mustard greens, if possible, as they are the most tender. You can use less water in making the dressing and create a creamy sauce for pasta or grains.

Prep time: 10 minutes

Makes 6 servings, 1½ cups dressing

Salad

½ **bunch mustard greens**

½ **head green leaf lettuce**

½ **bunch red radishes, sliced**

1 **handful alfalfa sprouts**

Dressing

½ **pound silken tofu**

2 **tablespoons brown rice vinegar**

1 **tablespoon snipped fresh dill**

   or 1 teaspoon dried

2 **tablespoons extra-virgin olive oil**

¼ **-plus cup water**

Wash mustard greens and lettuce by placing leaves in a sink full of cold water. Drain and repeat. Spin or pat dry. Tear greens into bite-size pieces and place in a large salad bowl with radishes and sprouts on top. Set aside.

Put all ingredients for the dressing in a blender and blend until smooth and creamy. Dress salad with the dressing before serving and toss well. Any leftover dressing will keep in the refrigerator for about a week.

For babies 10 months and older: Reserve some of the tofu. Cut into cubes. Steam and serve cubes or mash.

Watercress Salad with Creamy Ginger Dressing

The dressing for this salad may seem a bit fussy, but trust me, it is excellent. It comes from a quiet vegetarian restaurant in Seattle called Silence-Heart-Nest. Watercress is rich in minerals and is usually free of pesticides as it grows easily and abundantly.

Prep time: 10 minutes
Makes 6 servings, ¾ cup dressing

Salad

1 bunch watercress, tough stems removed
½ head red leaf lettuce
1 cucumber, thinly sliced

Dressing

2 tablespoons chopped ginger
2 teaspoons chopped celery
½ teaspoon maple syrup
6 tablespoons extra-virgin olive oil
3 tablespoons toasted sesame seeds
⅛ teaspoon white pepper
⅛ teaspoon celery seed
½ teaspoon ketchup
3 tablespoons soy sauce
3 tablespoons brown rice vinegar
3 tablespoons water

Wash watercress and lettuce by placing leaves in a sink full of cold water. Drain and repeat. Spin or pat dry. Tear greens into bite-size pieces and place in a large salad bowl. Add cucumber and set aside.

Place ginger, celery, maple syrup, oil, sesame seeds, pepper, celery seed, and ketchup in a blender and blend. Add soy sauce, vinegar and water; blend again until creamy. Before serving, toss salad with about half of the dressing. The remainder of the dressing will keep in the refrigerator for at least a week. (It is great over plain cooked brown rice!)

For babies 6 months and older: This salad is a lovely accompaniment to Deep-Fried Millet Croquettes (page 144), and millet is a wonderful beginner grain for babies. Reserve some of the plain, cooked millet before deep-frying. Purée with water or breast milk and serve as cereal.

Greek Salad

This is the perfect accompaniment to a feast of Hummus (page 114) and Middle Eastern Falafel (page 160) in a pita.

Prep time: 10 minutes
Makes 3 to 4 servings

> 3 tablespoons extra-virgin olive oil
> 1 tablespoon brown rice vinegar
> 1 teaspoon honey or agave nectar
> Sea salt
> Freshly ground pepper
> 1 cucumber, peeled
> 16 (about ½ cup) pitted kalamata olives, halved
> 1 plum tomato, cut into wedges
> ½ pound feta, cut into cubes

Whisk together oil, vinegar, honey, and salt and pepper to taste in a salad bowl. Cut cucumber in half lengthwise; seed it with a spoon, and dice into half-moon slices. Add olives, cucumber, tomato, and feta to salad bowl and toss gently.

☞ **For babies 10 months and older:** Serve this salad with hummus or falafel, and reserve some of the cooked chickpeas for mashing.

Spinach Salad with Balsamic Vinaigrette

This hearty salad goes with just about any main dish you could dream of adding dark, leafy greens and flavor too. Leftover vinaigrette works well on grain or bean salads for lunch boxes.

Prep time: 10 minutes
Makes 6 servings, ⅓ cup dressing

Dressing

2 tablespoons balsamic vinegar
1 teaspoon maple syrup
¾ teaspoon Dijon mustard
¼ teaspoon freshly ground pepper
3 to 4 tablespoons extra-virgin olive oil

Salad

1 bunch spinach, washed well, dried, stems removed
⅓ cup Sweet Glazed Nuts (page 118)
¼ small red onion, sliced in thin half or quarter moons

Place all dressing ingredients except oil in a large salad bowl and stir to mix. Add oil a little at a time, whisking it into the other ingredients so that it incorporates nicely.

Wash spinach by placing leaves in a sink full of cold water. Drain and repeat. Spin or pat dry. Tear spinach into bite-size pieces. Place in a large salad bowl. Add glazed nuts and red onion to spinach. If you don't like the sharpness of raw red onion, soak slices in cold, salted water for 5 minutes before adding.

Dress salad just before serving.

For babies 6 months and older: This salad makes a completely satisfying meal served with a thick soup or stew, such as Three Sisters Stew (page 157). Remove some of the cooked squash from the stew, purée, and serve to baby.

Triple "A" Salad
(Avocado, Arame, and Almonds)

This is one of Mary Shaw's very popular whole foods salad recipes. My students love this salad served with Yakisoba (page 150) or Sweet Potato and Shrimp Tempura (page 171). Mary was an inspirational teacher at Bastyr University for many years and currently runs a cooking program for the Ashland Food Co-op in Ashland, Oregon.

Prep time: 15 minutes
Makes 4 servings

Salad

- ¼ cup raw almonds
- 4 cups salad greens
- ⅛ cup arame, soaked in 1 cup water
- 1 ripe avocado, peeled and pitted

Dressing

- 1 tablespoon sesame oil
- 2 tablespoons toasted sesame oil
- 3 tablespoons brown rice vinegar
- 2 tablespoons brown rice syrup
- 2 teaspoons Dijon mustard
- ½ teaspoon sea salt
- 2 teaspoons poppy seeds

Preheat oven to 350°F. Roast the almonds on a dry cookie sheet for 7 to 10 minutes, or until aromatic. Coarsely chop and set aside.

Wash the salad greens in a sink full of cold water. Spin or pat dry. Drain arame and add to the greens.

Combine all the dressing ingredients in a large salad bowl, using a whisk to incorporate. Add greens and arame. Toss to combine just before serving. Slice avocado in long strips and gently fold into salad. Garnish with cooled roasted almonds.

🥄 **For babies 6 months and older:** This one's easy—some mashed ripe avocado rich in vitamin A and E is just the right food for baby.

Creamy Coleslaw

This has the familiar look and taste of traditional coleslaw but is not so sloppy with mayonnaise. The lemon gives it a fresher taste. Serve it with Sloppeh Joes (page 165) for a new twist on traditional fare. Or go classic and serve with Lemon- and Herb-Roasted Chicken (page 177) and Pressure-Cooked Garlic Mashed Potatoes (page 209).

Prep time: 5 to 10 minutes
Makes 6 servings

Salad

3 cups shredded green cabbage
  (about ¼ head)
1 cup shredded red cabbage
1 carrot, grated
1 scallion, finely chopped

Dressing

3 tablespoons mayonnaise
2 tablespoons freshly squeezed lemon juice
1 teaspoon maple syrup
1 teaspoon tamari or shoyu
Freshly ground pepper

Combine cabbages, carrot, and scallion in a bowl. Toss together and set aside.

Combine dressing ingredients in a small bowl and blend with a whisk or a fork until mixed well. Pour dressing over vegetables and toss again.

For babies 6 months and older: This recipe works well with Dilled Brown Rice and Kidney Beans (page 102) to make a simple summer meal. Reserve some of the plain, cooked rice before adding the beans and dressing and purée it with a pinch of grated carrot reserved from the slaw.

Variation for children: Serve separate little piles of the grated or shredded vegetables before adding dressing.

Susan's Succulent Supper Salad

My friend Susan Wilson made up this feast of a salad that gets raves in my classes. Served with soup and/or bread and a spread, it is a most satisfying meal. I've used romaine, spinach, and arugula, but any combination of wild greens and salad greens works fine.

Prep time: 20 minutes

Makes 8 servings; 4 servings if used as a main course

Salad

½ head romaine lettuce

1 bunch spinach

½ bunch arugula

1 cup chopped red cabbage

1 tart apple, cut in bite-size pieces

1 ripe avocado, cut in bite-size pieces

¼ cup raisins

¼ cup toasted pumpkin seeds

3 scallions, finely sliced

1 or 2 fresh tomatoes, cut in wedges

⅔ cup cooked chickpeas

Dressing

¼ cup extra-virgin olive oil

3 tablespoons balsamic vinegar

2 teaspoons Dijon mustard

2 teaspoons maple or brown rice syrup

1 clove garlic, minced

⅛ teaspoon paprika

¼ teaspoon tamari or shoyu

Wash lettuce and greens by placing leaves in a sink full of cold water. Drain and repeat. Spin or pat dry. Tear greens into bite-size pieces and place in a large salad bowl. Add all other salad ingredients. Set aside.

Put all ingredients for dressing in a small bowl or jar and whisk together or shake vigorously. Dress salad just before serving and toss well.

For babies 6 months and older: Reserve a slice or two of avocado, mash or blend, and serve.

For babies 10 months and older: Steam a few apple slices and serve with a tablespoon of raisins.

Variation for children: Serve separate piles of raisins, apples, pumpkin seeds, and avocado.

Lime Cabbage Slaw

I like serving this simple slaw with enchiladas or in tacos. Its slightly sharp flavor goes nicely with beans and cheese.

Prep time: 10 minutes
Makes 4 servings

> 2 to 3 tablespoons extra-virgin olive oil
> 2 tablespoons lime juice
> 1½ cups shredded cabbage
> 2 leaves romaine, rolled and cut in thin strips
> ¼ cup chopped red onion
> Sea salt
> Freshly ground pepper

Put oil and lime juice in a small salad bowl and whisk together. Add cabbage, romaine, and onion. Toss with dressing. Season with salt and pepper just before serving.

For babies 6 months and older: Serve this slaw with a slice or two of avocado on top. Mash or purée a few slices of avocado for baby and serve.

Grilled Vegetable Salad with Sweet Poppy Seed Dressing

Vegetarians take heart! Summer grilling is for you, too! Grilled vegetables are delicious whether served over rice, in a pocket pita, or in this incredible salad. Thanks to Susan Wilson for the inspiration.

Prep time: 30 minutes
Makes 8 servings, ⅔ cup dressing

Salad

- 1 eggplant, cut into ½-inch rounds
- 1 red pepper, cut into large wedges
- 1 onion, cut into large wedges
- 1 summer squash, cut into long, fat strips
- 1 zucchini, cut into long, fat strips
- 10 big mushrooms
- Extra-virgin olive oil
- 8 cups salad greens
- 1 to 2 ounces feta cheese, crumbled

Dressing

- 4 tablespoons extra-virgin olive oil
- 3 tablespoons brown rice vinegar
- 2 tablespoons maple syrup
- 1 tablespoon Dijon mustard
- 2 teaspoons poppy seeds
- 1 tablespoon snipped fresh dill or 1 teaspoon dried

Heat up your grill (a small hibachi works fine). While grill is heating, brush both sides of each vegetable piece with a light coat of oil. Place vegetable pieces on hot grill and cook a few minutes on each side, until the vegetables just start to brown. Set aside grilled vegetables.

Wash salad greens by placing leaves in a sink full of cold water. Drain and repeat. Spin or pat dry. Tear greens into bite-size pieces and place in a large salad bowl. Cut grilled vegetables into bite-size pieces and add them to salad greens. Crumble feta on top.

Whisk all ingredients for dressing together or shake in a small jar. Dress and toss salad before serving. Save any leftover grilled vegetables to make sandwiches the next day.

For babies 6 months and older: Reserve some slices of zucchini and summer squash. Steam until soft and purée or mash for baby.

Variation for children: You may want to make a shish kebob and grill vegetables instead of serving salad. Grilled vegetables can also be served with a dip. Lemon Tahini Sauce (page 231) or Tofu Dill Dressing (page 197) work well.

Dulse Salad with Lemon Tahini Dressing

If you're looking for added iron in your diet, search no more. Dulse, a dark red sea vegetable, contains 11 grams of iron per ¼ cup. To find out more about dulse or tahini, see Appendix B, "Identifying, Purchasing, and Storing Whole Foods." Serve this salad to your favorite pregnant or nursing mom with a bowl of warm Split Pea Soup with Fresh Peas and Potatoes (page 127).

Prep time: 15 minutes, 1 hour to marinate
Makes 4 servings, ¾ cup dressing

Salad

1 cup dry dulse
1 red onion, sliced in very thin rounds
1 to 2 stalks celery, cut in bite-size pieces
1 tablespoon brown rice vinegar
Pinch of sea salt
4 red leaf lettuce leaves

Dressing

¼ cup tahini
2 tablespoons extra-virgin olive oil
1 clove garlic
Juice of 1 lemon
½ teaspoon tamari or shoyu
⅓ cup water

Soak the dulse in cold water. Clean the soaked dulse well, removing any small pebbles. Pat dry. Combine dulse, red onion, and celery with vinegar and salt; refrigerate for an hour or so.

Combine all ingredients for dressing in a blender and blend until smooth. Serve the salad on a lettuce leaf with 1 tablespoon of dressing on top. Leftover dressing will keep in the refrigerator for a week and is excellent as a sauce on brown rice.

For babies 6 months and older: Toast dulse in a 250°F oven for 12 to 15 minutes. Crumble toasted dulse into flakes and store in a sealed jar. Sprinkle flakes into baby's cereal or other foods to make them iron fortified.

Rosemary- and Garlic-Roasted Potatoes

Roasted potatoes are heavenly. Serve them for brunch with Green Eggs (No Ham) (page 92) or for dinner with Nori-Wrapped Wasabi Salmon (page 168). The time involved is just roasting in the oven, not you in the kitchen.

Prep time: 45 minutes
Makes 4 servings

> 12 small red potatoes, halved
> 5 to 6 cloves garlic
> 2 tablespoons fresh rosemary leaves
> 3 tablespoons extra-virgin olive oil
> Sea salt
> Pepper

Preheat oven to 450°F. Wash red potatoes, scrubbing off any dirt and removing any eyes, and cut into halves. At this point you have the option of boiling the pieces in water for about 3 minutes. This will hasten your roasting time. Place potatoes (quick-boiled or not) in a baking dish.

Chop garlic and rosemary leaves together until very fine. Put oil in a small bowl and add garlic, rosemary, salt, and pepper. Drizzle over potatoes and shake pan to coat. Roast for 45 to 60 minutes (time depends on the size of the potatoes) until potatoes are tender inside, browned on the outside.

🥣 **For babies 10 months and older:** Smash a few potatoes with a fork and serve!

Potato Gratin

This recipe was inspired by another that I found in a little book called Gourmet Underway *by The Resource Institute in Seattle.*

Prep time: 50 minutes
Makes 4 to 6 servings

>   **4 to 6 red potatoes, sliced ¼-inch thin**
>   **2 teaspoons extra-virgin olive oil**
>   **1 red pepper, sliced thin**
>   **1 large onion, sliced thin**
>   **2 cloves garlic, minced**
>   **¼ cup freshly grated Parmesan cheese**
>   **Freshly ground pepper**

Preheat oven to 350°F.

Place sliced potatoes in a steamer basket and steam 10 minutes, or until edges are limp. Heat oil in skillet. Add pepper, onion, and garlic; sauté a few minutes.

Layer steamed potatoes and vegetables in a casserole. Cover and bake 30 to 40 minutes. Uncover the casserole and top with Parmesan and pepper. Turn oven up to 400°F and bake until the top is brown, approximately 10 minutes.

For babies 6 months and older: Put some of the steamed potatoes in a separate baking dish and bake 30 to 40 minutes. Remove and purée with water or breast milk.

Pressure-Cooked Garlic Mashed Potatoes

Most of you probably have your own method of making mashed potatoes, but you can save time and intensify flavor by using a pressure cooker. Use small Yellow Finn or red potatoes and leave the skins on to increase the nutrient value.

Prep time: 15 to 20 minutes
Makes 4 servings

> **6 to 8 Yellow Finn or red potatoes (about 2 pounds)**
> **1 cup water**
> **½ teaspoon sea salt**
> **5 cloves garlic, peeled and left whole**
> **2 tablespoons milk or half-and-half**
> **1 to 2 tablespoons butter**
> **Sea salt and pepper to taste**

Wash and scrub potatoes; cut each in half. Put potatoes, water, salt, and garlic in pressure cooker and secure lid. Bring heat up to high until pressure comes up. Lower heat slightly and pressure-cook for 10 minutes.

Allow pressure to come down undisturbed or drizzle cool water over top of pot until pressure comes down. Drain excess water. Add milk, butter, salt, and pepper to hot potatoes and whip with a hand mixer or mash with potato masher until smooth.

🥣 **For babies 10 months and older:** Use plain yogurt instead of milk to mash potatoes and serve some to baby.

Fresh-Baked Breads and Muffins

Homemade Whole Grain Bread
Whole Grain Bread Variations
Lemon Cranberry Scones
Sweet Squash Corn Muffins
Pumpkin Pecan Muffins
Date Walnut Cinnamon Rolls
Marilyn's Best Pizza Dough
Holly's Pilgrim Stuffing

Homemade Whole Grain Bread

Jeff Basom, the chef at Bastyr University in Seattle, shares his unique way of making bread. Jeff's bread is economical and nutritious, and children love the soft, light texture. Using leftover grains or cereal as a starter dough is a beautiful example of the transformative quality of whole foods.

Prep time: Fermenting the starter dough takes 24 hours; the kneading, rising, and baking take 3 to 3½ hours
Makes 2 loaves

Starter Dough
2 cups cooked whole grains
2 cups water
¼ cup olive oil or melted butter
1 tablespoon sea salt
1 tablespoon yeast
1 cup whole wheat flour (more or less)

Blend grains and water in a blender or food processor until creamy; pour into a large mixing bowl. Mix in oil, salt, and yeast. Add enough flour to make the mixture look like thick-cooked cereal. Cover the bowl with plastic wrap or a damp towel and leave for 12 to 24 hours at room temperature. Once the dough is fermented, it can be refrigerated for up to a week before using to make bread.

To Make the Bread
¼ cup maple syrup or honey
2 cups whole wheat flour
3 to 4 cups unbleached white flour or whole wheat flour

After 12 to 24 hours, add sweetener to starter dough and stir. Stir in whole wheat flour. As you add the white flour, the mixture will be too difficult to stir. Knead it by hand in the bowl and continue to add white flour. When dough is less sticky, transfer it to a floured surface and knead 10 to 15 minutes, or until dough is soft and springy, but not too sticky.

Wash and dry mixing bowl and oil it. Place dough in bowl, cover, and let rise in a warm place 1½ to 2 hours.

To make the loaves, lightly oil 2 loaf pans. Divide dough in half. Punch down and shape the dough using the following instructions (children love to help with this part).

Flatten half of the dough into a square on your working surface. Press all of the air out of the dough by vigorously slapping the dough with the palms of both hands.

Fold the flattened dough into a triangle and press it down again.

Fold two corners into the center and press again.

Fold the top point into the body of the dough and press it down again.

Pick up the dough with both hands and begin rolling it into itself. This stretches the outside of the dough and creates a tight roll with no air pockets. Seal the seam by flattening it with the heel of your hand.

Shape the dough into a nice loaf and place in the pan seam side down. Repeat punching down and shaping with the other half of the dough.

To Bake the Bread

1 teaspoon water
1 teaspoon maple syrup or honey
1 teaspoon butter, melted
¼ teaspoon sea salt

Mix water, syrup, butter, and salt in a small cup or bowl and coat the top of each loaf with this mixture. Cover and let rise in pans for 45 to 60 minutes until the loaves have doubled in size. Test the bread for readiness. If you press the dough and it wants to stay in, but still has a little spring, it's ready to bake.

Preheat oven to 350°F. Bake 45 to 50 minutes. Bread will come out of pans after 5 minutes of cooling. Let it cool 30 minutes before slicing (if you can wait!).

Whole Grain Bread Variations

Here are four delicious versions of Jeff's bread. Follow general directions for Homemade Whole Grain Bread with these more specific ingredients.

WHOLE WHEAT AND RICE BREAD

A practical use of leftover rice. Extra cooked oatmeal works just as well.

Starter Dough
2 cups cooked brown rice
2 cups water
¼ cup cold-pressed vegetable oil
1 tablespoon sea salt
1 tablespoon yeast
1 cup whole wheat flour (more or less)

To Make the Bread
Starter Dough
¼ cup barley malt
2 cups whole wheat flour
3 to 4 cups unbleached white flour or whole wheat flour

ORANGE MILLET RAISIN BREAD

The juice and dried fruit make this variation sweeter.

Starter Dough
2 cups cooked millet
1 cup water
1 cup orange juice
¼ cup cold-pressed vegetable oil
1 tablespoon sea salt
1 tablespoon yeast
1 cup whole wheat flour (more or less)

To Make the Bread
Starter Dough
¼ cup barley malt or maple syrup
2 cups raisins
1 teaspoon ground cinnamon
2 cups whole wheat flour
3 to 4 cups unbleached white flour or whole wheat flour

QUINOA GARLIC HERB BREAD

This savory variation is delicious with soups.

Starter Dough
2 cups cooked quinoa
2 cups water
¼ cup extra-virgin olive oil
1 tablespoon sea salt
1 tablespoon yeast
1 cup whole wheat flour (more or less)

To Make the Bread
Starter Dough
6 cloves garlic, minced very fine
1 tablespoon chopped fresh basil
2 tablespoons chopped fresh parsley
2 tablespoons chopped fresh cilantro
2 teaspoons chopped fresh rosemary
2 cups whole wheat flour
3 to 4 cups unbleached white flour or whole wheat flour

BEAN APPLE RYE BREAD

The beans and rye flour give this bread a hearty flavor and a darker color.

Starter Dough

2 cups cooked beans or 1 cup cooked beans and 1 cup baked winter squash
1 cup water
¼ cup cold-pressed vegetable oil
1 tablespoon sea salt
1 tablespoon yeast
1 cup whole wheat flour (more or less)

To Make the Bread

Starter Dough
⅓ cup apple butter
2 cups whole wheat flour
1 cup rye flour
2 to 3 cups unbleached white flour or whole wheat flour

For babies 6 months and older: Reserve part of the cooked brown rice, quinoa, or millet you are using for the Starter Dough. Put it in a blender with a little breast milk or water and purée.

For babies 10 months and older: Reserve part of the cooked grains, beans, or squash you are using for the Starter Dough. Put it in a blender with a little breast milk or water. Well-cooked whole beans can also be used for finger food.

Lemon Cranberry Scones

These are simple to make and quite versatile. Any dried fruit can be substituted for the cranberries to create a different flavor. Alternative milks such as soy or rice with a squeeze of lemon added can be used instead of buttermilk.

Prep time: 45 minutes
Makes 8 scones

> 2 cups whole wheat pastry flour
> ¼ cup unrefined cane sugar or brown sugar
> 2 teaspoons nonaluminum baking powder
> ½ teaspoon baking soda
> ½ teaspoon sea salt
> 6 tablespoons chilled butter
> ¾ cup dried cranberries
> 1 tablespoon lemon zest
> ¾ cup buttermilk
> ½ teaspoon lemon extract

Preheat oven to 350°F. Mix flour, unrefined cane sugar, baking powder, baking soda, and salt together in a large bowl or food processor. It helps to pregrind the coarse unrefined cane sugars (like Sucanat) in a coffee mill or blender. Cut in the butter with a fork or add in bits while pulsing the food processor until the mixture is crumbly or pebbly. Transfer to a large mixing bowl if a food processor was used.

Add cranberries and zest and stir. Pour in the buttermilk and lemon extract and stir until the mixture holds together.

Gather the dough onto a floured surface and knead a few times. Pat out into an 8-inch circle and cut into 8 wedges. Place on a greased baking sheet and bake for 25 minutes. Cool on a rack.

For babies 10 months and older: Add a few dried cranberries to baby's cereal while it is cooking. Make sure the cranberries are very soft. Run through the blender before serving.

Sweet Squash Corn Muffins

These corn muffins are perfect served with a bowl of hot soup. The cooked winter squash imparts vitamin-rich sweetness and keeps the muffin moist. Baked red garnet yams are divine to use in this recipe.

Prep time: 30 minutes
Makes 12 regular muffins

> 1½ cups cornmeal
> 1½ cups whole wheat pastry flour or barley flour
> 2 teaspoons nonaluminum baking powder
> ½ teaspoon sea salt
> 1 cup baked and mashed winter squash or red garnet yam
> ½ cup water or milk
> ½ cup butter, melted
> ½ cup maple syrup
> 2 eggs
> 2 tablespoons pumpkin seeds, for topping

Preheat oven to 375°F. Lightly oil muffin tins or line with paper muffin cups. Mix cornmeal, flour, baking powder, and salt together in a large bowl; set aside.

Put mashed squash or yam in a blender with water (there's your food for baby!) and blend until smooth. Add butter, maple syrup, and eggs and pulse a few times to blend.

Add wet ingredients to dry mixture and mix with a minimum of strokes. Fill muffin cups full with batter. Decorate top of each muffin with a few pumpkin seeds. Bake 25 to 30 minutes. Top of muffin will crack slightly when done.

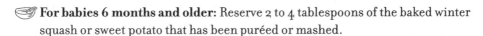 **For babies 6 months and older:** Reserve 2 to 4 tablespoons of the baked winter squash or sweet potato that has been puréed or mashed.

For babies 10 months and older: Toast some pumpkin seeds in a dry skillet until they puff up and pop. Grind these to a meal and use a ½ teaspoon or so added to baby's cereal for flavor and nutrients.

Pumpkin Pecan Muffins

Baked sugar pie pumpkin or buttercup squash is delicious in this recipe. These muffins make excellent snacks or breakfast food. They are also a nice accompaniment to White Bean and Kale Minestrone (page 132) or other savory soups.

Prep time: 45 minutes
Makes 12 muffins

2 cups whole wheat pastry flour
1 cup unbleached white flour
1 tablespoon baking powder
1 teaspoon sea salt
1 teaspoon ground cinnamon
½ teaspoon ground cloves
½ teaspoon ground cardamom
½ cup unrefined cane sugar
   or brown sugar

½ cup butter
¼ cup molasses
¼ cup honey
1 cup mashed, cooked pumpkin
   or winter squash
½ cup milk or water
2 eggs
2 teaspoons vanilla extract
½ cup pecans, chopped

Preheat oven to 375°F. Lightly oil muffin tins or line with paper muffin cups. Mix together flours, baking powder, salt, spices, and unrefined cane sugar in large bowl; set aside.

Melt butter in a small saucepan. Add molasses and honey to warm butter and stir together. Put cooked pumpkin or squash in blender, add butter mixture and milk; blend until smooth. Add eggs and vanilla and pulse to blend.

Add wet ingredients to dry mixture and fold gently, using a minimum of strokes. Fold pecans into batter. Fill muffin cups full with batter. Bake 25 to 30 minutes.

For babies 6 months and older: Reserve 2 to 4 tablespoons of the baked pumpkin or winter squash used in the muffins. Purée with a little breast milk or water.

Date Walnut Cinnamon Rolls

This recipe was inspired by The Sweet Life: Natural Macrobiotic Desserts *by Marcea Weber (Japan Publications, 1981). I chose to find a happy whole food medium between intensely sweet conventional pastry and Marcea's macrobiotic version. The dates add whole food sweetness and moisture. These are wonderful for holiday breakfasts or brunches.*

Prep time: 2½ hours
Makes 2 dozen cinnamon rolls

Dough
1½ **cups apple juice, divided**
1 **tablespoon yeast**
2 **tablespoons honey or agave nectar**
2 **beaten eggs**
2 **cups whole wheat pastry flour**
1 **cup unbleached white flour**
½ **cup butter, melted**
½ **teaspoon sea salt**
1 **teaspoon vanilla extract**
2 **teaspoons ground cinnamon**
1 **tablespoon lemon zest**

Filling
1 **cup pitted dates**
2 to 3 **cups apple juice, divided**
2 to 3 **cups raisins**
⅔ **cup walnuts, chopped**
4 to 6 **tablespoons unrefined cane sugar**
Ground cinnamon

Icing
½ **cup sour cream**
2 to 3 **tablespoons honey or agave nectar**
1 **teaspoon vanilla extract**

Warm ½ cup of the apple juice in a small pan. Transfer to a large mixing bowl and add yeast and honey. Stir and set aside for 5 minutes until mixture bubbles.

Add eggs and enough flour to form a thin batter. Beat until smooth. Clean sides of bowl, cover with a damp cloth, and let dough rise in a warm spot until doubled, about 30 minutes.

While dough is rising, make filling. Place dates in a small pan and cover with apple juice. Heat to a simmer, cover, and cook until liquid is absorbed, about 20 minutes. Let cool. Purée in blender and set aside. Place raisins in a bowl and cover with 1 cup of the apple juice. Soak at least 15 minutes to soften and plump. Discard excess juice.

Return to dough. Beat in butter, salt, vanilla, cinnamon, and zest. Begin adding flour to yeast mixture. When it is too hard to stir, place on a lightly floured surface and knead until smooth. Clean and oil bowl. Place dough in it, cover, and let rise in a warm place until doubled, about 45 minutes.

Preheat oven to 350°F. On a lightly floured board, roll out half the dough to a rectangle. Spread half of the date purée, strained raisins, and walnuts on the dough. Sprinkle with unrefined cane sugar and cinnamon. Roll up from the side like a jelly roll. Cut into 1-inch slices and place cut side up on an oiled cookie sheet or in muffin tins. Repeat with the other half of the dough. Bake for 15 minutes.

While rolls are baking, place all ingredients for icing in a small bowl and whisk together well. When rolls have baked 15 minutes, spoon some of the icing on top of each roll and bake another 10 to 15 minutes.

For babies 10 months and older: Add a teaspoon or two of softened dates to baby's cereal.

Marilyn's Best Pizza Dough

I learned how to make pizza dough properly from my dear friend Marilyn McCormick, who runs the PCC Cooks classes in Seattle. Under her leadership, this unique educational program has flourished, with classes becoming wildly popular. The dough is easy to make, is delicious, and can be used for a variety of savory dishes—including pizza!

Prep time: 30 minutes to make dough and pizza, 2-plus hours for rising time
Makes dough for six, 8-inch pizzas

> 2 teaspoons yeast
> 2 cups lukewarm water
> 1 tablespoon extra-virgin olive oil
> 1 teaspoon sea salt
> 3 cups whole wheat pastry flour
> 2¾ cups unbleached white flour

To make the dough, combine yeast in lukewarm water in a large mixing bowl. Let rest for 10 minutes while yeast comes to life. Gently stir in olive oil. Mix salt and whole wheat pastry flour, and whisk in a little at a time. Beat for a minute or two until mixture is stretchy and elastic. Stir in unbleached white flour to make a soft dough. Cover and let rise 1 to 2 hours.

To make the pizza, deflate, divide, and shape dough into 5 to 6 balls. Each will make an 8-inch pizza crust. (At this point, the dough could be frozen for later use). Cover and let rest 15 minutes to relax dough.

Preheat oven to 500°F. Shape each ball into a flat round by using your fingertips to make little tapping indentations rather than pulling or stretching the dough. Place on a baking sheet liberally dusted with cornmeal or rice flour. Top each pizza with favorite sauce and toppings. Place on lowest rack in your oven. An 8-inch pizza will cook in about 6 minutes.

For babies 6 months and older: Use zucchini slices for pizza topping. Reserve some and steam; purée and serve.

Holly's Pilgrim Stuffing

My dear friend Holly and I make this stuffing almost every Thanksgiving. My family begs for it. The better the bread that you use, the better the stuffing will be. Choose bread that is savory or neutral, not sweet. Ask a friend to help and make a lot—it is so good.

Prep time: 1½ hours
Makes enough to stuff two, 12- to 15-pound turkeys or fill one 9 x 13 baking dish

8 to 10 whole chestnuts	1 cup fresh cranberries
8 tablespoons unsalted butter	¼ to ½ cup water
1 onion, chopped	Fresh thyme
1 loaf whole grain bread, cut into small cubes	Fresh marjoram
	Fresh sage (lots), chopped
3 to 4 stalks celery, chopped	Sea salt
1 apple, chopped	Pepper (lots)

Preheat oven to 400°F. Cut an X on the flat side of each chestnut. Place in a baking dish and bake about 20 minutes, until the shell comes away from the meat. Set aside and let cool.

Melt butter in a large skillet. Add onion and sauté until soft.

Put bread cubes in a large bowl. Add celery, apple, and cranberries, and toss. Add butter and onions and work butter into the bread mixture.

In the skillet used for butter and onion, heat water. Pour this over bread mixture and work in with your hands. Peel chestnuts, cut into pieces and add. Add all herbs, salt, and pepper. Taste the mixture. Make sure the taste pleases you. If needed, add more seasonings.

Stuffing is ready to be put into the turkey cavity. You can also put it in a covered 9 x 13 baking dish and bake at 350°F for about 45 minutes to use as a side dish.

🥄 **For babies 6 months and older:** Steam some apple slices until they are soft and mash into applesauce.

Refreshing Relishes, Convenient Condiments

Tahini Oat Sauce with Scallions
Almond Ginger Drizzle
Coconut Peanut Sauce
Sweet Pepper Relish
Yogurt Cucumber Topping (Raita)
Lemon Tahini Sauce
Cucumber Jalapeño Relish
Fresh Corn Salsa
Tofu Ginger Garlic Dressing
Honey Ginger Elixir
Mango Salsa
Pumpkin Seed Parsley Garnish
Cranberry Apple Relish
Homemade Curry Paste
Ghee

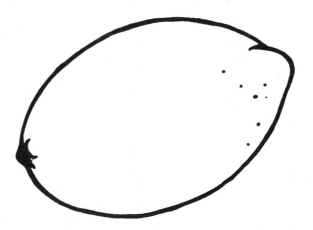

Tahini Oat Sauce with Scallions

This creamy, simple-to-make sauce is just the thing to serve over whole grains or whole grain noodles or s over brown rice with cooked greens and beans or fish to complete the meal.

Prep time: 20 minutes
Makes 1 cup

> ¼ **cup rolled oats**
> 1 **cup water**
> ½ **teaspoon sea salt**
> 2 **tablespoons tahini**
> 1 **tablespoon tamari or shoyu**
> 1 **tablespoon water**
> 1 **scallion, finely chopped**

Put the oats, water, and salt in a small pan; bring to a boil. Lower heat, cover, and simmer 10 to 12 minutes. Put oat mixture in a blender with tahini, tamari, and water; blend until smooth. Return to pan, adding scallion. Gently reheat, if necessary, before serving.

☞ **For babies 6 months and older:** Cook twice the amount of oatmeal, reserve for baby's meals. Purée with a little water or breast milk if too thick.

Almond Ginger Drizzle

A sensuous topping for grains or vegetables. I especially like it served over kasha. You can substitute different nut butters to create slight variations in taste. A Microplane grater is a very useful kitchen gadget to have on hand for recipes that call for freshly grated ginger.

Prep time: 5 minutes
Makes 1 cup

¼ cup creamy almond or cashew butter
2 teaspoons maple syrup
2 tablespoons tamari or shoyu
1 tablespoon brown rice vinegar
1 teaspoon grated ginger
1 to 2 teaspoons hot pepper oil
⅓ cup water

Put all ingredients in a small pan on low heat. Using a whisk, mix ingredients until smooth and warm. Mixture will thicken so you may want to thin it with a little water. Serve immediately over grains, beans, or cooked vegetables.

For babies 10 months and older: Stir a half teaspoon of almond butter into baby's warm whole grain cereal for added calories and other nutrients.

Variation for children: Omit hot pepper oil and offer as a dipping sauce for raw vegetables.

Coconut Peanut Sauce

A simple variation on the preceding recipe gives the sauce more of a Thai flavor. This sauce is sensational on cooked greens or noodles, essential as a dip for Fresh Vegetable Spring Rolls (page 119).

Prep time: 5 minutes
Makes 1 cup

> ¼ cup creamy peanut butter
> 2 teaspoons maple syrup*
> 2 tablespoons tamari or shoyu
> 1 tablespoon brown rice vinegar
> 2 teaspoons grated ginger*
> 1 to 2 teaspoons hot pepper oil
> ½ cup coconut milk

Place all ingredients for sauce together in a small saucepan over medium to low heat. Whisk until smooth. Stir gently until sauce begins to thicken. Add water if needed to get desired consistency. Serve immediately.

☞ **For babies 10 months and older:** Stir a teaspoon or two of coconut milk into baby's warm whole grain cereal for added calories and other nutrients.

---

* *Or use 1 heaping tablespoon Honey Ginger Elixir (page 234) and omit ginger and maple syrup.*

Sweet Pepper Relish

This brightly colored concoction is easy to make, keeps well in the refrigerator, and adds a zesty flavor and crispy texture to anything. Amazing served with cheese and crackers. I like it on sandwiches or next to rice and other grains. Also fabulous plopped on top of Squash- and Raisin-Stuffed Chicken Breasts (page 176).

Prep time: 10 to 15 minutes
Makes 1 cup

> 1 cup finely diced red, orange, or yellow bell pepper
> 1 jalapeño pepper, finely diced
> 3 tablespoons sugar
> 3 tablespoons unfiltered apple cider vinegar
> Pinch of sea salt

Place peppers in a clean jar. Add sugar, vinegar, and salt, and stir to mix. Put a lid on the jar and keep in the refrigerator for up to two weeks. The flavors deepen with time.

For babies 10 months and older: Try some of this relish on a sandwich made with French Lentil Dijon Spread (page 113). When making the spread, reserve plain cooked lentils and purée with a little water for baby.

Yogurt Cucumber Topping (Raita)

There are many recipes for this classic topping for curry dishes. This one is adapted from one of my all-time favorite cookbooks, Sundays at Moosewood Restaurant *by The Moosewood Collective (Fireside Books, 1990). Buy yogurt that has active cultures and no fillers added (such as nonfat milk solids or pectin).*

Prep time: 5 minutes, plus 30 minutes chilling time
Makes 1½ cups

> 1 cup plain whole milk yogurt
> ½ cucumber, peeled, seeded, and diced
> 1 clove garlic, minced
> 2 tablespoons finely chopped cilantro or mint
> ½ teaspoon ground cumin
> Pinch of cayenne
> Salt to taste

Combine all ingredients in a small bowl. Chill for 30 minutes before serving.

For babies 10 months and older: Serve a teaspoon of plain yogurt mixed with cooked vegetables.

Lemon Tahini Sauce

This dressing is so versatile it is worth making up a regular batch to have around. I love it as a topping on brown rice or soba noodles, or as a lively salad dressing. Tahini is a creamy paste made of crushed, hulled sesame seeds. Look for it with other nut butters or Middle Eastern foods.

Prep time: 5 minutes
Makes 1½ cups

    ½ cup tahini
    ¼ cup extra-virgin olive oil
    Juice of 1½ lemons
    1 clove garlic
    2 teaspoons tamari or shoyu
    Pinch of cayenne
    ¾ cup water

Place all ingredients except water in a blender or processor; blend until smooth. Add enough water to get desired consistency. Allow mixture to set for a half hour if possible to allow flavors to meld. Taste for salt and add more tamari if needed. Sauce will keep in the refrigerator for 10 to 14 days.

☙ **For babies 10 months and older:** Add a little tahini to baby's cereal for extra calories and other nutrients.

Cucumber Jalapeño Relish

This recipe was created by one of my students, Heather Kraetsch. It is simple yet adds a zesty flavor and groovy texture to meals. Try it plopped into a Middle Eastern Falafel (page 160) sandwich, snuggled up next to Caribbean Lime Halibut (page 169), or as a topping on French Lentil and Potato Stew (page 135).

Prep time: 5 to 10 minutes
Makes 4 small servings

> ½ medium cucumber, peeled, seeded, and diced
> 1 small jalapeño pepper, seeded and minced
> 1 scallion, minced
> ¼ white onion, diced
> ¼ cup chopped cilantro
> 1 tablespoon lime juice
> 1 tablespoon brown rice vinegar
> 2 tablespoons sugar

Place all ingredients in a bowl. Gently stir until sugar has dissolved. Allow mixture to marinate at least 20 minutes. Can be made in advance and stored in a sealed container in the refrigerator.

☙ **Variation for children:** The jalapeño gives this topping a lot of heat! Take an extra cucumber, dice it, and blend with scallion, onion, lime juice, vinegar, and sugar for a less fiery version.

Fresh Corn Salsa

This is fabulous in late summer/early fall when you can cut sweet corn kernels right off the cob. Frozen corn can be quickly blanched and used when fresh corn is not in season. Use with Tempeh Tacos (page 159), Black Bean Tostados (page 161), Dr. Bruce's Awesome Grilled Salmon (page 166), or use as a topping on any bean soup.

Prep time: 5 to 10 minutes
Makes 4 small servings

> 1 ear of corn, shucked, kernels removed with knife
> 1 serrano or jalapeño pepper, seeded and minced
> ½ ripe avocado, sliced into cubes
> ¼ red onion, diced
> 2 tablespoons fresh cilantro
> Juice of 1 large lime
> ½ teaspoon ground cumin
> ½ teaspoon freshly ground pepper
> ½ teaspoon salt

Place all ingredients in a bowl. Allow mixture to marinate at least 20 minutes. Can be made in advance and stored in a sealed container in the refrigerator.

For babies 6 months and older: The tried-and-true mashed avocado works well.

Tofu Ginger Garlic Dressing

This lively dressing is delicious served on pasta, rice, kasha, cooked greens, steamed vegetables, and green salads. Try it as a dip for Deep-Fried Millet Croquettes (page 144).

Prep time: 5 minutes
Makes 1 cup

> ½ pound silken tofu
> 1 teaspoon grated ginger
> 2 cloves garlic, minced
> 2 tablespoons extra-virgin olive oil
> 2 tablespoons lime juice
> 2 teaspoons tamari or shoyu
> ¼ cup water

Place all ingredients in a blender; blend until smooth. This will keep in the refrigerator 4 to 5 days.

🥣 **For babies 10 months and older:** Cut up extra tofu into small cubes. Steam or drop into boiling water for a few seconds. Let cool and serve as finger food.

Honey Ginger Elixir

This little concoction is my latest indispensable ingredient. It can be used in any dish that requires freshly grated ginger and sweetener, like Coconut Peanut Sauce (page 228). A teaspoon of this can be added to teas and soups for a revitalizing brew. Use a Micropolane grater for ease in grating ginger.

Prep time: 15 minutes
Makes 1 cup

> ¼ cup peeled, grated ginger (6 inches ginger)
> ½ cup honey
> ½ cup water

Place all ingredients in a small pan over low heat, stirring to melt honey. Bring heat up to simmer and cook uncovered until mixture has reduced slightly (about 10 minutes). Pour into a clean jar and keep in the refrigerator for a few months.

🥣 **Variation for children:** Got a child with a scratchy throat or cough? Try a teaspoon of this on its own or mixed in some hot water.

Mango Salsa

This topping is wonderful served with grilled shrimp and rice. It's also fabulous with Huevos Rancheros (page 95) or Caribbean Lime Halibut (page 169).

Prep time: 10 minutes, 30 minutes to marinate
Makes 6 servings

> **2 ripe mangoes**
> **1 bunch scallions, thinly sliced on diagonal**
> **2 jalapeño peppers, finely diced**
> **¼ cup finely chopped cilantro**
> **Juice of 2 limes (about 2 tablespoons)**

The mango has a flat, ellipse-shaped seed in it. Hold mango vertically and cut from the top down on both sides, just missing the seed. You will have two, bowl-shaped halves. Discard the middle section with the seed. Push up from the skin side turning the bowl inside out and score the meat of the mango in a crisscross pattern on each half. Cut the cubes off the skin.

Mix mango cubes with all other ingredients in a bowl. Let mixture sit about 30 minutes in refrigerator to mingle flavors.

☞ **For babies 6 months and older:** Blend some of the mango pieces to serve baby as a perfect beginner food.

Pumpkin Seed Parsley Garnish

This garnish adds a great texture and sharp flavor to smooth dishes like soup. Sprinkle some on Rosemary Red Soup (page 128) or use instead of sesame seeds on Sweet Rice Timbales (page 147). The fresh parsley adds dark, leafy green nutrients as well as digestibility to any dish it's served with.

Prep time: 5 minutes
Makes around ¾ cup

> ½ cup pumpkin seeds
> 2 cloves garlic
> ¼ cup parsley
> ¼ teaspoon sea salt
> 3 to 4 tablespoons olive oil

Heat a dry skillet to medium. Add pumpkin seeds and keep them moving with a wooden spoon. After a few minutes they will begin to pop, puff up, and give off a nutty aroma. Remove from heat.

Place toasted pumpkin seeds with all other ingredients in a food processor and pulse a few times until you have a coarse mixture. The toasted seeds, garlic, and parsley can also be finely chopped by hand.

For babies 10 months and older: Grind a few toasted pumpkin seeds before adding other ingredients, then add to any food you are puréeing for baby to add healthful fats and vitamins.

Cranberry Apple Relish

An adaptation of a recipe from Natural Foods Cookbook *by Mary Estella (Japan Publications, 1985) that uses apple juice and maple syrup to add sweetness to tart cranberries. Try a little of this relish as a side dish to Lemon- and Herb-Roasted Chicken (page 177), a natural served with Holly's Pilgrim Stuffing (page 223).*

Prep time: 30 minutes
Makes 2½ cups

1½ cups cranberries
1 cup chopped apples
½ cup currants
1 teaspoon orange zest
¼ cup maple syrup
¼ teaspoon sea salt
1 cup apple juice or water
¼ cup chopped walnuts

Place cranberries, apples, currants, zest, maple syrup, salt, and juice in a large saucepan. Cover and bring to a boil. Reduce heat, remove cover, and simmer 20 to 25 minutes until excess liquid has evaporated. Remove from heat. Add walnuts. Serve at room temperature. This will keep in a sealed container in the refrigerator 3 to 4 days.

For babies 10 months and older: If your baby has teeth, reserve some apple slices, steam until soft, let cool, and serve as finger food.

Homemade Curry Paste

My life is so much easier with a jar of this in the refrigerator. Jeff Basom created this multiuse flavoring for soups, beans, and all sorts of vegetable dishes. This handy product for busy cooks will keep months in the refrigerator. It also makes a great holiday gift.

Prep time: 20 to 25 minutes
Makes 2 cups

1 cup extra-virgin olive oil	2 tablespoons whole mustard seeds
1 pound onions, finely chopped	2 teaspoons allspice
¼ cup whole cumin seeds	1 teaspoon cardamom
¼ cup whole coriander seeds	4 teaspoons ground cinnamon
1 teaspoon whole fenugreek seeds	¼ cup turmeric
1 teaspoon whole cloves	2 teaspoons cayenne
2 teaspoons black peppercorns	¼ cup peeled, finely chopped ginger

Heat oil in a 2-quart pot. Add onions and sauté until very soft.

While the onions are cooking, grind the following whole spices to a fine powder in a coffee or spice grinder: cumin, coriander, fenugreek, cloves, peppercorns, and mustard. Add to onions. Add the remaining spices and fresh ginger to the onion mixture; let it cook about 5 minutes while stirring. Store in a sealed jar(s) in the refrigerator, where it will keep for several months.

For babies 10 months and older: I love to use this paste to make French Lentil and Potato Stew (page 135). Remove some of the cooked potatoes and carrots from the soup, purée, and serve.

Ghee

Thought in the East to have many virtues, ghee is believed to take on and magnify the properties of food it is combined with, making the food more nutritious. Ghee is sometimes used in my recipes in place of oil, especially in foods that contain Indian spices. Ghee imparts a buttery flavor but can hold a much higher temperature than butter without scorching.

Prep time: 15 minutes
Makes about 1 cup

½ pound unsalted butter
1 clean 8-ounce jar with lid

Put butter in a saucepan. Heat until it begins to boil, then turn heat to low. White foam (from the milk solids) will accumulate on the top. Use a small strainer and begin gently skimming solids off the top without disturbing the bottom. As you continue this process, the liquid in the bottom of the pan will begin to appear clear and golden. When all the water is boiled out of the butter, the cooking will sound like hissing, and the bubbling will stop. Remove from heat and let cool a few moments. Pour the ghee into the jar. It will solidify as it cools. Store in the refrigerator.

For babies 6 months and older: Ghee is a wonderful product to use in place of oil in curry dishes. Use ghee to make Curried Lentils and Cauliflower (page 158). Reserve a small portion of soft cauliflower, purée with a little water or breast milk, and serve to baby.

Simple Sweet Desserts

One-Trick Fruit Desserts
Gingerbread People
Lemon Raspberry Thumbprint Cookies
Oatmeal Chocolate Chip Walnut Cookies
Halloween Cookies (Wheat-Free)
Rapunzel's Triple Chocolate Brownies
Chocolate-Dipped Coconut Macaroons
Fruitsicles
Apricot Kudzu Custard
Raspberry Yogurt Parfait
Winter Fruit Compote with Vanilla Nut Cream
Summer Fruit Ambrosia with Vanilla Nut Cream
Pear Plum Crisp
Apple Pie with Butter Crust
Gracie's Yellow Birthday Cake
Carrot Cake with Apricot Glaze
Mary's Buttermilk Chocolate Cake
Strawberry Sauce
Carob Butter Icing
Yummy Yam Frosting
Banana Cream Frosting
Pomegranate Granita

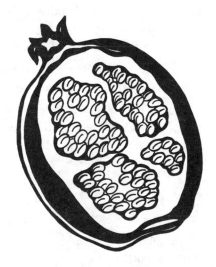

One-Trick Fruit Desserts

These four fruit desserts look like they might be kind of plain-Jane. They're not! Heat intensifies the sweetness in apples, pears, plums, and bananas and softens the texture, resulting in very sensuous desserts. Ripe mango is sweet and soft all on its own; blended with yogurt, it is heavenly.

Baked Apples

Prep time: 45 minutes
Makes 4 apples

> 4 **Honeycrisp or Fuji apples**
> **¼ cup raisins**
> **½ teaspoon ground cinnamon**
> **¾ cup apple juice**
> **1 tablespoon butter**

Preheat oven to 400°F. Wash apples and remove core from the top, leaving bottom intact. Using a peeler, take off a piece of skin around the top next to the core to prevent apples from bursting while they bake. Place apples in baking dish.

Stuff each apple with raisins, sprinkle with cinnamon, and fill with apple juice. Top each apple with a dab of butter. Bake 30 to 40 minutes, depending on how tender you wish to have the apples.

Pressure-Cooked Plum Sauce

Prep time: 15 minutes
Makes about 2 cups

> **4 to 5 cups pitted sliced plums (1½ to 2 pounds)**
> **4 to 6 tablespoons apple juice**
> **⅛ teaspoon sea salt**
> **Sucanat or other unrefined cane sugar**

Place plums, juice, and salt in pressure cooker. Bring heat to high until pressure gauge rises. Lower heat and pressure-cook 5 minutes.

Allow pressure to come down. Remove lid. Taste the plums. If you feel the mixture needs to be sweeter, add a teaspoon or two of Sucanat and reheat, stirring constantly, until it dissolves. Purée in a blender or serve as is, depending on whether you want a smooth or chunky consistency.

Poached Pears

Prep time: 15 minutes
Makes 4 small servings

> **½ cup fruit juice**
> **2 tablespoons mirin**
> **2 tablespoons unrefined cane sugar***
> **2 pears, halved and cored**
> **1 teaspoon kudzu or arrowroot**
> **2 tablespoons water**

Combine juice, mirin, and sugar in a 2-quart saucepan. Bring to a boil, then lower heat to a simmer. Stir constantly, until crystals dissolve completely, about 2 minutes.

Add pears to pan face down, turn heat to a very low simmer, cover, and poach until tender, about 10 minutes. Using a slotted spoon, remove fruit from pan, set aside. Keep the poaching liquid in the pan.

Combine starch with water in a small bowl. Bring poaching liquid to a simmer. Stir starch mixture into poaching liquid, stirring constantly. As soon as mixture thickens and clears, remove from heat.

To serve, place each ½ pear on a small plate or in a bowl and spoon sauce over the top.

Caramelized Bananas

Prep time: 15 minutes
Makes 4 small servings

> **2 tablespoons butter**
> **2 tablespoons Sucanat or brown sugar**
> **2 tablespoons mirin or rum**
> **1 teaspoon vanilla extract**
> **⅛ teaspoon ground nutmeg**
> **2 bananas**

Preheat broiler. Peel bananas and cut lengthwise. Heat butter, sugar, mirin, vanilla, and nutmeg in a small saucepan until melted. Stir to blend.

Place banana halves in a lightly oiled baking dish, cut side down. Pour glaze over bananas and broil until sugar bubbles and bananas are lightly browned (about 5 minutes). These bananas are divine.

---

*   *You can use 2 tablespoons of Honey Ginger Elixir (page 234) instead of the cane sugar and have Gingered Poached Pears!*

Mango Lassi

Prep time: 5 minutes
Makes 2 servings

1 ripe mango
1 cup vanilla yogurt
Pinch of ground cardamom
2 to 4 ice cubes

The mango has a flat, ellipse-shaped seed in it. Hold mango vertically and cut from the top down on both sides, just missing the seed. You will have two bowl-shaped halves. Discard the middle section with the seed. Push up from the skin side turning the bowl inside out and score the meat of the mango in a crisscross pattern on each half. Cut the cubes off the skin.

Put mango cubes with all other ingredients in a blender and blend until smooth. Using 2 ice cubes renders a dessert that can be eaten with a spoon. If you want the lassi thin enough to suck through a straw, add more ice cubes or a little water to thin it out.

For babies 6 months and older: Easy-as-can-be baby food can be made from cooked fruit. Apply the heat and not the other stuff and you have soft mushed apple, pear, plum, or banana purée. Ripe mango blended with a little water is just right for baby.

Gingerbread People

Children love making and decorating these tasty little cookie people. Unrefined cane sugar is a naturally processed sweetener where the juice from organically grown sugar cane is simply extracted and dehydrated. Sucanat (which stands for "sugar cane natural") and Rapadura are two brand names for this product.

Prep time: 15 to 20 minutes
Makes 8 to 15 people, depending upon thickness

¼ **cup unsalted butter, softened**
¼ **cup unrefined cane sugar**
 or brown sugar
¼ **cup brown rice syrup***
¼ **cup blackstrap molasses**
1 **tablespoon freshly grated ginger***
2½ **cups whole wheat pastry flour**
½ **cup unbleached white flour**
1 **teaspoon baking soda**
¼ **teaspoon ground cloves**
½ **teaspoon ground cinnamon**
½ **teaspoon sea salt**
¼ **to ½ cup orange juice**

Decorations

Raisins
Papaya bits
Peanuts
Dried cranberries

Preheat oven to 350°F. In a large mixing bowl, blend butter and sugar until creamy. Add rice syrup, molasses, and ginger; mix well.

In a separate bowl, combine flours, baking soda, cloves, cinnamon, and salt.

Add dry mixture to wet ingredients a little at a time. Add orange juice as needed to achieve a pliable dough that can roll. Work in the last of the flour mixture with your hands.

Lightly oil a cookie sheet and roll the dough directly onto it. Cut out figures with a cookie cutter or make up your own shape. Remove scraps of dough between cutouts to make more cookies. Add decorations before baking. Bake 8 minutes or longer depending upon thickness of dough.

---

* *2 tablespoons of Honey Ginger Elixir (page 234) can be used to replace the ginger and 1 tablespoon of the brown rice syrup.*

Lemon Raspberry Thumbprint Cookies

These delicious and fun-to-make cookies are perfect with afternoon tea. Variations in flavor can be made by substituting different nuts and jams. I love cherry preserves and blackberry jam too!

Prep time: 30 minutes

Makes 24 cookies

> **2 cups whole wheat pastry flour**
> **1 cup almonds, ground into fine meal**
> **2 teaspoons baking powder**
> **1 tablespoon lemon zest**
> **½ teaspoon sea salt**
> **10 tablespoons unsalted butter, melted**
> **½ cup maple syrup**
> **2 teaspoons almond extract**
> **½ teaspoon lemon extract**
> **Raspberry preserves (fruit-sweetened)**

Preheat oven to 350°F. Combine flour, almonds, baking powder, zest, and salt in a large mixing bowl; set aside.

In a separate bowl mix butter, maple syrup, and extracts.

Add wet ingredients to dry and mix well, kneading a little. Form dough into balls and flatten to make circles. Place on lightly oiled cookie sheet. Indent each cookie with your thumb or your child's thumb and put ½ teaspoon preserves in the imprint. Bake 15 minutes, or until edges turn golden.

Oatmeal Chocolate Chip Walnut Cookies

These cookies are very easy to make and take very little time. Great for packing in a lunch box as a special treat.

Prep time: 20 minutes
Makes 1 dozen 3-inch cookies

> **1½ cups rolled oats**
> **1 cup whole wheat pastry flour**
> **¼ teaspoon sea salt**
> **½ cup maple syrup**
> **½ cup unsalted butter, melted**
> **1 teaspoon vanilla extract**
> **⅓ cup chopped walnuts**
> **⅓ cup chocolate chips**

Preheat oven to 350°F. Combine oats, flour, and salt together in a large bowl; set aside.

In a separate bowl mix together maple syrup, butter, and vanilla.

Add wet ingredients to dry mixture and mix well. Stir in nuts and chips.

With moist hands form dough into 3-inch cookies and place on a lightly oiled cookie sheet or one lined with parchment paper. Bake for 15 to 20 minutes, or until edges turn golden.

Halloween Cookies (Wheat-Free)

The children at the Briar Rose Kindergarten in Seattle happily devoured these Halloween cookies with a swirl of Yummy Yam Frosting (page 261) on top, a healthy harvest treat designed by Rita Carey. Barley flour and spelt flour substitute well for wheat flour in most recipes.

Prep time: 25 to 30 minutes
Makes 2 dozen cookies

> 1 cup barley flour
> 1 cup spelt flour
> ½ teaspoon baking soda
> 1 teaspoon ground cinnamon
> ½ teaspoon ground ginger
> ¼ teaspoon ground nutmeg
> ¼ teaspoon allspice
> ¾ cup puréed, cooked pumpkin, winter squash, or sweet potato
> ¾ cup unrefined cane sugar or brown sugar
> ¼ cup apple butter
> 6 tablespoons butter, melted

Preheat oven to 350°F. Combine flours, baking soda, cinnamon, ginger, nutmeg, and allspice in a large mixing bowl; set aside.

In a separate bowl, combine pumpkin, sugar, apple butter, and butter.

Add wet ingredients to dry mixture.

Drop by tablespoons onto a lightly oiled cookie sheet. Bake 15 minutes.

Rapunzel's Triple Chocolate Brownies

The Rapunzel food company (www.rapunzel.com) makes fine chocolate products: cocoa powder, baking chocolate, chocolate chips, and a less-refined granulated sugar product called Rapadura. They are stellar in their dedication to offering high-quality organic products. They honor the Hand in Hand fair trade program, which ensures farmers in developing countries are paid fairly. If you haven't tried their products before, make a date with these brownies.

Prep time: 35 minutes
Makes 12 brownies

> **2 ounces semisweet chocolate**
> **¼ cup butter, melted**
> **¾ cup Rapadura or other unrefined cane sugar**
> **½ cup whole wheat pastry flour**
> **¼ cup cocoa powder**
> **½ teaspoon baking soda**
> **Pinch of sea salt**
> **2 eggs**
> **½ cup semisweet chocolate chips**

Melt chocolate and butter; set aside and let cool.

Grind Rapadura in a small grinder to get a finer texture. In a large mixing bowl, combine Rapadura, flour, cocoa powder, baking soda, and salt; set aside.

Beat eggs until foamy. Combine cooled chocolate/butter with eggs and whisk together.

Add wet ingredients to dry and stir to blend. Fold in chocolate chips and spread mixture into lightly oiled 8 x 8-inch pan. Bake 20 to 25 minutes.

Chocolate-Dipped Coconut Macaroons

These are a great sweet treat for adults or children that have problems with wheat or flour. Be sure to have a good plan for how you will use the precious yolk from the egg. The honey adds sweetness while the rice syrup hardens when cooled, helping the macaroon stay together.

Prep time: 30 minutes
Makes 2 dozen 1½-inch macaroons

> ½ cup honey
> 2 tablespoons plus 2 teaspoons brown rice syrup
> 1 egg white
> 3½ cups shredded unsweetened coconut
> ⅛ teaspoon sea salt
> ½ teaspoon almond extract
> ½ teaspoon vanilla extract
> 4 ounces semisweet chocolate (baking chocolate)

Preheat oven to 350°F. Grease a cookie sheet or line with parchment paper.

Lightly oil a glass measuring cup and put honey and rice syrup in it. Place cup in a small pan of simmering water until it is less viscous.

Whip egg white to stiff peaks with a hand mixer.

Put coconut and salt in a large mixing bowl. Stir extracts into warm honey. Pour the honey into the coconut, stirring well until you have a crumbly mixture. Fold in egg white.

With moist hands, make small mounds and place them side by side on the cookie sheet (they will not spread). Bake 15 to 20 minutes, or until lightly browned. Allow to cool to room temperature.

Melt chocolate in the top of a double boiler, stirring occasionally. Dip half of each macaroon into the melted chocolate or frost the top half with a knife. Let chocolate set until firm before serving (brief refrigeration will hasten this process).

Fruitsicles

You can buy Popsicle holders in the summertime at most stores that carry toys or kitchenware. Dream up an endless variety of frozen treats to delight sun-soaked children and adults.

Prep time: 5 minutes for making pops, 2 hours for freezing
Makes 4 fruitsicles, depending on size of holders

Juicesicles

1 cup juice (raspberry, grape, cherry, tropical)

Pour in holders and freeze.

Creamy Orange Vanilla Pops

¾ cup orange juice
¼ cup vanilla yogurt
1 teaspoon vanilla extract

Combine all ingredients in a blender, pour into holders, and freeze.

Banana Raspberry Pops

1 banana
⅓ cup raspberries
½ cup water

Combine all ingredients in a blender, pour into holders, and freeze.

Melonsicles

2 cups of melon chunks (cantaloupe, honeydew, watermelon)
¼ cup water

Combine all ingredients in a blender, pour in holders, and freeze. If using watermelon, remove seeds, and omit water.

Note how much liquid it will take to fill your Popsicle holders. Each of these recipes makes one cup of liquid, which fills four of the common cylindrical-style holders. Freeze for at least 2 hours. Run warm water on the outside of the holder until the pop pulls out easily. You can also use ice-cube trays to make iced fruit cubes for children to suck.

Apricot Kudzu Custard

Kudzu, from the root of the kudzu plant, looks like broken chalk. It can be dissolved in cool or room temperature liquid and can be used as a natural thickener. Kudzu is thought to have an overall calming effect on the body, especially the digestive system. Tahini, a sesame seed paste, is used to give the custard a slightly nutty flavor. This sweetly soothing dessert or snack is easy to prepare. Fit for company with a little Maple Butter Nut Granola (page 82) or a dollop of Vanilla Nut Cream (page 254) on top.

Prep time: 5 to 10 minutes
Makes 4 servings

> 2 tablespoons kudzu
> 2 cups apricot juice
> 2 teaspoons tahini
> 1 teaspoon vanilla extract

Dissolve the kudzu in cold or room temperature apricot juice. Put mixture in a small pan over medium heat, stirring constantly. As mixture simmers, it becomes clear and thick. Once this happens, remove from heat. Add tahini and vanilla; mix well. Serve immediately; custard will get rubbery if allowed to cool to room temperature.

☞ **For babies 10 months and older:** Serve a small amount as is.

Raspberry Yogurt Parfait

This recipe uses the natural jelling agent agar to thicken liquid. Agar is a tasteless sea vegetable that looks like small, translucent flakes. Agar thickens at room temperature, unlike gelatin, which must be chilled. By using both agar and kudzu as thickeners you get a much smoother, creamier dessert.

Prep time: 20 minutes to make, 1 hour to gel
Makes 6 to 8 servings

> 1 quart raspberry juice or nectar
> ¼ cup agar flakes
> 1 tablespoon kudzu dissolved in ¼ cup water
> 2 tablespoons maple syrup or agave nectar
> 1 teaspoon vanilla extract
> 2 cups vanilla yogurt
> Fresh raspberries

Put juice and agar in a 2-quart saucepan over medium heat; bring to a boil. Lower heat and simmer 10 minutes. Add dissolved kudzu in water, stirring mixture constantly until smooth and clear. Remove from heat. Add maple syrup and vanilla; stir again. Pour into a 9 x 13-inch pan and let gel at room temperature or in the refrigerator for an hour.

Put gelled mixture into a blender or food processor and blend for a few seconds until smooth. Layer the gel, yogurt, and raspberries in clear glasses to make a refreshing parfait.

Fruit Compote with Nut Cream

...raditionally been used in winter when fresh fruit was unavailable. This compote is a tummy-warming treat that's perfect for cold weather. Vanilla Nut Cream also makes a wonderful topping for cakes and gingerbread.

Prep time: 35 minutes
Makes 4 servings

Compote
½ cup dried apricots
¼ cup pitted prunes
1 apple, sliced
1 pear, sliced
1 cinnamon stick
⅛ teaspoon ground nutmeg
1 cup apple juice

Vanilla Nut Cream
½ cup raw, unsalted cashews
3 tablespoons maple syrup
2 teaspoons vanilla extract
Water

Combine apricots, prunes, apple, pear, cinnamon stick, nutmeg, and juice in a medium-sized pan; bring to a boil. Lower the heat and simmer, covered, for 20 to 30 minutes, until all the fruit is soft. Remove cinnamon stick.

Grind nuts to a fine meal in a small grinder (or in your blender if it is powerful). Put ground cashews, maple syrup, and vanilla in a blender. With blender running, add water a little at a time until you have a thick creamy consistency. Put compote in individual serving bowls and top with Vanilla Nut Cream.

☙ **For babies 10 months and older:** Reserve some of the cooked fruit and purée. Serve in very small amounts: a teaspoon with your baby's cereal.

Summer Fruit Ambrosia with Vanilla Nut Cream

And here is the summertime version of Winter Fruit Compote. Use any fresh berries or other seasonal fruit. This little combo is so simple and yet extraordinarily delightful.

Prep time: 15 minutes
Makes 4 servings

> ¼ cup thawed orange juice concentrate
> 2 tablespoons sugar
> 1 kiwi, peeled and sliced
> 1 cup sliced ripe banana
> 1 cup fresh sliced strawberries
> Vanilla Nut Cream (page 254), for garnish

Combine orange juice concentrate and sugar in a medium bowl. Add kiwi, banana, and strawberries, tossing gently.

Spoon fruit into each of 4 glasses; top with Vanilla Nut Cream.

Pear Plum Crisp

This wonderful dessert uses the fruits of the season. It is easy to double for a large gathering. The recipe is easily adapted for strawberries and rhubarb in the spring or peaches and blueberries in the summer.

Prep time: 1 hour and 20 minutes
Makes 8 servings

1 cup rolled oats
½ cup whole wheat pastry flour
½ teaspoon sea salt
¼ cup butter, melted
6 tablespoons maple syrup, divided
⅓ cup chopped nuts

2 tablespoons water
1 teaspoon ground cinnamon
¼ teaspoon ground nutmeg
2 teaspoons vanilla extract
5 cups sliced pears and plums
(about 3 pears and 5 plums)

Preheat oven to 350°F. Mix oats, flour, and salt together in a bowl. Add butter and 4 tablespoons of the maple syrup; mix well. Stir in nuts and set aside.

In small bowl combine water, the remaining 2 tablespoons maple syrup, spices, and vanilla; set aside.

Put fruit in a lightly oiled pie pan or an 8 x 8-inch baking dish. Pour the liquid mixture over the fruit and toss gently. Spoon the oat-nut mixture evenly on top of the fruit. Cover and bake 40 to 45 minutes. Uncover and bake 10 minutes more to crisp the topping.

🥄 **For babies 10 months and older:** Remove some of the baked pear and plum from the bottom of the crisp. Purée and serve.

Strawberry Rhubarb Crisp

Substitute 1 pint strawberries, washed, trimmed, and sliced, and 1 stalk rhubarb, diced, for the plums and pears. Toss fruit with 1 tablespoon tapioca, 1 tablespoon orange juice, and ¼ cup unrefined cane sugar or brown sugar instead of the water-maple syrup combination in the original recipe before placing in a lightly oiled pie plate or baking dish. Bake 30 minutes covered, 10 minutes uncovered.

Peach Blueberry Crisp

Substitute 1 pint blueberries and 3 cups sliced peaches for the plums and pears. Sprinkle 1 tablespoon tapioca over the fruit before adding liquid mixture and tossing. Bake 30 to 40 minutes covered, 10 minutes uncovered.

Apple Pie with Butter Crust

I adapted this recipe from a combination of sources, mostly from a pie-making class I took many years ago. One year, when my daughter was turning 10, she requested a coed birthday party at the skating rink. Instead of traditional cake, she wanted apple pies. I will never forget her blowing out candles on a pie and all those overheated kids happily eating big slices between rounds on the rink.

Prep time: 1 hour

Makes two, 9-inch pie crusts and an 8-slice pie

Crust

- 1 cup whole wheat pastry flour
- 1 cup unbleached white flour
- ½ teaspoon sea salt
- 8 tablespoons cold, unsalted butter
- 4 tablespoons unrefined coconut oil
- ¼ cup ice water

Filling

- 5 to 7 tart apples
- ½ cup unrefined cane sugar or brown sugar
- ⅛ teaspoon sea salt
- 1 tablespoon arrowroot
- ½ teaspoon ground cinnamon
- ⅛ teaspoon ground nutmeg

Make your crusts first and chill for at least 30 minutes. Put flours and salt in a food processor and pulse 20 seconds. Add chunks of butter and coconut oil and pulse until mixture resembles coarse meal. Add ice water, drop by drop, through the feed tube with the machine running until dough forms a ball and holds together. Remove dough from processor and form into a rough ball, and then transfer to a lightly floured surface.

If you do not have a food processor, use a pastry cutter or two table knives, and cut butter into chilled flour until it resembles coarse meal with pea-size pieces of butter. Sprinkle in water, stirring dough with a fork until it begins to hold together.

Give dough several quick kneads until it becomes smooth. Divide in half, shape into 2 balls, and flatten each ball slightly to make a disk. Wrap each disk in plastic wrap. Refrigerate for at least 30 minutes and up to 8 hours before using.

Preheat over to 350°F. Peel apples if desired. Quarter, core, and cut apples into thin slices. Combine sugar, salt, arrowroot, and spices and sprinkle over apples. (Amounts of sweetener and spices are variable. The amounts given make for a mildly sweet, lightly spiced pie.) Toss gently until apples are evenly coated.

Roll out half of your pie crust dough on a floured surface. Fold in half and in half again. Gently place in pie pan, unfold, and press in. Place apples in layers in bottom pie shell. Cover pie with upper crust, crimp the edge of the two crusts together, and trim. Prick the top of the pie so that steam can release. Bake until edges of crust are golden, about 45 to 50 minutes.

Gracie's Yellow Birthday Cake

Cooked millet gives this cake its moist texture and yellow color. My friend Ralfee made four layers of this cake for her birthday, using apricot jam between the layers and Carob Butter Icing (page 261) on top— divine! When my daughter was little, she loved it served on a pool of Strawberry Sauce (page 260) with fresh sliced strawberries on top.

Prep time: 50 to 55 minutes
Makes an 8-inch, 2-layer cake or 18 cupcakes

> 1½ cups unbleached white flour
> ½ cup whole wheat pastry flour
> 1 teaspoon nonaluminum baking powder
> 1 teaspoon baking soda
> ½ teaspoon sea salt
> 1½ cups cooked millet (see page 60)
> 1¼ cup orange juice
> ½ cup butter, melted, or coconut oil
> ½ cup maple syrup
> 2 teaspoons vanilla extract
> 2 eggs, separated

Preheat oven to 350°F. Lightly oil and flour two 8-inch cake pans. Sift flours, baking powder, baking soda, and salt together in a large mixing bowl; set aside.

Put millet and juice in blender; blend until smooth. Add butter, maple syrup, and vanilla to the millet purée in a blender; pulse briefly. Add egg yolks to millet purée and pulse again.

Add wet ingredients to dry mixture and mix well.

Place egg whites in a separate glass or metal bowl and beat until peaks form. Fold egg whites into batter. Pour into cake pans. Bake 30 to 40 minutes, or until cake begins to pull away from edge of pan. Let cool in pans for 10 minutes before removing. Wait until completely cool before icing.

For babies 6 months and older: Reserve some extra cooked millet and purée some with water. Warm slightly before serving.

Carrot Cake with Apricot Glaze

This familiar cake looks quite elegant when you decorate the top with fresh raspberries or with a few fresh flowers and date halves. This cake is also delicious frosted with Yummy Yam Frosting (page 261) or a traditional cream cheese icing instead of the apricot glaze. Double the recipe to make a two-layer cake.

Prep time: 1 hour
Makes 8 servings

Cake

1¼ cup whole wheat pastry flour
1 teaspoon baking soda
1 teaspoon sea salt
1 teaspoon ground cinnamon
¼ teaspoon ground cloves
½ cup butter or coconut oil
½ cup honey
2 eggs
1 cup grated carrot
1 tablespoon lemon zest
⅓ cup chopped walnuts
⅓ cup currants

Glaze

1 tablespoon kudzu
½ cup apricot juice or nectar
1 tablespoon freshly squeezed lemon juice
1 tablespoon honey or agave nectar

To make the cake, preheat oven to 350°F. Lightly oil a 9-inch cake pan. Sift together flour, baking soda, salt, and spices in a mixing bowl; set aside.

Melt butter and honey over low heat. Add eggs and whisk together. Add wet ingredients to dry mixture and mix well.

Fold in carrot, zest, nuts, and currants. Pour batter in pan; tap on counter to release air bubbles and bake for 30 minutes, or until knife inserted in center of cake comes out clean. Remove and let cool.

To make the glaze, dissolve kudzu in juice in a small pan. Heat mixture on medium heat, stirring constantly, until it becomes clear and thick (5 minutes). Remove from heat, add lemon juice and honey; stir well. Spread over the top of cake.

For babies 6 months and older: Reserve some extra carrot. Slice and place in a small covered baking dish; bake while the cake is baking. Mash or blend and serve.

Mary's Buttermilk Chocolate Cake

I learned how to make this incredible cake from my dear friend Mary Shaw. The recipe is easy to make and turns out a beautiful cake every time. For a dairy-free version substitute 1 cup soy milk with 1 tablespoon lemon juice added for the buttermilk and use melted coconut oil in place of butter.

Prep time: 45 minutes
Makes two, 8-inch layers

> 2½ cups whole wheat pastry flour
> ¼ cup organic cocoa powder
> ½ teaspoon sea salt
> 1 teaspoon baking powder
> 1 teaspoon baking soda
> 1 cup buttermilk
> ½ cup butter, melted
> 1 cup maple syrup
> 1 tablespoon vanilla extract

Preheat oven to 375°F. Lightly oil two 8-inch cake pans. Mix flour, cocoa, salt, baking powder, and baking soda together in a bowl. In a separate bowl, combine remaining ingredients and stir into flour mixture. Pour batter into cake pans. Bake for 30 minutes.

Strawberry Sauce

This is a beautiful, simple sauce that can be used to make a lovely presentation. Serve cake on a pool of this or put sauce in a squeeze bottle and squeeze out a design on top of your favorite cake, pudding, or frozen dessert.

Prep time: 10 minutes
Makes 1 cup

> 1 pint strawberries
> 1 teaspoon lemon or orange juice
> 1 tablespoon maple syrup, honey, or agave nectar

Wash and trim strawberries. Place all but 4 to 5 strawberries, juice, and maple syrup in blender; blend until smooth. Use at once or refrigerate until used. Will keep several days in the refrigerator. Use remaining strawberries for garnish.

Carob Butter Icing

Carob was so popular in the '70s and the answer to everyone's chocolate addiction. Carob has its own personality and needn't be regarded as chocolate's poor cousin. Use 1½ cups icing to ice the top and sides of two 8-inch layers of cake or one 9 x 13-inch cake.

Prep time: 10 minutes
Makes 1½ cups icing

> ½ **cup maple syrup**
> ½ **cup carob powder, sifted**
> ¼ **cup creamy cashew or almond butter**
> ⅛ **teaspoon sea salt**
> 2 **to 3 tablespoons apple or orange juice**
> 2 **teaspoons vanilla extract**

Heat the maple syrup in a small saucepan. Stir in the carob powder and heat, stirring constantly, until mixture begins to simmer. Add cashew butter, salt, and juice; stir with a whisk until smooth. Remove from heat and add vanilla. Add a bit more juice if too thick so that cake will ice easily. Ice cooled cake immediately.

Yummy Yam Frosting

This naturally sweet, beautiful golden-orange frosting comes from the creative mind of Rita Carey. Use it to top cookies, cupcakes, quick breads, graham crackers, or gingerbread people. This recipe makes enough to frost 2 dozen cookies or a one-layer cake.

Prep time: 5 minutes
Makes ¾ to 1 cup frosting

> 1 **cup mashed baked yams**
> ¼ **cup softened cream cheese or soft tofu (2 ounces)**
> 1 **tablespoon melted unsalted butter**
> 2 **tablespoons maple syrup or agave nectar**
> 1 **teaspoon lemon or orange juice**

Place yams, cream cheese, butter, maple syrup, and juice in a bowl and cream together. Purée with a hand mixer or in a food processor to a smooth, spreadable consistency.

For babies 6 months and older: Reserve some extra baked yam. Mash well and serve.

...a Cream Frosting

...opping that can be used for dairy lovers or it can be dairy-free. By using sweet banana as
...create creamy icings that children love to lick. This icing works well on Mary's Buttermilk
...nocolate Cake (page 260) or Pumpkin Pecan Muffins (page 219). One cup of frosting is plenty for a dozen
cookies or muffins.

Prep time: 10 minutes
Makes about 1 cup

>   **6 ounces silken tofu or cream cheese**
>   **½ ripe banana**
>   **2 tablespoons honey**
>   **2 teaspoons almond or cashew butter**
>   **½ teaspoon vanilla extract**
>   **2 tablespoons pineapple juice or water**

Blend tofu, banana, honey, almond butter, and vanilla in a blender or food processor. Add enough juice to get a smooth consistency. If using cream cheese, a hand
mixer may work better than the blender. Refrigerate frosting if not using right away.
Store leftover goodies topped with this frosting in the refrigerator.

For babies 6 months and older: Guess where the other half of the ripe banana
goes? Mash and serve.

Pomegranate Granita

Granita is a classic Italian dessert that is very versatile and easy to make. It makes the ultimate cooling summer dessert. This version was inspired by several online recipes, Odwalla's new pomegranate juices, and a (fuzzy) recollection of a student's final presentation.

Prep time: 3 hours and 5 minutes
Makes 6 servings

> **1 ½ cups pomegranate berry juice**
> **1 ½ cups water**
> **6 tablespoons agave nectar or sugar**

Mix juice, water, and agave well with a whisk. Pour mixture into a 9 x 13-inch baking dish. Cover tightly with plastic wrap and freeze approximately 45 minutes, or until icy at edge of pan. Whisk to distribute frozen portions evenly. Cover and freeze again until icy at edge of pan and overall texture is slushy, about 45 minutes. Stir the granita with a fork and return to the freezer. Stir the granita every 30 to 45 minutes, using a fork, until completely frozen (about 3 hours total).

Using a fork, scrape granita down length of pan, forming icy flakes. When served, the granita should look like a fluffy pile of dry, red crystals. To serve, scoop flaked granita into tall goblets or parfait glasses. Serve immediately with iced teaspoons.

Daily Drinks and Brews

Water
Lemon Water
Sparkling Fruit Juice
Bubbly Fruit Tea
Ginger Tea
Cranberry Ginger Cider
Chai Tea
Hot Mocha Milk
Banana Milk
Nut Milks

Water

Our bodies require water. You can save both money and calories by quenching your thirst with plain water. Some parents habitually give juice or soda to a thirsty child. Try offering water first, especially if your child drinks juice and then won't eat. It's important to keep the attention at mealtime on eating, not drinking. Save juices, teas, milks, and other drinks for between-meal snacks. For everyday meals, serve water or no drinks. Avoid ice water with food. Cold drinks can halt the body's warm digestive process.

Lemon Water

This is my favorite drink first thing in the morning. It is also nice served with summer meals. I keep a pitcher of lemon water in the refrigerator during hot weather.

Makes 1 quart

½ lemon, sliced
1 quart water

Put lemon slices in a pitcher of water. Let set 10 to 20 minutes. Refrigerate or drink at room temperature.

Sparkling Fruit Juice

Instead of giving your child pop or soda, try this more healthful sparkling beverage.

Makes 1 quart

2 cups fruit juice
2 cups mineral water

Combine ingredients in a pitcher.

Bubbly Fruit Tea

Another delicious way to dilute fruit juice for youngsters.

Makes 1 quart

> **1 cup fruity hibiscus herbal tea**
> **1 teaspoon honey**
> **1½ cups fruit juice**
> **1½ cups mineral water**

Put a bag of red zinger or other hibiscus tea in a cup and cover with boiling water. Add honey and stir. Allow tea to cool. Combine with juice and mineral water in a pitcher; serve cold.

Ginger Tea

Ginger tea is the perfect remedy for a winter cold. Ginger warms the body and increases circulation. Ginger tea is also a very soothing drink to give someone who has an upset stomach or nausea. For a quick version simply stir a heaping tablespoon or two of Honey Ginger Elixir (page 234) into hot water with a squeeze of lemon.

Makes 2 cups

> **2 cups water**
> **1-inch piece fresh ginger, sliced thin**
> **Freshly squeezed lemon juice**
> **Maple syrup or honey to taste (optional)**

Simmer water and ginger 10 to 20 minutes. Strain and pour into cups. Add a squeeze of fresh lemon to each cup. Stir in sweetener, if desired.

Cold Remedy Ginger Tea

When a cold is coming on, use a piece of ginger the size of the ill person's thumb in the 2 cups of water. Simmer until the liquid is reduced by half, which will take about an hour. Remove from heat and add lemon and honey. This is very strong medicine!

Cranberry Ginger Cider

The perfect drink to warm visitors on a chilly night. Serve it in glass mugs so folks can enjoy the deep red color. Float an orange slice on top. For a quick method, add 1 tablespoon of Honey Ginger Elixir (page 234) to warm cider.

Prep time: 20 minutes
Makes 4 cups

> 2 cups cranberry juice
> 2 cups apple cider
> Eight, ¼-inch slices fresh ginger
> ½ teaspoon orange zest
> Orange slices, for garnish (optional)

Place juice, cider, ginger, and zest in a medium pan. Bring heat up and simmer 15 minutes. Remove pieces of ginger. Garnish each cup with an orange slice, if desired. Serve warm.

Chai Tea

This drink (which I was first introduced to as "Yogi Tea") is filled with many warming spices. It is wonderful on cold winter days. Children love its sweet taste. Traditionally, this tea is made with black tea. I have omitted it because children don't need the caffeine. Sometimes I add a little green tea in the last 5 minutes.

Makes 4 to 5 cups

> 4 cups water
> 10 whole cloves
> 12 whole cardamom pods
> 12 whole black peppercorns
> 2 cinnamon sticks
> 4 slices fresh ginger, ¼-inch thick
> 1 cup milk
> Honey to taste

Bring water, spices, and ginger to a boil in a pot. Cover with a lid, lower heat, and simmer 30 to 45 minutes. Add milk, bring to a boil again. Turn heat off. Strain into cup and stir in sweetener.

Hot Mocha Milk

Cafix is a dry powder made from grains, figs, and other natural ingredients that dissolves in hot water. It has a coffeelike flavor with no caffeine—safe for children!

Makes 1 cup

½ teaspoon Cafix or other grain beverage
½ teaspoon cocoa powder
½ cup boiling water
1 teaspoon honey or sugar
½ cup milk

Put Cafix and cocoa powder in a cup. Fill cup halfway with boiling water. Stir in sweetener. Fill cup to top with milk.

Banana Milk

A fun recipe that older children can make by themselves.

Makes 2½ to 3 cups

1 ripe banana
2 cups milk (cow, nut, or soy)
2 teaspoons vanilla extract

Blend all ingredients in a blender and serve.

Nut Milks

Nut milks, a nutritious and versatile group of foods, taste good on cereals or fruit desserts. You can use them to replace cow's milk in any recipe. Nut milks can be kept in the refrigerator for a couple of days although they may separate and need to be reblended. Here are ideas for three nut milks; the possibilities are limitless.

All variations make 2 cups

Almond Sesame Milk

¼ cup almonds
¼ cup sesame seeds
2 cups water, divided
1 tablespoon maple syrup or brown rice syrup

Place nuts in blender with a few tablespoons of the water and blend until you have a paste. Add the rest of the water and sweetener; blend again. For smoother milk, pour the contents of the blender through a fine strainer lined with cheesecloth to remove nut pulp. Pick up the ends of the cheesecloth and squeeze pulp to remove all the milk.

Almond Cashew Milk

¼ cup almonds
¼ cup cashews
2 cups water, divided
3 pitted dates

Place nuts in blender with a few tablespoons of the water and blend until you have a paste. Add the rest of the water and dates; blend again. For smoother milk, pour the contents of the blender through a fine strainer lined with cheesecloth to remove nut pulp. Pick up the ends of the cheesecloth and squeeze pulp to remove all the milk.

Nut Butter Milk

2 tablespoons creamy almond, sesame, or cashew butter
2 cups water
1 tablespoon honey

Place nut or seed butter in a blender with the other ingredients. Blend until smooth.

APPENDIX A: Have It Your Way: Flour, Fat, Milk, Sweetener, and Egg Substitutions

FLOUR
Replacing white flour with whole grain flour

Whole grain flour contains bran and tends to absorb more liquid than white flour. If you replace white flour with whole grain flour in equal amounts, your dish may come out too dry. Use less flour when making this substitution.

Replace 1 cup white flour with ⅞ cup whole grain flour.

Replacing gluten flour with a nongluten flour

Wheat, kamut, spelt, rye, and barley all contain gluten. For the family member who is gluten intolerant or gluten sensitive, a substitution needs to be made. Karen Robertson's lovely book *Cooking Gluten-Free!* (Celiac Publishing, 2003) offers several formulas. I find that formulas with bean flours give baked goods a funny, beany taste and prefer this simpler one.

Replace 1 cup gluten flour with ¾ cup brown rice flour, 3 tablespoons potato starch, 1 tablespoon tapioca flour, and ½ teaspoon xanthan gum.

FAT

Notice whether the fat in your recipe is solid or liquid. When you replace a liquid fat with a solid fat (e.g., canola oil with butter), melt the solid fat to get the correct measurement. It is tricky to replace a solid fat with a liquid fat (e.g., replacing Crisco with olive oil). You will need to examine how the fat is used in the recipe and experiment. If you need to make a dairy-free recipe, you can substitute coconut oil for butter.

MILK

Soy, rice, or Nut Milks (page 271) can be substituted for cow's milk in any recipe.

SWEETENER
Replacing a granulated sweetener with a liquid sweetener

When replacing a granulated sweetener with a liquid sweetener (e.g., replacing white sugar with maple syrup), reduce liquid content in the recipe by ¼ cup. If no liquid is called for in the recipe, add 3–5 tablespoons of flour for each ¾ cup of liquid concentrated sweetener. Heat thick syrups before working with them by setting the jar in hot water for 5–10 minutes. Be sure to oil measuring utensils used with the thick syrups.

Because of a natural starch-splitting enzyme, the malted sweeteners (brown rice syrup and barley malt) may liquefy the consistency of the mixture. This is more likely if eggs are in the recipe. Boiling the malt syrup for 2 to 3 minutes before using can prevent this. Let it cool slightly before adding to the recipe.

Replacing a liquid sweetener with a granulated sweetener

When replacing a liquid sweetener with a granulated sweetener (e.g., replacing honey with Sucanat), increase the liquid content of the recipe by ¼ cup or reduce the flour by 3 to 5 tablespoons. The dried or granulated natural sweeteners tend to absorb liquid. Check your dough or batter to see if it resembles the texture you are used to and consider adding an extra tablespoon of water or oil if it seems dry. Adding extra moisture is especially important if you are also substituting white flour with whole grain flour in the recipe. Whole grain flours, because of their fiber, also absorb moisture.

EGGS

I don't recommend replacing eggs in a recipe unless there is an allergy or a commitment to being vegan. Dietary cholesterol is not the threat we once thought it was, and current research does not support eliminating it. Eggs are unequaled in their ability to bind. They also add high-quality protein and fat to baked goods and desserts, which helps balance the high-carbohydrate content.

Two eggs equal approximately ½ cup of liquid and fat. One option is to simply increase the liquid and fat in the recipe by ¼ cup each. Another choice is to use ½ cup of fruit or vegetable purée. This can be handy if you want to get more fruits and vegetables in your family's diet. Dates, bananas, applesauce, sweet potatoes, or yams are a few choices. The texture will be softer than if the dish was made with eggs.

A third option is to grind 2 tablespoons of flaxseed, add 6 tablespoons boiling water, let mixture set 15 minutes, then whisk with a fork. This will replace two eggs in any recipe for baked goods. The flax will also significantly increase the fiber content. There is also a product called Ener-G Egg Replacer that works—as its name indicates.

APPENDIX B: Identifying, Purchasing, and Storing Whole Foods

Most major cities have many fine natural foods grocery stores where you can purchase whole foods and whole foods products. A surprising number of national supermarket chains now carry grains and beans in bulk, tofu and tempeh, alternative sweeteners, whole grain products, and organic produce. Ask your local grocer to stock items you wish to buy regularly. This is how change begins.

Buying foods in bulk whenever possible reduces waste from unnecessary packaging. When buying packaged products, support manufacturers that use recyclable packaging. Unprocessed foods tend to be more fragile because they still contain life. Pay attention to the manufacturer's recommendations for storage written on labels. Always check the expiration date on perishable products before purchasing them.

If you do not live near a natural foods store, consider gathering a few interested friends together and starting a food-buying club. Write or call the companies listed below to find out about their catalogues and mail order services.

Eden Foods Inc., 701 Tecumseh Road, Clinton, MI 49236, 1-888-424-3336, www.edenfoods.com

Goldmine Natural Foods, 7805 Arjons Drive, San Diego, CA 92126, 1-800-475-3663, www.goldminenaturalfood.com

Mountain Ark, 146 Londonderry Turnpike #10, Hooksett, NH 03106, 1-888-392-9237, www.mountainark.com

United Natural Foods, New Customer Inquiry, Western Region, 15965 E. 32nd Avenue, Aurora, CO 80011, 1-800-522-7633, ext. 54243, www.unfi.com

Walnut Acres, 4600 Sleepytime Dr., Boulder, CO 80301, 1-800-434-4246, www.walnutacres.com

In addition, the Organic Trade Association has a Web site that catalogues many producers of organic products at www.theorganicpages.com.

Agar, a sea vegetable, is a natural jelling agent that can be used in place of animal gelatin. Agar thickens at room temperature, unlike gelatin, which must be chilled. One-quarter cup of agar gels a quart of liquid. Agar is sold in bars and small packages of translucent flakes; flakes are easier to measure. Look for agar in the macrobiotic section of your natural foods store. Store agar in a sealed container in a cool, dark place.

Amaranth is a whole grain that looks like tiny yellow, brown, and black seeds. It was an important food source for the Aztecs. Amaranth has a very good nutritional profile. It is unusually high in lysine—the amino acid most grains are low in. This makes amaranth high in protein (15 to 18 percent). It also contains more calcium, vitamin A, and vitamin C than most grains, making it a good food for those with elevated needs. Amaranth has a flavor similar to graham crackers without the sweetness. When cooked it has the texture of gelatinous cornmeal mush. Store whole grains in airtight containers where they will keep for 6 to 9 months.

Arame, a sea vegetable, is finely shredded, cooked, and then naturally sun dried. When reconstituted, it looks like small, black threads. Its milder flavor makes it a useful introductory sea vegetable. Look for it dried and packaged, in the macrobiotic section of your natural foods store or Asian markets. Store in a sealed container in a cool, dark place, where it will keep indefinitely.

Arrowroot comes from a tropical plant whose tuberous root is dried and ground into a fine powder. Arrowroot, a natural thickener, can be substituted for cornstarch in equal measure. Whole-foods cooks prefer arrowroot or kudzu's natural method of preparation over cornstarch, which is bleached and chemically treated during processing. Arrowroot can substitute for kudzu to thicken liquids. Arrowroot keeps indefinitely in a sealed container on the shelf.

Baking powder, non-aluminum. See Non aluminum baking powder.

Balsamic vinegar is an Italian red wine vinegar with a lower-than-average acidity. Its sweet, mellow flavor comes from being aged in wood; it is a distinctive addition to dressings and marinades. Vinegars store on the shelf indefinitely.

Barley is a chewy whole grain. One-third of the barley grown in this country is used to make beer, and most of the rest is used for animal feed. **Hulled barley** is whole grain barley with only the outside hull removed. **Pearled barley** is a refined product, similar to white rice, where the hull, other outside layers, and the germ of the grain are removed. Store whole grains in airtight containers, where they will keep for 6 to 9 months.

Barley malt is a complex carbohydrate sweetener made by cooking soaked, sprouted barley until the starches in the grain are broken down and converted into maltose. Barley malt is dark and thick and has a maltlike taste. Sorghum or rice syrup can be substituted for barley malt. Be careful when using barley malt in a recipe that includes eggs. Check the instructions in "Replacing a liquid sweetener with a granulated sweetener" (page 274). Refrigerate after opening.

Brown basmati rice is a long, slender grain with a distinctly aromatic flavor. Basmati rice is popular in Indian and Pakistani cultures. It can be stored in an airtight container on the shelf for 6 to 9 months.

Brown rice syrup, a naturally processed sweetener, is made from soaked and sprouted brown rice cooked with an enzyme that breaks the starches into maltose. Rice syrup has a light, delicate flavor. It looks similar to honey but is less sweet. Substitute rice syrup in equal amounts for honey, maple syrup, or barley malt. To enhance pouring, place rice syrup in a pan of hot water before using. Refrigerate after opening.

Brown rice vinegar is a mild, delicate vinegar made from fermented brown rice. It is less acidic than most vinegars; you can substitute apple cider vinegar for brown rice vinegar. Vinegars store on the shelf indefinitely.

Bulgur is parboiled, dried, and cracked whole wheat. Store whole grains in airtight containers, where they will keep for 6 to 9 months.

Carob is an evergreen tree with edible pods. The pulp of the pods is ground into carob powder or carob flour, which is naturally sweet, low in fat, high in calcium, and caffeine free. **Carob powder**

can be stored on the shelf in an airtight container for 6 to 12 months. Sift before using if lumpy. **Carob chips** come unsweetened and malt sweetened. Some chips contain dry milk, and most contain palm kernel oil, which is high in saturated fat. Look for carob products made without palm kernel oil, or use them sparingly.

Chipotle chiles are smoked, dried jalapeño peppers. Look for them in the ethnic foods section of your grocery store. Store on the shelf in a closed container.

Coconut oil is a saturated fat that is solid at temperatures under 76°F. It has a long shelf life, is very stable (unlikely to become rancid), and is safe to store at room temperature. Coconut oil is a great alternative to shortening. It can also replace butter in baked goods.

Cold-pressed vegetable oils are oils that have been extracted by mechanical means rather than using heat and solvents; however, there is no legal standard for this term. Many companies that produce cold-pressed oil guarantee that their oil was not heated at any point to over 110°F. With the exception of olive oil, most cold-pressed oils are polyunsaturated, making them susceptible to heat, light, and air. All oils should be stored in the refrigerator.

Couscous is actually a tiny pasta made from coarsely ground and steamed wheat. It is usually made from refined wheat, though whole wheat couscous is becoming more commonly available.

Store whole grains in airtight containers, where they will keep for 6 to 9 months.

Dairy products can be healthful used in moderate amounts. Some consumers prefer to buy raw milk products, as homogenization and pasteurization alter nutrient composition and digestibility. When buying raw milk products or any dairy products, buy from organic dairies. Check the pull date on all dairy products before purchasing and discard after that date.

Dulse is a sea vegetable extremely high in iron (14 mg per ¼ cup) and other minerals. The dark red, dried leaves can be soaked for 5 minutes and added to soups or salads. Dulse is also sold dried and broken into tiny bits as **dulse flakes** or **granulated dulse**. Sprinkle on most any food for a nutritional boost. Dulse will store indefinitely in an airtight container in a cool, dark place.

Eggs are best stored in their carton in the refrigerator. Keeping them in their carton prevents moisture loss. For more on purchasing eggs, see page 14 in "Shopping for Sustenance." See Appendix A, "Have It Your Way: Flour, Fat, Milk, Sweetener, and Egg Substitutions" for a description on how to substitute.

Essene bread is a naturally sweet, moist, flourless bread. Sprouted grains are crushed, hand-shaped, and then slowly baked at low temperatures. The Essenes were a sect of monks living in early biblical times, and this method of bread-making is attributed to them. Sprouted wheat bread comes in several flavors and is found in the refrigerated or frozen food section of most natural foods stores.

Extra-virgin olive oil comes from the first pressing of the olives and is the highest-quality olive oil. I use extra-virgin olive oil for dressings and light sautéing. Purchase oils in small bottles made of dark glass and use them within a few months to avoid spoilage. Most cooks recommend refrigeration for oils. Hold bottle under warm water for 30 seconds to restore free-flowing qualities.

Fish should be purchased as fresh as possible, stored in the refrigerator, and used within 24 hours. Look for fish that has firm flesh, a high sheen, and no offensive odors. For more on purchasing fish, see page 15 in "Shopping for Sustenance."

Flaxseeds are seeds from the flax plant. The oil in the seeds is rich in essential fatty acids, and flaxseed oil is sold as a nutritional supplement. It is easier and more effective to buy whole flaxseed and grind them in a small coffee grinder before adding them to cereals and yogurts and such. In this way, the oils are fresher and you also receive the benefits of the high fiber content of the seed. Store flaxseeds in a sealed container in a cool, dry place.

Flour. See Spelt, Unbleached white flour, Whole wheat flour, Whole wheat pastry flour, and Whole grain flours. Store all flours in a cold, dry place for 1 to 2 months, in the refrigerator for 6 months, or in the freezer for up to 12 months.

Ghee is clarified butter used in traditional Indian cooking. The milk proteins in the butter are removed and only the fat remains. Unlike butter, ghee can hold high heat without scorching. For more information and instructions on how to make ghee, see page 239. Refrigerate homemade ghee.

Herbs are the leaves of certain temperate-climate plants that can be used fresh or dried to add wonderful, distinctive flavors to whole foods. Fresh herbs have more flavor and more nutritional value. Store dried herbs in closed containers made of dark glass, away from heat and light. Dried herbs keep their flavor for about 6 months. Substitute 1 teaspoon dried herbs for 1 tablespoon fresh herbs. Some herbs have medicinal effects and are not appropriate for pregnant or nursing moms; for instance, sage can reduce the flow of breast milk. Refer to *Wise Woman Herbal for the Childbearing Year* by Susun S. Weed (Ash Tree Publishing, 1986) for more information.

High-heat safflower oil comes from safflower seeds that have been selectively bred so that there is more oleic acid, making the oil more stable and higher in monounsaturated fats. This change allows the oil to hold a higher heat than regular safflower oil, making it suitable for deep-frying. Refined safflower oil is pale yellow and, like other refined oils, is bland and tasteless.

Hijiki, of all the sea vegetables, is the richest in calcium. Its thick, black strands have a firm texture and look striking with other colors. As with several other sea vegetables, soak in cold water before using. The strong taste can be moderated by cooking hijiki in apple juice and by combining it with other vegetables. Store hijiki in a sealed container in a cool, dark place, where it will keep indefinitely.

Hulled barley. See Barley.

Kasha is roasted buckwheat groats. It is a brown-colored grain with angular edges. Buckwheat is actually the seed of a plant related to rhubarb that originated in Russia. Store whole grains in airtight containers, where they will keep for 6 to 9 months.

Kombu is a dark green sea vegetable sold in thick strips. It contains glutamic acid, which acts as a tenderizer when added to cooking beans. As with other sea vegetables, kombu is mineral rich. Store kombu in a sealed container in a cool, dark place, where it will keep indefinitely.

Kudzu or kuzu, from the root of the kudzu plant, looks like broken chalk. The kudzu plant grows wild in the southern United States, but there is no American company producing and marketing it. Natural food distributors import packaged kudzu from Japan, making it very pricey. Kudzu can be dissolved in cool or room temperature liquid and used as a thickener. The thickened liquid will have a smooth, glossy appearance. In macrobiotic practice, kudzu is recommended for its soothing effect on the digestive system. You can substitute arrowroot for kudzu. Look for kudzu in the macrobiotic section of your natural foods store. Kudzu will keep indefinitely stored in a sealed container on the shelf.

Maple syrup is made from the boiled sap of sugar maple trees. About 40 gallons of sap (from nine trees) make 1 gallon of syrup. Maple syrup is available in three grades: A, B, or C, determined by the temperature used and length of time cooked. The lighter the color, the better the quality (and the more expensive). Store in a cool location to prevent fermentation and crystallization. During hot weather, refrigerate. Freezing maple syrup may damage flavor.

Millet is a small, round, golden grain that continues to be a major food source in Asia, North Africa, and India. Store whole grains in airtight containers, where they will keep for 6 to 9 months.

Mirin, a versatile sweet cooking wine, is made from sweet brown rice and contains no additives. Dry sherry may be substituted for mirin. Store mirin in a closed container in a cool, dry place.

Miso is a salty paste made from cooked and aged soybeans. The soybeans are mixed with various grains and other ingredients to produce different flavors. The longer miso is aged and the darker its color, the stronger and saltier the taste. Miso is traditionally used as a soup base, but it can also be used in spreads, dressings, dips, or as a substitute for salt. Unpasteurized miso contains beneficial enzymes and organisms that aid in digestion. Refrigerated miso will keep indefinitely.

Mochi is made from sweet brown rice that has been cooked, pounded into a paste, and then compressed into dense bars. Mochi requires cooking. When broken into squares and baked at 400°F for 10 minutes, it puffs up and gets gooey inside. It can also be grated and melted into foods. Refrigerate opened packages and eat within one week. Extra packages can be stored in the freezer and thawed in about 2 hours.

Molasses, a by-product of sugar refinement, has a strong bittersweet flavor. Only blackstrap molasses has appreciable amounts of iron and calcium. Barley malt or sorghum can be substituted for molasses. Molasses will keep for up to 6 months in a sealed container in a cool place; however, refrigeration is safest.

Non-aluminum baking powder is recommended for use as a leavening agent in non–yeast baked goods. Stored in a closed container in a cool, dry place, non-aluminum baking powder will keep indefinitely.

Nori, a dried and rolled sea vegetable, resembles dark green or black paper. While nori is most commonly used in making sushi, it can also be eaten directly from the package by lightly toasting and crumbling onto foods. Store in the freezer in a freezer bag to preserve freshness.

Nuts and seeds are best bought and stored in their shell, for flavor as well as freshness. Because of their oil content, nuts and seeds are subject to rancidity. Store shelled nuts and seeds in an airtight container in the refrigerator for up to 3 months or in the freezer for 12 months.

Oils are described individually under their specific names. They should be used sparingly. Extra-virgin olive oil and unrefined sesame oil are the highest-quality oils. These are the least processed and least likely to go rancid. Unrefined oils usually have a darker color and retain some of the flavor of their origin. Refined oils are pale, odorless, and tasteless because they have been bleached and deodorized during the refining process. For more on purchasing fats and oils, see page 17 in "Shopping for Sustenance." Store oils in dark glass in the refrigerator and use within 6 months.

Potato starch is a gluten-free flour made from cooked, dried, and ground potatoes. It can be used as a nongrain thickener in place of cornstarch or as part of a gluten-free flour mix. Liquids thickened with potato starch should never be boiled. This starch will keep indefinitely on the shelf.

Poultry is recommended for consumption as a protein dish. Three to 4 ounces daily is ample for most; more can be consumed by those with elevated needs. For more on purchasing poultry, see page 15 in "Shopping for Sustenance." Purchase organically raised poultry to feed your family, as factory-produced poultry is notorious for being laden with antibiotics, hormones, and other undesirable toxins. Fresh poultry can be kept 1 to 2 days in the refrigerator, best if used within 24 hours.

Quinoa (*keen-wah*) was cultivated in Peru for thousands of years. This staple food of the Incas has been rediscovered and is now grown in the United States. Quinoa contains all eight amino acids, making it a complete protein. It also contains appreciable amounts of calcium and iron. Store whole grains in airtight containers, where they will keep for 6 to 9 months.

Radicchio is a small burgundy- and white-colored head of lettuce leaves. The leaves have a slightly sharp taste.

Ramen is a dry block of quick-cooking pasta. The cooked noodles are curly.

Ramen is made from a variety of flours and usually comes packaged with a packet of dry seasonings to be used in cooking. Look for ramen made from whole grain flours.

Rice syrup. See Brown rice syrup.

Sea salt is refined sodium chloride from sea water. Although potassium iodide (iodine) is in commercial table salt for people with no access to seafood or sea vegetables, dextrose (a type of sugar), sodium bicarbonate, and other unwanted additives are also added in processing. High-quality sea salt contains none of these additives. Salt-related health problems come from consuming processed foods to which large amounts of sodium have been added (such as diet soft drinks), not from small amounts of salt used in cooking. Small amounts of high-quality salt are beneficial to our health and vastly improve the flavor of whole grains and legumes. For more on purchasing salt, see page 17 in "Shopping for Sustenance."

Sea vegetables are purchased dried and are available in packages or occasionally in bulk. Look for sea vegetables in the macrobiotic section of your natural foods store or in Asian markets. Sea vegetables should be stored in sealed containers in a cool, dark place. Properly stored, they will keep indefinitely. See Arame, Dulse, Hijiki, Kombu, Nori, and Wakame for information about specific sea vegetables.

Shiitake mushrooms have a dark brown cap, a beige underbelly, and a tough stem. When cooked they have a delicious savory taste and a chewy texture. It is said that shiitake mushrooms are a natural source of interferon, a protein thought to boost the immune system. The mushrooms are sold fresh, which is best, or they can be purchased dried and packaged. Store fresh mushrooms in a paper bag in the refrigerator.

Shoyu is made from soybeans, wheat, water, and sea salt, but unlike commercial soy sauces shoyu does not contain sugar, monosodium glutamate (MSG), and other additives. Both shoyu and tamari are naturally brewed and aged and used to flavor dishes. Tamari is similar to shoyu but contains little or no wheat. Store shoyu or tamari in a sealed container on the shelf indefinitely.

Soba is a traditional type of Japanese noodle made principally from buckwheat.

Sorghum is a syruplike sweetener with a rich, dark taste. It is made by concentrating the juice of crushed and boiled sorghum stems. The sorghum plant is a relative of millet. Barley malt can be substituted for sorghum. Refrigerate after opening.

Soy beverage or soy milk, best known by commercial names such as WestSoy and EdenSoy, is a high-protein alternative to cow's milk. Manufacturers of soy beverages have succeeded in producing delicious milks from soybeans in many flavors. Do not substitute soy milk for infant formula as it does not contain all of the necessary nutrients for growing babies. For more on soymilk see page 49 in "What Should I Give My Child to Drink?" Soy beverages usually come in aseptic packages that require refrigeration after opening.

Spelt was a staple grain in biblical times. Spelt is easier to digest than whole wheat and makes a suitable substitution for wheat in baked goods. It is sold as flour, flakes, and in its whole form. Store whole grains in airtight containers, where they will keep for 6 to 9 months.

Spices are the whole or ground buds, fruits, flowers, barks, or seeds of usually tropical-zoned plants. In traditional Indian cooking, spices are sautéed in butter or ghee to enhance their flavor before added to a dish. To maintain optimum potency, spices should be stored in closed containers made of dark glass away from heat and light and used within 6 months.

Sucanat. See Unrefined cane sugar.

Tahini is a creamy paste made of crushed, hulled sesame seeds. Seeds used for tahini are either raw, toasted, or lightly toasted, each giving the tahini a slightly different flavor. Sesame is uniquely resistant to rancidity, perhaps why it has been enjoyed by many cultures for centuries. Look for it with other nut butters or Middle Eastern foods. Refrigerate after opening.

Tamari is a naturally brewed soy sauce made from soybeans, water, and sea salt. Tamari and shoyu are interchangeable. Also see Shoyu.

Tapioca flour is a grain-free flour derived from cassava root. It is a starchy, slightly sweet white flour. Tapioca flour can be used to thicken liquids. If stored in a cool, dark place, all types of tapioca will keep indefinitely.

Tempeh, originally an Indonesian food, is made from soybeans that have been cooked and split to remove the hull. A culture is added to the cooked beans, which age for several days before forming into a solid piece, which can be cut and sliced. This high-protein food can be baked, boiled, fried, or steamed. Store tempeh in the refrigerator and use within one week. Tempeh can also be frozen for up to 6 months; allow 1 hour to thaw.

Toasted sesame oil has a darker appearance and nuttier taste than plain sesame oil and delivers a lot of flavor in small amounts. Store in the refrigerator.

Tofu is soybean curd made from the "milk" of soybeans. Tofu's low calories, relatively high protein, and bland flavor make it a versatile ingredient. A variety of textures are available: firm, soft, and silken. Soft or silken tofu works well for dressings and desserts, while firm tofu holds its shape well for stir-fries and marinated dishes. Tofu can be purchased in bulk and in packages. Be sure to note the expiration date on packages. Cover bulk tofu and packaged tofu that has been opened in fresh water and store in the refrigerator in a sealed container. Change the water daily and use within a week. To freshen tofu, drop in boiling, salted water for a few minutes; remove and use.

Udon noodles are traditional Japanese noodles made from a combination of whole wheat, brown rice, and white flours.

Umeboshi plums come from Japanese apricots that are picked green and pickled in sea salt with shiso leaves. Their unique salty-sour taste adds zip to recipes.

Umeboshi plum paste is a purée made from pitted umeboshi plums. Plums and paste will keep indefinitely stored in a sealed container on the shelf. A pinch of sea salt in 1 tablespoon of lemon juice can be substituted for 1 plum or 2 teaspoons of paste although it doesn't produce quite the same flavor.

Umeboshi plum vinegar is the leftover juice from the umeboshi plum-pickling process. The salty-sour taste gives a lift to soups and salad dressings and eliminates the need for salt in a recipe. Stores indefinitely in a sealed container in a cool, dry place.

Unbleached white flour is flour that has had the bran and germ removed in a refining process. But unlike regular white flour, it has not been bleached. When used in combination with whole grain flours, this flour gives muffins, crusts, and cakes a lighter texture. Store in an airtight container in a cool, dry place for up to a year.

Unrefined cane sugar is a generic name I have used for granulated products derived from sugar cane juice. Sucanat is a trade name for organically grown, dehydrated cane juice. Another brand name is Rapadura. I prefer to use these products, which are less refined than regular white sugar and retain the mineral-rich molasses from the cane juice. They resemble brown sugar in appearance and taste, though less sweet. Substitute dried cane juice in equal proportions for white or brown sugar. Store on the shelf.

Vegetables and fruits should be purchased frequently and used within a few days to ensure freshness. Fresh produce is best; frozen produce is a distant second. Use your senses when shopping for produce. Fresh fruit should have a fragrant smell, and fresh vegetables should look perky, with rich color. Store ripe fruits and vegetables separately in the refrigerator. Tropical fruits and citrus fruits, including tomatoes and avocados, do well at room temperature. Potatoes, onions, garlic, and winter squashes prefer an unrefrigerated location; store them in a cool, dark place. Cut the leaves from root vegetables, as the flow of sap continues to the leaves at the expense of the root. Most fresh produce benefits from storage in open plastic bags. Wash, dry, and reuse your plastic bags to avoid waste.

Wakame is a green, leafy sea vegetable high in calcium and other minerals. A small amount expands when soaked; after soaking, remove the main rib or stem and cut leaves into small pieces. Often used in soups, wakame can also be toasted and ground into a condiment. Store in a sealed container in a cool, dark place indefinitely.

Wheat berries are whole wheat kernels. They can be purchased as soft red winter wheat or hard winter wheat berries. Store all whole grains in airtight containers, where they will keep for 6 to 9 months. Wheat berries can be planted in a container with soil and watered regularly to make wheat grass.

Whole grains, such as brown rice, buckwheat, oats, quinoa, and millet, can be stored in airtight containers at room temperature. Unground whole grains will keep this way for 6 to 9 months. Whole grain pastas stored in airtight containers will keep over a year.

Whole grain flours, including whole wheat, barley, brown rice, buckwheat, and spelt flour, should be stored in airtight containers, where they will keep for 2 months at room temperature, 6 months in the refrigerator, and a year in the freezer. The essential oils in grains are released when grains are ground into flour, making them more susceptible to spoilage.

Whole wheat flour is ground from hard winter wheat and contains more gluten than whole wheat pastry flour, making it a suitable choice for yeasted breads. See Whole grain flours for storage information.

Whole wheat pastry flour is ground from soft spring wheat and has less gluten, making it better for whole grain cakes, crusts, and unyeasted breads. See Whole grain flours for storage information.

APPENDIX C: Meal Plans Using Recipes from This Book

1. Chipotle Navy Bean Soup (legume, vegetable)
   Sweet Squash Corn Muffins (whole grain, vegetable, B12)
   Spinach Salad with Balsamic Vinaigrette (green vegetable, digestive)

2. Quinoa (whole grain)
   Szechwan Tempeh (legume, digestive)
   Becky's Braised Greens (green vegetable)
   Mango Salsa (fruit, digestive)

3. Peasant Kasha, Potatoes, and Mushrooms (whole grain, vegetable)
   Nori-Wrapped Wasabi Salmon (animal protein)
   Massaged Kale and Currant Salad (green vegetable, digestive)

4. Bok Choy and Buckwheat Noodles in Seasoned Broth (whole grain, green vegetable, legume, digestive)
   Sweet Potato and Shrimp Tempura (animal protein)

5. Nut Burgers (grain, nut)
   Fresh Corn Salsa (digestive)
   Red Lentil Soup with East Indian Spices (legume, vegetable)
   Quick Boiled Greens (green vegetable)

6. Brown Rice (grain)
   Curried Lentils and Cauliflower (legume, vegetable)
   Watercress Salad with Creamy Ginger Dressing (green vegetable, digestive)

7. Polenta (whole grain, B12)
   White Bean and Kale Minestrone (legume, green vegetable)
   Fresh Corn Salsa (digestive)

8. Ben's Friday Pancakes (whole grain)
   Homemade Applesauce (fruit)
   Green Eggs (No Ham) (animal protein, green vegetable)
   Chai Tea (digestive)

9. Quick Lemon and Garlic Quinoa Salad (whole grain, green vegetable)
   Rainbow Trout Poached in Herbs (animal protein)
   Pressure-Cooked Beets with balsamic vinegar (vegetable, digestive)

10. Soba Noodles (whole grain) with Coconut Peanut Sauce
    Thai Steak Salad over Soba (animal protein, green vegetable, digestive)
    Poached Pears (fruit)

11. Tomato Basil Soup (vegetable)
    Lemon- and Herb-Roasted Chicken (animal protein)
    Emerald City Salad (whole grain, green vegetable, digestive)

12. Rice Balls Rolled in Sesame Salt (whole grain)
    Cynthia's Hearty Vegetable Miso Soup (legume, green vegetable, digestive)
    Triple "A" Salad (green vegetable, digestive)

13. Golden Spice Rice with Chickpeas (whole grain, legume)
    Greens in Cashew Curry Sauce (green vegetable)
    Yogurt Cucumber Topping (digestive, B12)

14. Huevos Rancheros (animal protein, whole grain, vegetable)
    with shredded lettuce, avocado, sour cream (digestive, green vegetable)

15. Cream of Asparagus Soup with Dill (vegetable, whole grain)
    Tofu Kale Supper Pie (legume, whole grain, green vegetable)
    Luscious Beet Salad with Toasted Pumpkin Seeds (vegetable, digestive, B12)

16. Baked Chicken with Mushrooms and Rosemary (animal protein)
    Pressure-Cooked Garlic Mashed Potatoes (starchy vegetable)
    Sweet Apple Walnut Kale (green vegetable, fruit, digestive)

17. Pan-Fried Tofu and Greens with Almond Ginger Drizzle (legume, green vegetable)
    Brown Rice (whole grain)
    Cucumber Jalapeño Relish (digestive)

18. Middle Eastern Falafel (legume) with shredded lettuce (green vegetable)
    Whole wheat pita (whole grain)
    Lemon Tahini Sauce
    Greek Salad (vegetable, digestive, B12)

19. Quinoa (whole grain)
    Dr. Bruce's Awesome Grilled Salmon (animal protein)
    Grilled Vegetable Salad with Sweet Poppy Seed Dressing (green vegetable, vegetable, digestive)

20. Rosemary Red Soup (legume, vegetable)
Pumpkin Seed Parsley Garnish (digestive)
Whole Wheat and Rice Bread (whole grain) and butter (B12)
Susan's Succulent Supper Salad (green vegetable, vegetable)

21. Thai Coconut Chicken Soup (animal protein, green vegetable, digestive)
Asian Noodle Salad with Toasted Sesame Dressing (whole grain, vegetable)

22. Golden Mushroom Basil Soup (starchy vegetable)
Salmon and Rueben Sandwich (whole grain, animal protein, vegetable, digestive)

23. Spinach Feta Quiche (animal protein, green vegetable, whole grain)
Mustard Greens Salad with Tofu Dill Dressing (vegetable, digestive)

24. Orange-Glazed Salmon Kebobs with Yogurt Garlic Dip (animal protein, digestive)
Sweet Rice Timbales (whole grain)
Garlic-Sautéed Greens (green vegetable)

25. Black Bean Tostados (whole grain, legume)
Lime Cabbage Slaw (green vegetable, digestive)

26. Split Pea Soup with Fresh Peas and Potatoes (vegetable, legume)
Romaine Chop Salad with Basil Dressing (green vegetable, B12, digestive)
Whole Grain Bread with butter (whole grain)

27. Squash- and Raisin-Stuffed Chicken Breasts (animal protein, starchy vegetable)
Sweet Pepper Relish (digestive)
Massaged Kale and Currant Salad (green vegetable)

REFERENCES

WHOLESOME FAMILY EATING

Ballantine, Rudolph. 1978. *Diet and nutrition*. Honesdale, PA: The Himalayan International Institute. 55, 59, 128–30.

Bray, George A., Samara Joy Nielsen, and Barry M. Popkin. 2004. Consumption of high-fructose corn syrup in beverages may play a role in the epidemic of obesity. *The American Journal of Clinical Nutrition*. 79: 537–43.

Colbin, Annemarie. 1986. *Food and healing*. New York: Ballantine Books.

David, Marc. 2005. *The slow down diet: Eating for pleasure, energy, and weight loss*. Rochester, VT: Healing Arts Press.

Ensminger, Audrey H., M. E. Ensminger, James E. Konlande, and John R. K. Robson. 1983. *Food and nutrition encyclopedia, vol.2*. Clovis, CA: Pegus Press. 1460–67.

Guthrie, Helen. 1986. *Introductory nutrition*. St. Louis: Times Mirror/Mosby College Publishing.

Haas, Elston. 1981. *Staying healthy with the seasons*. Millbrae, CA: Celestial Arts.112.

McGee, Harold. 1984. *On food and cooking*. New York: Macmillan Publishing Co.

Morningstar, Amadea, and Urmila Desa. 1990. *The ayurvedic cookbook*. Santa Fe, NM: Lotus Press. 260–61.

The National Center on Addiction and Substance Abuse at Columbia University. 2006. *The importance of family dinners*. New York: National Center on Addiction and Substance Abuse.

Nestle, Marion. 2006. *What to eat*. New York: North Point Press.

Pitchford, Paul. 1993. *Healing with whole foods*. Berkeley, CA: North Atlantic Books.

Pollan, Michael. 2006. *The omnivore's dilemma*. New York: Penguin Press.

Robertson, Laurel, Carol Flinders, and Brian Ruppenthal. 1986. *The new Laurel's kitchen*. Berkeley, CA: Ten Speed Press. 415–16, 461–87.

Tortora, Gerard J., and Bryan H. Derrickson. 2006. *Principles of anatomy and physiology, 11th edition*. New York: Wiley.

INCLUDING BABY

Brode, Michelle. 2001. Cultural aspects of starting solids. *New Beginnings*. 18:64–65.

Chow, Marilyn P., Barbara A. Durand, Marie N. Feldman, and Marion A. Mills. 1984. *Handbook of pediatric primary care*. New York: John Wiley & Sons.

Dewey, Kathryn, and Camila Chaparro. 2005. Delayed umbilical cord clamping boosts iron in infants. nutrition.ucdavis.edu/news.htm.

Dorfman, Kelly. 1987. All about feeding babies. *Mothering*. Fall:33–39.

Fallon, Sally, with Mary G. Enig. 2000. *Nourishing traditions*. Winona Lake, IN : New Trends Publishing.

Firkaly, Susan Tate. 1984. *Into the mouths of babes*. White Hall, VA: Betterway Publications.

Forsyth, J. S., et. al. 1999. A randomized controlled study of the effect of long chain polyun-saturated fatty acid supplementation on stool hardness during formula feeding. *Archives of Disease in Childhood*. 81:253–56.

Gardner, Joy. 1987. *Healing yourself during pregnancy*. Freedom, CA: The Crossing Press. 28–37.

Goldsmith, Judith. 1990. *Childbirth wisdom*. Brookline, MA: East West Books.

Government of South Australia, Child and Youth Health. 2007a. Bottle-feeding additions to baby formulas. www.cyh.com.

———— 2007b. Bottle-feeding soy infant formulas. www.cyh.com.

Harnett-Robinson, Roy. 1988. Interview by the author. August.

Hu W., I. Kerrige, A. Kemp. 2004. Reducing the risks for food allergic children in schools and preschools. *Journal of Pediatrics and Child Health*. 40:672–73.

Isolauri, E., et al. 2002. Functional foods and probiotics: Working group report of the First World Congress of Pediatric Gastroenterology, Hepatology, and Nutrition. *Journal of Pediatric Gastroenterology and Nutrition*. 35: S106–09.

Kenda, Margaret Elizabeth, and Phyllis S. Williams. 1982. *The natural baby food cookbook*. New York: Avon Books.

La Leche League International. 1981. *The womanly art of breastfeeding*. New York: Plume, New American Library. 288–89.

Liebman, Bonnie. 1990. Baby formulas: Missing key fats? *Nutrition Action Newsletter*. 17: 8–9.

Makrides, M., R. A. Gibson, K. Simmer. 1993. The effect of dietary fat on the developing brain. *Journal of Pediatrics and Child Health*. 29:409–10.

Mohrbacher, Nancy, and Judy Torgus. 2003. *The new La Leche League leaders handbook*. Franklin Park, IL: La Leche League International.

Mohrbacher, Nancy, and Julie Stock. 1991. *The breastfeeding answer book*. Franklin Park, IL.: La Leche League International.

Palmer, Gabrielle. 1993. *The politics of breastfeeding, 2nd edition*. Kitchener, ON: Pandora Press.

Price, Weston. 2000. *Nutrition and physical degeneration: A comparison of primitive and modern diets and their effects*. La Mesa, CA: Price-Pottenger Nutrition Foundation.

Pryor, Karen. 1973. *Nursing your baby*. New York: Pocket Books. 52–53.

Royal Prince Alfred Hospital, Allergy Unit. Allergy information sheets. www.cs.nsw.gov.au/rpa/allergy.

Saavedra, J. M. et. al. 1998. Effect of long term consumption of infant formulas with Bifi-dobacteria and S. thermophilus on stool patterns and diaper rash in infants. *Journal of Pediatric Gastroenterology and Nutrition*. 27: 483.

Viljanen, M., E. Savilahti, T. Haahtela, K. Juntunen-Backman, R. Korpela, T. Poussa, T. Tuure, M. Kuitunen. 2005. Probiotics in the treatment of atopic eczema/dermatitis syndrome in infants: A double-blind placebo-controlled trial. *Allergy*. 60:494–500.

RAISING HEALTHY EATERS

Bray, George A, Samara Joy Nielsen, and Barry M. Popkin. 2004. Consumption of high-fructose corn syrup in beverages may play a role in the epidemic of obesity. *The American Journal of Clinical Nutrition*. 79:537–43.

Caughlan, Goldie. 1992. What's a mother to do? *PCC (Puget Consumer's Co-op) Sound Consumer*. March: 228.

Hannaford, Carla. 1995. *Smart moves: Why learning is not all in your head*. Scotland: Ladder of Learning.

Ianelli, Vincent. 2003. Fruit juice: How much is too much? pediatrics.about.com/cs/nutrition/a/fruit_juice.htm.

Jacobson, Michael F. 2005. Liquid candy: How soft drinks are harming Americans' health. www.cspinet.org/sodapop?liquid_candy.htm.

King, Jonathan. 1985. Is your water safe to drink? *Medical Self Care*. 44–57.

Kirkendall, Donald. 2004. Common myths about nutrition among soccer players. www.usyouthsoccer.org/coaches/70077.html.

K-State Research and Extension. 1998. Do kids need sports drinks? www.oznet.ksu.edu/humannutrition/_timely/sportdrink.htm.

Lair, Cynthia, and Scott Murdoch. 2002. *Feeding the young athlete: Sports nutrition made easy for players and parents*. Seattle: Moon Smile Press.

Leach, Penelope. 1989. *Your baby and child*. New York: Alfred A Knopf, Inc.

Mayo Clinic. 2006. Water: How much should you drink every day? www.mayoclinic.com/health/water/NU00283.

Michael Fields Agricultural Institute. 2004. Case study: Appleton Central Alternative Charter High School's nutrition and wellness program. www.michaelfieldsaginst.org/programs/food/case_study.pdf .

Oski, Frank. 1983. *Don't drink your milk!* Syracuse, NY: Mollica Press, Ltd. 24–27.

Pearce, Joseph Chilton. 1985. *Magical child matures*. New York: E. P. Dutton.

Pope, Sharon. 1988. Good nutrition for the very young. *PCC (Puget Consumer's Co-op) Sound Consumer*. 181:1,3,6.

Schardt, David. 1993. The problem with protein. *Nutrition Action Healthletter*. 20:5.

———— 2004. Sweet nothings: Not all sweeteners are equal. *Nutrition Action Healthletter*.

Riedler, J., C. Braun-Fahrländer, W. Eder, M. Schreuer, M. Waser, S. Maisch, D. Carr, R. Schierl, D. Nowak, E. Von Mutius, the Alex study team. 2001. Exposure to farming in early life and development of asthma and allergy. *The Lancet*, 358 (9288):1129–33.

Smith, Lendon. 1979. *Feed your kids right*. New York: McGraw-Hill. 36.

Soffritti, Morando, et al. 2005. Aspartame induces lymphomas and leukemias in rats. *European Journal of Oncology*. 10:2.

Weed, Susun S. 1986. *Wise woman herbal for the childbearing year*. Woodstock, NY: Ash Tree Publishing.

RECOMMENDED READING

These are a few of the books that have been inspiring and helpful to me.

FOOD AND HEALTH

Ballantine, Rudolph, 1978. *Diet and nutrition*. Honesdale, PA: The Himalayan International Institute.

Carson, Rachel. 2002. *Silent spring*. Boston: Mariner Books.

Colbin, Annemarie. 1986. *Food and healing*. New York: Ballantine Books.

David, Marc. 1994. *Nourishing wisdom*. New York: Harmony/Bell Tower.

——— 2005. *The slow down diet: Eating for pleasure, energy, and weight loss*. Rochester, VT: Healing Arts Press.

Fallon, Sally, with Mary G. Enig. 2000. *Nourishing traditions*. Winona Lake, IN : New Trends Publishing.

Flaws, Bob. 1998. *The tao of eating*. Boulder, CO: Blue Poppy Press.

Haas, Elston M., 1981. *Staying healthy with the seasons*. Millbrae, CA: Celestial Arts.

——— 2006. *Staying healthy with nutrition*. Millbrae, CA: Celestial Arts.

Katz, Sandor Ellix. 2003. *Wild fermentation*. White River Junction, VT: Chelsea Green Publishing.

McGee, Harold. 2004. *On food and cooking: The science and lore of the kitchen*. New York: Simon and Schuster.

Nestle, Marion. 2003. *Food politics*. Berkeley, CA: University of California Press.

——— 2006. *What to eat*. New York: North Point Press.

Pitchford, Paul. 1993. *Healing with whole foods*. Berkeley, CA: North Atlantic Books.

Pollan, Michael. 2002. *Botany of desire*. New York: Random House.

——— 2006. *The omnivore's dilemma*. New York: Penguin Press.

Price, Weston. 2000. *Nutrition and physical degeneration: A comparison of primitive and modern diets and their effects.* La Mesa, CA: Price-Pottenger Nutrition Foundation.

Schmid, Ronald F. 1987. *Native nutrition*. Rochester, VT: Healing Arts Press.

COOKING

Bastyr University Press. 2004. *From the Bastyr kitchen*. Seattle: Bastyr University Press.

Colbin, Annemarie. 1989. *The natural gourmet*. New York: Ballantine Books.

Cook's Illustrated Editors. 2006. *834 kitchen quick tips: Techniques and shortcuts for the curious cook*. Boston: America's Test Kitchen.

Estella, Mary. 1985. *The natural foods cookbook*. Tokyo and New York: Japan Publications.

McCarty, Meredith. 1989. *Fresh from a vegetarian kitchen*. Eureka, CA: Turning Point Publications.

Moosewood Collective. 1990. *Sundays at Moosewood*. New York: Fireside.

Robertson, Laurel, Carol Flinders, and Brian Ruppenthal. 1986. *The new Laurel's kitchen*. Berkeley, CA: Ten Speed Press.

Rombauer, Irma S., and Marion Rombauer Becker. 2006. *Joy of cooking, 75th anniversary edition*. New York: Simon and Schuster.

Weber, Marcea. 1981. *The sweet life*. Tokyo and New York: Japan Publications.

Wood, Rebecca. 1997. *The splendid grain*. New York: William Morrow and Company, Inc.

BREASTFEEDING, BABIES, AND CHILDREN

Firkaly, Susan Tate. 1984. *Into the mouths of babes*. White Hall, VA: Betterway Publications.

Gardner, Joy. 1987. *Healing yourself during pregnancy*. Freedom, CA: The Crossing Press.

Goodwin, Mary T., and Gerry Pollen. 1974. *Creative food experiences for children*. Washington, DC: Center for Science in the Public Interest (CSPI).

Kenda, Margaret Elizabeth, and Phyllis S. Williams. 1972. *The natural baby food cookbook*. New York: Avon Books.

Kitzinger, Sheila. 1991. *Breastfeeding your baby*. New York: Alfred A. Knopf.

La Leche League International. 1981. *The womanly art of breastfeeding*. New York: Plume, New American Library.

Mason, Diane, and Diane Ingersoll. 1986. *Breastfeeding and the working mother*. New York: St. Martin's Press.

Mendelsohn, Robert S. 1984. *How to raise a healthy child in spite of your doctor*. Chicago: Contemporary Books, Inc.

O'Mara, Peggy. *Mothering*. Santa Fe, NM. www.motheringmagazine.com.

Palmer, Gabrielle. 1993. *The politics of breastfeeding, 2nd edition*. Kitchener, ON: Pandora Press.

Weed, Susun S. 1986. *Wise woman herbal for the childbearing year*. Woodstock, NY: Ash Tree Publishing.

Yaron, Ruth. 1998. *Super baby food, 2nd edition*. Archbald, PA: F. J. Roberts Publishing Company.

WEB SITES

Here is a list of Web sites mentioned in this book:

www.bastyr.edu: Bastyr University School of Natural Medicine.

www.bastyr.edu/bookstore: Bastyr University School of Natural Medicine bookstore.

www.celiac.com: Center for finding resources for those requiring gluten-free diets.

www.celticsalt.com: Grain and Salt Society.

www.certifiedhumane.com: Certification program for raising animals humanely.

www.eatwild.com: How to find local grass-fed food such as eggs, dairy, and meat.

www.localharvest.org: How to find a community-supported agriculture (CSA) farm in your area.

www.mbayaq.org: Monterey Bay Aquarium Web site, with information about sustainable fisheries.

www.oregoncountrybeef.com: Country Natural Beef, an independent brand of beef produced by a cooperative of ranchers.

www.pregnancy.org: Resource for all aspects of pregnancy.

www.purcellmountainfarms.com: Resource for interesting heritage beans and gourmet food.

www.ranchogordo.com: Resource for interesting heritage beans.

www.rapunzel.com: The Rapunzel food company, producers of high-quality sugars, cocoa, chocolate, and other food products.

INDEX

D

ABOUT THE AUTHOR

photo by Howard Petrella

Cynthia Lair is a nationally recognized expert on whole foods cooking. In 1987 she graduated as a Certified Health and Nutrition Counselor from the Health and Nutrition Program in New York City. Since 1994, she has been on the faculty of Bastyr University's School of Nutrition and Exercise Science. More recently, she became a Clinical Associate for the University of Washington School of Nursing.

In 1994 she released her landmark cookbook *Feeding the Whole Family*. The second edition, revised and distributed under her independent publishing venture Moon Smile Press, was released in 1998, and has sold more than 35,000 copies. It has received praise from such organizations as La Leche League International, *Vegetarian Journal*, and *NAPRA ReView*. Her most recent book, *Feeding the Young Athlete: Sports Nutrition Made Easy for Players and Parents*, was released in 2002.

In addition to her two books, Lair has written articles for such magazines as *Living Without*, WSYSA's *Play On!*, and the *Well-Being Journal*, and is a featured columnist in *Mothering*.

Combining a background in acting and improvisational theater with her work in food and cooking, Cynthia is the host of Cookus Interruptus (www.cookusinterruptus.com), a humorous online cooking show that features many of the recipes in this book.

She lives with her husband and daughter in Seattle, WA.

Peggy O'Mara is the mother of four adult children and has been the editor and publisher of *Mothering* for 27 years. Her books include *Natural Family Living*, *Having a Baby Naturally*, and *A Quiet Place*.